WHAT READERS

Jamie's mom Krista wouldn't listen to people who said no. "No, he'll never get better." "No, you can't help him." Her book covers everything from fighting to keep her son from disappearing into Autism, to marital stress, to threats to her own health, and other life-altering struggles. She describes how to find physicians, therapists, schools, and even offers healthy family friendly recipes. Mainly, she talks about persistence and success! Her countless examples of advocating for her son, and her tireless search for experts and answers, give hope and motivation to every parent.

—Jay Gordon, MD, FAAP

Meet Jamie Now illuminates the extraordinary accomplishments of a resourceful, creative woman who holds her family together through the strains of the insurmountable task she undertakes: to dedicate herself to finding new ways to help her autistic son while barely maintaining her own health and sanity. She reveals every reader's inner strength by discovering her own. Persuasive in its simple honesty, this book is tender, wrenching, funny, and uplifting—nearly impossible to put down.

But more than that, *Meet Jamie Now* is a gift.

—Kathryn Lynn Davis,
New York Times bestselling author

Meet Jamie Now is an inspiring story of a mother who refused to let a doctor(s) determine her child's success in life. As a mother of a child with cerebral palsy, I could not put this book down. I truly felt as if I was with Krista on her journey, with both tears and celebrations. As an owner of a specialized therapy clinic, I will put this book on every parents must read list. Thank you Krista for taking the time to share your story and Jamie's incredible recovery.

—Lynette LaScala, CEO and
Founder NAPA Center

"*Meet* Jamie *Now* is an inspiring, groundbreaking account of autism and the endless-seeming journey for a cure. Krista's courage and commitment to medical and holistic approaches for Jamie's future well-being will help motivate a new generation of parents to search for and attain alternative protocols.

As a mother to a child with cerebral palsy, I have found strength and perseverance in Vance's story. It is a gripping, must-read."

—Bizzie Gold, Celebrity Trainer and
Wellness Expert

Meet Jamie Now

A Life Free of Autism

Krista Vance

Rose Junky
PUBLISHING

Published by Rose Junky Publishing
www.meetjamienow.com

ISBN-13: 978-0-9848625-0-4 (paperback)
ISBN-13: 978-0-9848625-1-1 (ebook: ePub)
ISBN-13: 978-0-9848625-2-8 (ebook: Kindle / mobi)

Printed in the U.S.A.

Photography credits: Brittany Hanson: pages 320 and 321. Harry Langdon: pages 199 and 239. Elizabeth Messina: cover, back cover photos, and photos on pages 293, 303, 304, 307, 308, 310, 311, 317, 322, 323, and 331. Rose photographs: iStockphoto © Matspersson0, white rose, pp. i. xii; iStockphoto © Chrisgramly, rose (modified), p. ii; iStockphoto © Caziopeia, rose (modified), p. iv, vi; iStockphoto © Liliboas, white rose, p. viii; iStockphoto © Dtv2 , red roses, pp. ix, x, 18, 39, 57, 71, 93, 97, 118, 120, 171, 217,233, 257, 261, 285, 291, 292, 302, 305, 306, 318, 320, 338, 342, 350; iStockphoto © Petegar, red roses, pp. 25, 26, 40, 91, 115, 161; iStockphoto © Ranasu, pink rose, pp. 37, 72, 76, 108, 131, 148, 166, 177, 191, 239, 321, 136, 347.
Photo-manipulation by RD Studio

Editing by Melissa Stein, Kathryn Davis, Kathy Kaiser and Kathleen Erickson

Book design by DesignForBooks.com

I dedicate this book to my children, Jack, Jamie, Sofia, and Gabriella, the loves of my life. You inspire me, energize me, and make me laugh and cry. You've helped keep my mind and heart open to challenges, always discovering new possibilities ahead. I love deeper every day because of each of you. I am so grateful you chose me as your mom.

Also, to Heather Anderson. I could not have written this book without your tireless energy, sense of humor, and compassion. I am grateful for the time you took away from your family to help me, for your warm spirit, and for your kindness. I can't put into words how much your work on this book meant to me.

Contents

Acknowledgments

I am eternally grateful to Dr. Terry Grossman, Dr. Gary Klepper, Dr. Luc Maes, and Dr. Max Collins. I will always, for the rest of my life, be indebted to you for your efforts, and I am forever in awe of your abilities. You shared my vision and belief in Jamie's potential. When you find people like these—whose minds are open, who are intelligent, and who know how to listen and respond—you have found a priceless gift. These caregivers are truly compassionate and genuinely concerned about the people they treat. I was dissatisfied with the treatment we received from many of the doctors who crossed our path, but I know that there are a greater number of doctors out there doing incredible work for people.

To all the doctors in all the emergency rooms we visited in the first ten years of Jamie's life: Thank you! Thank you from the bottom of my heart for saving my son every time, and thank you for all the medicines that kept him alive.

I want my mom to know how grateful I am for what she went through to have my brothers, my sister, and me.

She sacrificed so much for us. I appreciate how my mom and dad raised me and stuck by me. They gave me love and support through trials and tribulations. I am lucky enough to have received their incredibly strong will and ability to persevere. Thanks, Mom. (I also learned how to hyperstress about things. Thanks, Mom!)

To my brothers and sister, I love you so much and am so grateful that we are a family.

To Robert Vance, DO, for your resources, which helped me so much.

To Janet Berlin: Your special talent helped me cope with all the many emotions that surfaced in me.

And to James, thank you for helping me bring forth such beautiful children into this world.

Thank you, everyone. With this book I acknowledge that you helped me to save a life.

Foreword

I began reading *Meet Jamie Now* last night at bedtime and couldn't wait to pick it up and start again when I awoke this morning . . . and I didn't stop reading until I'd finished! You are in for a rare treat, for this is one of those extraordinary books that you cannot put down. If you're interested in the story of how a dedicated mother worked indefatigably to find a cure for her son's autism, consider reading this book. If someone in your family is affected with autism or an autistic spectrum disorder, consider this book required reading.

According to the Centers for Disease Control and Prevention, autistic spectrum disorders—which include Asperger's syndrome, attention deficit disorder, pervasive developmental delay, and autism itself—are estimated to affect 1 in every 88 children (and 1 in 54 boys) in the United States. Some authorities feel that these figures are low. Whatever numbers you believe, it is clear that this spectrum of disorders affects millions of individuals worldwide.

Despite the fact that autism is a relatively common condition, the enormous degree of difficulty experienced by author Krista Vance in obtaining adequate treatment for Jamie's autism suggests that the overwhelming majority of patients are receiving suboptimal care. Although *Meet Jamie Now* is mostly the story of what the Vance family went through in dealing with and helping an autistic child, this book can also be used as a guidebook to what treatments may be of benefit.

Shortly after Jamie developed autistic symptoms, Krista found that "mainstream medicine had already thrown in the towel." She was told that autism is a lifelong diagnosis and that little can be done. Krista was unwilling to accept this. She "couldn't let him go through life with autism." Quoting Robert Frost, Krista says that she "was willing to do anything to get him well, even if it meant taking a journey on the road 'less traveled.'" She took inspiration from other parents who had had the courage to go down less-traveled roads themselves.

And what a strange and wondrous journey it turned out to be! Along their way, Krista and Jamie encountered fairy godmothers and princes in the form of astute nutritionally based chiropractors, complementary physicians, and physical, occupational, and speech therapists. There were also some perils along the way. If Krista had not taken control when Jamie was in severe respiratory distress, this story might not have had a happy ending. But the true enemy in this story is the disorder of autism itself, and the real heroes are Jamie and his family, who ultimately prevail.

I believe that parents of an autistic child will do anything within their power to help that child get better. Yet the treatment that pediatricians and other health care providers have to offer is often woefully inadequate. In medical school, students are taught to rely on FDA-approved treatments, which are based upon randomized, double-blind, placebo-controlled trials. These trials are physicians' gold standard when making medical decisions. This approach may work for patented prescription drugs, but with the price for FDA approval now in excess of $900 million, this was not an option for the nonpharmaceutical therapies that Jamie required in order to get better. Who is going to pay for a randomized, double-blind, placebo-controlled trial on the use of a gluten- and dairy-free diet for autism? Or a generic drug, such as nystatin, for the systemic candida infections that are common in these children? Or the blue light diode or fish oil or vitamin B6 or any of the other interventions that were part of Jamie's recovery? No one can afford to perform those trials on these interventions, and the time has come for medical practitioners to look at evidence-based results for therapies such as these, which have so much potential to help and so little potential for harm.

Krista doesn't shy away from controversial topics. Take mercury, for instance. There is considerable debate about the possible contribution of mercury toxicity to autism. The speculation is that thimerosal, a mercury-containing preservative that was in common use in vaccines until 2001, may be a causative agent. Although Krista proceeded with caution in vaccinating her children, she was Rh-negative and had received eight thimerosal-containing RhoGAM injections prior to and during giving birth. She came to believe that mercury and other toxic metals had affected Jamie negatively, and that belief led her to research and pursue chelation therapy for him.

I was one of the physicians who worked with Krista and Jamie early in the course of his illness, when he was still profoundly affected. I witnessed the early signs of improvement as he began his journey to recovery. In more than thirty years of medical practice, I have found that little can match the joy and professional satisfaction I experience when a child recovers from a devastating illness, and I am grateful for the opportunity to have played a part in Jamie's recovery.

I know you will enjoy this book, which is the story of a family's struggles after one of their members falls chronically ill. Krista shares her heartfelt emotions, her doubts and triumphs, and her victories and struggles: four years without a full night's sleep, thirty-six hospital visits in ten years, worries about the financial burden of Jamie's treatments, and travel throughout the country to seek out the best therapies. But the nicest part of this story is that after all of the ups and downs, it has such a happy ending. So fasten your seatbelt and enjoy the roller-coaster ride as you . . . meet Jamie now!

Terry Grossman, MD
Denver, Colorado
September 2013

CHAPTER

1

The "A" Word

While I stared at the texture of the white walls, my eyes were drawn to the only photo hanging on it, that of a healthy child frolicking through tall green grass. Ironically, the photo saddened me. I felt anxious, worried about what was coming. I thought about reading a magazine to pass the time, but I couldn't focus. With each passing minute, my stress level deepened, and pediatrician George Allen, MD, was taking forever to come back to the examination room. What was taking so long? After he had seen my son Jamie, I had expected him simply to tell me what was wrong and how I could fix it.

Leaning my head against the wall, I remembered what life had been like before I became a mother, when worrying was something only other people did. I was living a young girl's dream, working as an actress, soaking up the Hollywood lifestyle.

I never could have imagined being in a situation where I was constantly in and out of doctors' offices with my own sick child. Before my life with my husband, James, my biggest concerns consisted of choosing between The Ivy on Robertson and The Ivy at the shore for lunch, and deciding what to wear. Quite often, I actually believed the world revolved solely around me! I traveled on a moment's notice, stayed up all night, or slept all day whenever I wanted. I loved having that kind of freedom—but deep inside burned a strong desire to have children.

After James and I had married, I wasn't sure what kind of mother I would make. Sometimes when my sister-in-law plopped her toddler in my lap so I could watch her for a few moments, the little girl and I would look at each other awkwardly, waiting for something to happen. Moments like those made me wonder how my life would be with children in it. I couldn't picture it clearly, but I definitely had a vision of a family of my own.

My impressions of motherhood came mainly from my close group of celebrity friends in L.A. Their children's lives didn't differ much from my own childhood, with nannies who roamed only designated parts of the house and were rarely seen by visitors. Those moms' pristine homes displayed no evidence of little kids: no plastic toys strewn across living room floors, no juice cups in the kitchen, no crayons on the table.

Outside that elite world, I did see a different kind of mother, the kind that pushed a stroller in which wriggled a toddler with sticky, melted-chocolate–covered fingers and a red Kool-Aid–covered mouth. But I couldn't relate to that kind of mother. She didn't seem happy; she looked frustrated and worn out. When I had kids, would I look like that, too? It was impossible to imagine.

The reality of having sick children or children with developmental problems was entirely foreign to me. When I was growing up, I never knew any kids with Down syndrome or any kind of chronic illness; I scarcely knew these conditions existed. I'd never even seen the inside of a hospital, as a patient or a visitor. Everyone around me was healthy and active, and I was naïve enough at the time to believe that the rest of the world lived like we did.

Not quite a decade had passed since the evenings I had been escorted out of a limo and down the red carpet by Steve, the high-profile Hollywood producer–director who was then my husband. We would enter yet another of the many award shows and elite parties we used to attend together. Inside, we mingled with the biggest Hollywood stars, major studio heads, and the town's hottest agents. Each week we would spend hours on movie sets, where it wouldn't be uncommon to chat with Cher or Whitney Houston between takes. On other occasions, I watched Steve direct studio-recording sessions with Tina Turner or listened to Patti LaBelle belt out her amazing vocals. Every activity centered on all that was attractive and glamorous, and, to be sure, it was a very charmed life.

Dr. Allen finally returned and I was thrust back into my current reality.

I could feel the anxiety rising up, rattling my insides. "I know Jamie's only nineteen months old, but something has really changed in him," I said. "What do you think is going on?"

Seeming to choose his words carefully and speaking not much above a whisper, Dr. Allen responded, "I don't want to alarm you . . . but . . . I think he has . . . the 'A' word."

"What?" I laughed nervously, confused by his cautious, indirect response.

"I think Jamie is *autistic*."

Autistic? Like the character Dustin Hoffman plays in *Rain Man*? What does that mean? Dr. Allen answered my questions the best he could. Then he gave me the names of specialists who could help with further diagnosis. As if attempting to fill the enormous hole in my chest, he placed an informational brochure in my hand. The seriousness of the diagnosis sank in slowly, and I began to feel like the world was closing in on me. I saw that Dr. Allen continued to speak, but his words dissipated as I felt myself sinking deeper into the haze.

Dr. Allen seemed genuinely concerned, and clearly wanted to help me understand what was happening with my son. But at the same time, I felt like he was not connected to the news, like he was used to treating sick kids and mine was just another child coming through his office.

Noticing my devastation, he continued in a measured tone, "Krista, I think you will find, as the mothers of my other autistic patients have, that there isn't a very optimistic outlook for this diagnosis. It will be easier simply to accept it. The reality is that, at this time, there is no cure. I'm sorry."

I don't know how I managed to get out of the doctor's office with my twin boys—Jack and Jamie—in tow, because

I felt an overwhelming lack of direction. I could only look up toward the sky in search of a Higher Power to answer my resounding question, "Why?!"

Once inside my car, I struggled to get it moving so I could work my way back home. I glanced at Jamie in the rear-view mirror. He had always been such an exceptionally pretty child. Looking at his beautiful yet empty eyes, I felt an indescribable pain in my heart. It was as though, in an instant, his future had been taken away. He would never be able to experience a life that included the joys of family, friends, playing sports, going to college, or having a wife and children of his own. The thought of it made me feel physically ill. I took my anguish out on the steering wheel, hitting it with my fists, hoping to beat back this reality.

How had we ended up here after all that we'd been through? I had worked so hard even to have children in the first place, suffering six failed pregnancies. Each time I had been faced with the possibility of life without children, I had chased the thought away.

Earlier, James and I had been living temporarily in Flagstaff, Arizona, learning some business training. One afternoon, while walking up the stairs at home, I experienced intense pain in my lower abdomen—so sharp that it knocked me to the ground. I called Philip Brooks, MD, my ob-gyn in L.A., and he told me to go to the hospital immediately. It was

February and a heavy winter storm was in full force outside; several inches of snow already lay on the ground. The hospital was about a half hour away when road conditions were good. James came home from work quickly to take care of me, and we worked our way through the treacherous weather in an old borrowed Ford Bronco.

At the hospital, emergency room doctors explained that they were unsure what was wrong with me. They administered a pregnancy test and it came back positive. I was pregnant! We were excited to hear the news in that moment, but our joy faded with the next breath as the doctors clarified the situation. Chances were that something was wrong with the pregnancy. The ultrasound results hadn't helped determine anything conclusive. The doctors believed exploratory surgery was the best avenue for discovering the source of my pain. An operation would be scheduled for first thing the next morning, but they couldn't tell me the name of the surgeon, because they didn't know yet. Yikes!

All this uncertainty eroded even further my low comfort level. James and I were also concerned because I had lost my left fallopian tube and ovary to a benign tumor years earlier; only the right side remained, and the surgery put me at risk of losing that as well. The doctors left the final decision to me, with the implication that there was no other option.

I struggled to decide whether to go ahead with the operation. Because my blood type was B– (B-negative) (Rh-negative), I was given RhoGAM. Regardless of the circumstances, and without knowing what type of blood James had, they brought the shot and gave it to me with no explanation. I didn't feel right about it, but at the time I trusted doctors and their knowledge of what was best for me more than I trusted my own intuition. Years later, people began to believe that the preservative in this particular shot was detrimental to fetuses. This was a lesson to me. Later on, I took a more active role in my own medical treatment.

Not knowing what to do at that moment, however, I called my mom for her usual support. She had always been an advocate for her own health as well as the health of her children. Her philosophy about medical treatment was a motivator for me. She would always search for the best doctor in a particular field, even if it took a lot of work and calling around the country to find him or her. Hanging up the phone from my conversation with my mom, I realized this was the perfect opportunity for me to step up and take control of my own health. The exploratory surgery the doctors were proposing carried the risk of my never being able to get pregnant, and I knew I had to do everything I could to make the right choice.

I got back on the phone and began calling. I was grateful to Dr. Brooks, who had identified several medical contacts in Arizona. I finally got hold of a specialist who happened to be out of town on business in New York. It was three in the morning for us, five in the morning on the East Coast. I was relieved by how helpful and friendly he was at such an early hour; it felt like a miracle that I had actually gotten in touch with someone who could provide a better alternative for me. His advice was to contact Alan Frederick, MD, a trusted fertility expert working out of a Phoenix hospital. I hung up the phone and never spoke to that doctor again, but I will always remember his kindness at a time when I really needed it.

In the morning my ultrasound was faxed to Dr. Frederick, and he recognized that the picture revealed an ectopic pregnancy, located in the fallopian tube. It took him only moments to determine the source of the problem, while I had been waiting hours for the local doctors to give me a solid diagnosis. These doctors were floored by Dr. Frederick's ability to read the ultrasound; they didn't even *try* to hide their reverence. It became glaringly obvious that I needed to get out of there and go to Phoenix as soon as possible. But how would I manage it?

Traveling by ambulance was too dangerous because of the storm, and would take too long in any case. The best option was to transport me by air ambulance. We were on our way shortly. My pain increased from intermittent to persistent with every bump in the road as the ambulance rushed to the airport. Once my gurney was rolled onto the plane, the flight nurse eased my suffering with an IV dose of morphine. I was quick to find my "happy place."

Then it was James's turn to battle uneasiness as he squeezed into the one small seat provided for an additional passenger. It was stuck in the back of the plane like an afterthought, without an ounce of comfort. After everyone was secure, the small, speedy airplane was off the ground and into the stormy skies, battling bumpy air all the way through the short flight from Flagstaff to Phoenix. I was high from the morphine, so the turbulence was of no concern to me, but James spent the entire flight trying to control his nausea and anxiety.

Once at the hospital, I was left to wait in a hallway near the operating room. I was beginning to feel like my emergency wasn't being treated like an emergency until James flagged down a passing medical staffer. At the mere mention of Dr. Frederick, I was immediately swept away like royalty to the intake room. Dr. Frederick walked in and greeted me warmly and confidently. I was pleased by my first impression of him.

After the initial meeting, the nurses wheeled me into the operating room, where I was troubled by the sight of several television sets airing the Super Bowl. My breathing changed to panting as I realized the doctors were actually planning to watch football during my surgery. The anesthesiologist hadn't even noticed my entrance because his eyes were already glued to the screen. I imagined them rooting for first downs while my reproductive parts lay waiting in distress.

I turned to Dr. Frederick and said, "You guys aren't really going to watch this game right now, are you?"

One of the surgeons said half-jokingly, "Aw, come on, Krista, it's the Super Bowl."

I played along, trying not to sound too worried. "Yeah, okay . . . but you are going to save my tube, right?"

The surgeons laughed and I tried to share their humor and nonchalance. Dr. Frederick looked straight at me and said, "I can't promise I can save it, but I'll do everything I can."

Though I still had concerns, I felt comforted, and strangely enough, even with the football announcer's voice in the background, I believed I was in the right hands.

Soon I was graced with the pleasure of leaving consciousness behind to the nurse's count of "5 . . . 4 . . . 3 . . .

2 . . ." In what felt like the very next moment, I was waking up in the recovery room and being greeted with the incredible news that Dr. Frederick had made good on his word; he had saved my fallopian tube. I was elated. Weeks later, after making a full recovery, I was ready to focus on getting pregnant again.

James and I tried hard to get pregnant. It became our favorite pastime. We made each attempt fun and playful, joking that "practice makes perfect." The more we practiced, the happier James became.

Meanwhile, I read every book I could find on conception, and we tested every touted "surefire" method. We tried it with the light on, in a swimming pool, hanging off the bed, lying sideways, and even with me staying horizontal for hours afterward. James did the whole underwear thing, trying different styles—whichever myth promised stronger swimmers—from Jockeys to boxers and eventually to no underwear at all. But month after month, the pregnancy test did not have that double line.

I was so envious as one by one our friends called with the happy news that they were expecting. We had become pregnant twice before without even trying, with the first ending in a miscarriage and the second an ectopic pregnancy. I couldn't understand why it wasn't happening for us, too.

During this time, we relocated to start our own business in Colorado. It was wonderful for us to have the romance of the Rocky Mountains around us. We enjoyed our life in Summit County, which—aside from the absence of children—was fulfilling and happy. We spent our winters skiing in

Keystone and Copper Mountain or visiting friends and dining out in Breckenridge. I found peace of mind by snowshoeing between the thick evergreens, running with our dogs—Emoi and Jaro—through the clean, untracked snow. And James and I enjoyed the warm-weather seasons by mountain biking the trails and hills around our home.

One snowy Sunday morning, while I was sipping a decaf latte at home, the word "fertility" in a newspaper article caught my eye. I read the article twice, absorbing every word. It was about William Schoolcraft, MD, a fertility doctor down in Denver. The article talked about his effective fertility procedures and his astounding success rate.

I called immediately, and they said there was a six-month wait for an appointment. Six months seemed like forever. I was still holding onto the hope of being a young mother. But I made the appointment and, fortunately, a cancellation allowed me to see the doctor three months earlier than expected.

I went to the first appointment by myself, since it only involved several ultrasounds and a blood draw. Dr. Schoolcraft came in to meet me and I liked him at once; he had a gentle demeanor and was obviously intelligent. I had known that he was accomplished for his age, but I was still surprised by how young he looked. The ultrasound results showed several cysts on my right ovary. It was helpful to learn that these cysts had probably kept me from ovulating over the last couple of years. That explained why all the research, all the positions, all the effort hadn't worked for us. The first thing the doctor wanted to do was remove the cysts, so we went ahead and scheduled the operation.

After the surgery, I had a four-week recovery period before I returned for another ultrasound. This study showed that three cysts had appeared in the place where the first two had been. I was completely distraught. Dr. Schoolcraft explained that this situation wasn't common, but that it wasn't unheard of either. He suggested that, after another surgery to remove the new cysts, we go right to in vitro fertilization (IVF). Apparently, he believed my body would continue to produce cysts, so we should pursue a more aggressive plan to get pregnant.

The goal of IVF was huge news. I had always thought of this procedure as intense and now it was going to happen to me. I was as nervous as I was excited. I had devoted my time and energy to trying to have children, and this might be my last chance. I would meet the challenge head-on, driven by my dreams of feeling a life growing inside me.

After six weeks of giving myself daily shots that left long-lasting bruises on my belly, my body was prepared for the embryos and the big day finally arrived for implanting them. On this incredibly important day, James managed to injure his ankle in his weekly basketball game. Sure, it was kind of funny when, as I was getting ready for our drive to Denver for the procedure, James hopped into the room on one foot and dropped down on the couch, plopping his grapefruit-size ankle up on the coffee table. But much more than amused, I was angry. I could see that he was in a lot of pain, and part of me felt bad for him, but I was more upset because I didn't understand his need to play at all on this particular morning.

Luckily, James's sister Rachel was visiting and was able to defuse the situation by getting us into the car and on our way to the appointment. Happy, anxious, excited, uncomfortable, and upset, we carried our bundle of emotions with us down the mountain from Summit County. We were late arriving at the Swedish Hospital. We explained it was because James had hurt his ankle, but it might also have been due to my need for a vanilla latte and the fact that Starbucks was busier than usual. Dr. Schoolcraft had been waiting for us. The nurses showed me to my room, where I changed into a hospital gown and lay down on the bed. Then Rachel and I realized James had disappeared. I wondered where he could possibly have gone—how could he have left my side already?

Dr. Schoolcraft came in to ask me if I wanted three or four embryos implanted. This was a big decision. Three eggs could result in twins or triplets, whereas four eggs could result in triplets or quadruplets. James needed to be with me. Several minutes earlier, Rachel had looked for and found him upstairs in the orthopedic surgeon's office he had apparently noticed on the way into the hospital. I couldn't imagine what he was thinking, but at the time I didn't know he was in a lot of pain. I only knew I was discouraged that we weren't together for this and that he was holding up a procedure that relied on precise timing.

Rachel had returned by the time the doctor came in to ask about the embryos, and she explained where James was. I was surprised when Dr. Schoolcraft, who was one of the nation's top reproductive doctors, declared, "I'll go ask him." In an instant, he had taken off down the hall. No one was more surprised than James to find that his fertility doctor had tracked him down in the X-ray room. Evidently, Dr. Schoolcraft interrupted the technician at work, confident that his business was more important, and explained the options for embryo choices. James thought three embryos would be best, and, after hearing the verdict, Dr. Schoolcraft was gone as quickly as he had entered, leaving James and the technician looking at each other in disbelief.

The doctor came back to my room and told us James's preference, and we all agreed. We decided to wait a little while for him to return, and, although I was concerned that he wouldn't make it, Dr. Schoolcraft seemed unworried. He reassured me, "He'll be here."

After a while, a couple of nurses came in with the embryologist, who was pushing a large device made mostly of glass (later referred to as "the incubator"). They showed us how the embryos were kept and invited Rachel to view them, an honor normally given to the father. Rachel glanced at me, not knowing what to do, and I nodded for her to go ahead and look. She described what she saw through the incubator's microscope. Three embryos were warming in the ambient air inside the glass machine: three egglike dots, each inside its own circle. It was a magic we couldn't explain or understand, and it brought tears to our eyes.

Soon Dr. Schoolcraft returned, ready to go—with or without James. It was time for the embryos to be implanted, and the doctor couldn't wait any longer. And then, right on cue, the door flew open and in rolled James in a wheelchair. He was a sight to everyone, dripping with sweat, knuckles cut and bleeding. As it turned out, his wheelchair was the kind designed to be pushed from behind. Without the special grips to get the wheels rolling, James had continually rammed his hands into the brakes as he tried to go faster. He had scraped his hands raw attempting to maneuver the wheels in the right direction. We all had to laugh at the situation—just one more event in our crazy day. But having James back in the room calmed us all, especially me. We were finally ready.

Dr. Schoolcraft proceeded by first turning a type of wand upside down, opening the incubator, and grabbing the eggs with it. We watched the remarkable process on the monitor. In moments, he said, "They're in!" and we all cheered joyfully.

The table I was lying on tilted back, so my head was down and my legs were elevated. I had to stay in this position for about an hour after the eggs were inserted. While I waited, Rachel pushed James back up to the orthopedic office. He was happy to have someone pushing this time to spare his wounded knuckles.

The blood rushed to my head as the minutes crept by. My bladder had been full from the start, as requested by the doctor, because it helped the view of the uterus. The nurse understood the urgency of my condition and checked in with me continually about my need to relieve myself. At one point, it seemed like a lot of time had passed since her last visit, and the pressure from my bladder took over my body. I started to worry irrationally that the tightening of my muscles was causing damage to the embryos. My concerns convinced me that I just needed to do it, so I went ahead and let go. What a strange feeling! Upon her return, the nurse found me lying in wet sheets.

"Don't worry about it. I won't tell anyone." She was especially nice, and that made me feel better. I spent the next two hours lying back in my newly changed bed, comfortable and happy. I touched my tummy with an extraordinary sense that my babies were inside me. I was tickled by the idea of the life growing there and I focused on connecting to them, sending them my love for the first time.

After a while and for the second time that day, the door flew open and there was James. He came in on crutches this time. I was too caught up in the excitement of this process to hold onto my anger, and I knew he had suffered enough. He held my hand, and we soaked up the thrill of our potential new life.

When the waiting period was over, we left the hospital, James on his crutches and I in my wheelchair. Rachel drove us back up to the mountains, where we would wait anxiously to see if the process had been successful.

I was on complete bed rest for three days. Because I wanted to do everything I could to make sure the eggs stayed in place, I stayed in bed even longer than I was supposed to, getting up only to use the bathroom. James was my resting partner, and we passed the time by watching TV and reading. Rachel ran to Starbucks or got us meals while we both lay in the living room. We laughed like two little kids, knowing she was working hard to fulfill our every request, especially since James had only joined me sympathetically in bed rest and really hadn't required any special treatment at all. But she was happy to help, and we were happy to let her.

Two weeks later, I took a blood test. They told me they would call the next day with the results. I was so anxious; I could hardly pass the hours. I tried to stay busy, going shopping and finding things to fill my day. As I was driving home with my friend Judy, they called me with the news. I called James right after I hung up, but I didn't share the results over the phone. I just told him he had to get home right away. He begged for confirmation of his suspicions, but I wouldn't give it to him.

When he returned from work, he knew the answer before he even asked the question. "You're pregnant, aren't you?"

"Yes!"

He swept me into his arms, and we hugged and kissed as tears came to our eyes.

I thought getting pregnant was the difficult part. I had absolutely no clue that the struggle was just beginning.

After the appointment with Dr. Allen, I returned home with the boys. I brought them inside and sat them down to play. Leaning against the kitchen counter, I could only rest my heavy head in my hands and sob. Jack noticed I was crying. He came over, touched my hand, and asked, "Mommy okay?"

Jack and Jamie looking so peaceful

CHAPTER

2

Growing Pains

As I looked into Jack's eyes, I felt the same calmness that spreads to everyone around him. He has always been my "little ray of sunshine." When I held him as a baby, he was content, just happy to be lying in my arms. Throughout his childhood, he was easy to care for and rarely ever sick. There was no need for worry when it came to Jack. He had a kind of internal peace and often elicited the term old soul. Being with him put me at ease. It might have been unfair, but I came to rely on Jack to stay strong when Jamie started struggling to stay healthy.

Jack and Jamie were born on December 15 at thirty-three weeks, and they remained hospitalized for seven weeks. I felt good during the pregnancy and gave birth to my twins naturally, but afterward I suffered from bleeding complications. I was held in the recovery room while, after only a quick touch from me, the babies were whisked away to receive attention for the issues arising from their premature birth.

I tossed and turned all that night, anxious to be with them after their long-awaited arrival. I wanted to hold their tiny hands and feel their soft skin, things I had dreamed about doing for years. In the wee hours of the morning, I found myself still wide-awake with anticipation. My emotions bounded here and there, and my mind raced as I went over and over my favorite baby-boy names. James had left it up to me to decide what to put on their birth certificates.

If I named the firstborn after James, he would feel more entitled than his brother. There seemed to be so many considerations when it came to the psychology of twins! On the other hand, I wanted to use my father's name. He had passed away at a young age when I was just a teenager, and giving our son his name felt like the perfect way to honor his memory. I mulled it over for hours and finally figured out how to balance all the important factors. I would name the firstborn Jack, after my father, and the second born Jamie, after James.

Eventually, it was time for the nurse to wheel me down the hall to the boys. Had I been able to get there on my own, I would have sprinted down the hall instead. I felt wonderful, even without any sleep. When we reached the NICU (Neonatal Intensive Care Unit), there was a group of nurses and doctors standing around Jamie. They saw me, instantly stopped what they were doing, and walked away with attempted casualness. Only one doctor remained.

I looked behind him to see Jamie lying beneath bright lights, his chin stretched in an upward position; it looked like he was being readied for CPR. I was confused about what was happening, and the doctor explained that Jamie needed to be intubated with a breathing machine. Apparently, he had been laboring to breathe for the last fifteen hours. Seeing my son this way was disturbing; there were numerous cords and wires hooked up to his tiny, new body. I understood, though, that it was meant to help him, and I tried not to get too upset about it. After five days, which was a long time for a premature baby to be intubated, the tube was removed. Jamie was then suited up with a plastic, bubblelike fixture that completely covered his head, holding an abundance of oxygen near his face. He eventually graduated to only a nasal cannula.

Jack's lungs were better developed and he hadn't needed to be intubated. But even he was strapped to an IV that had to be inserted into his head because they couldn't find a vein anywhere else. He has a scar there to this day, in addition to all the other scars he and Jamie both carry after the poking and blood-taking they endured from finger to toe those first several weeks.

Five days after the birth, I was released from the hospital, forced to leave Jack and Jamie behind. Tears streamed down my face as my mom drove me farther and farther away from the hospital. I ached with the pain of separating from my babies for the first time after carrying them for seven months. Like any new mother, I was having difficulty leaving them in the care of someone else, trusting the doctors and nurses who had been with them since birth. I had no choice: The boys needed to be in the hospital. I had to let go.

After a while, I got myself into a good routine. I would wake up and work out, trying to get my body back into shape. Then I would go to the hospital and spend my days touching the boys and watching them sleep. The nurses taught me their three-hour routine of changing newborn clothes, taking temperatures, changing diapers, and feeding. I tried to be there for every feeding, especially so I could hold my babies. I had started breast pumping to begin my milk flow, but I wasn't allowed to nurse yet because the work of being breastfed would cause the boys to burn too many calories. The doctors wanted to hold off to help with their weight gain. Instead, I held them skin-to-skin to ensure that they received physical stimulation from me, and also so they could feel the familiarity of my heartbeat. After they had been in the hospital for three weeks, I began nursing them for five minutes at a time. Those were welcome bonding moments for us.

I became rigorous about pumping, waking up through the night so my production was increased as much as it could be. The nurses told me the more I pumped, the more milk I would have, but every two hours was too much. This schedule really compromised my sleep, which probably ended up working against my goal in the end—as did the fact that I didn't know I needed to drink more water than usual. I wish the nurses had mentioned that little detail in their directions. It seemed like the more I pumped, the less milk I had. Eventually, the boys required more than I could produce, so I took advantage of the supplemental breast milk supply offered by the hospital's milk bank. It was wonderful that other mothers offered this precious resource to newborns.

James and I spent ten hours of Christmas day in the hospital. It was fun for us to bring the boys their first little gifts. Eventually, the nurses urged us to go out together while we had the chance. The boys were sleeping, and once the babies came home, things would be different. Should we go? Could we go? James and I took their advice and went to see a movie, something we hadn't done in months.

It happened to be the opening night for *Titanic*. I felt guilty taking this kind of time, but I knew it would be good for us. As strange as it felt, we went to the theater. *Titanic* was a three-hour film, and I sat crying through most of it. The boys never left my mind, but at the same time I enjoyed the escape of getting wrapped up in the story. The one thing that touched me deeply was the theme song, *My Heart Will Go On*. Celine Dion's voice was beautiful and the lyrics were so relevant to what was happening in our lives.

We went back to the hospital afterward, and I sang the song to my twins. From that point on, it became a love song for our children. My singing this particular tune seemed to mesmerize them, completely capturing their attention. It certainly wasn't because of my talent. Luckily for me, the boys had never heard Celine Dion perform it. For months, I would sing it to them when they cried and the sound always comforted them. I sang it for years afterward and I sing it to them still.

The next day, I was informed that Jamie and Jack were going to get routine hepatitis shots. The word *hepatitis* definitely carried negative implications, but I didn't know very much about the vaccine.

"Wait a minute. What is hepatitis exactly? I know there are different kinds, but how do you get it?" I asked the doctor.

"There are various strains, but hepatitis B is the biggest threat. It can be spread through sex, needle use, or blood transfusions."

The hairs lifted on the back of my neck. I thought, *There's no way!* Something felt wrong about giving the boys this vaccine. Why would you give a premature baby something like that?

I decided I really wanted to hold off until I could educate myself more. I voiced my feelings to the medical staff. Were their raised eyebrows a sign that they considered me a bad mother? Ultimately, I couldn't worry about what they thought; my gut feeling was a stronger influence.

Several weeks later, Jamie had progressed enough that the doctors were getting ready to release him, which was surprising because he'd had the harder time in the hospital. Doctors came in with the news and I was so excited—and really nervous, too. I questioned them closely: "Is his weight where it should be? Is his breathing strong enough?" They were satisfied with his growth, but he would be sent home with oxygen for the nighttime.

When I learned how to set him up on the oxygen machine, all of a sudden I felt the responsibility for his care, and the weight of that duty, shift to me. From the moment of their birth, the twins' well-being had been mostly in the hands of the hospital staff, whom I had come to know and trust. Now it would all be up to James and me. This realization was a scary one. I had spent months getting ready for this change, but, now that it had come, my confidence was shaky.

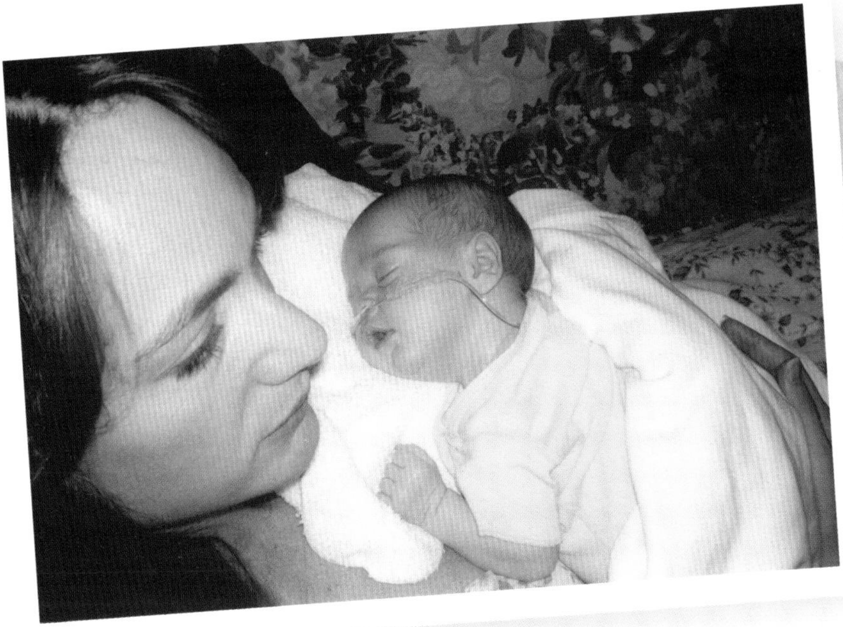

Jamie sent home with oxygen

Jack couldn't be released with Jamie because his blood cell count wasn't where it should be. There was talk of him needing either a blood transfusion or a special medication that would help his red blood cells multiply. I wanted to give a couple of pints of my blood for him to use because we shared the same blood type. At that time, there was a lot of concern about tainted blood donations. The doctors protested that I had lost too much blood during delivery. I argued with them for days, insisting that my blood, and only my blood, be given to Jack. They finally gave in and took my donation. As it turned out, the medication was effective enough and he didn't need the transfusion after all. It was

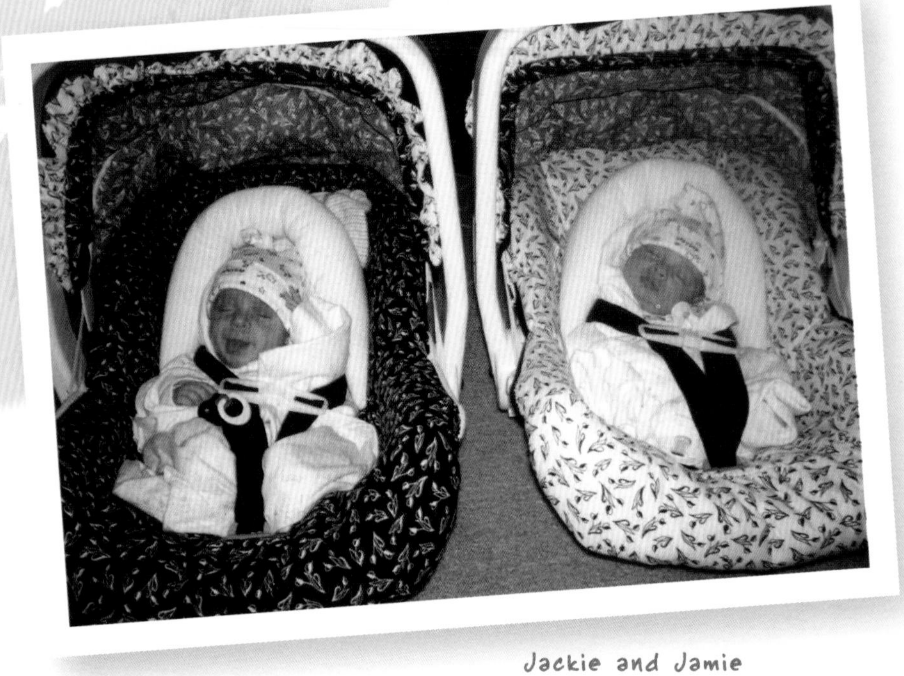

Jackie and Jamie

still worth it to me to play it safe, and I felt perfectly fine afterward.

Before the babies were born, we'd set ourselves up with temporary accommodations in Denver, and my in-laws had come to town to help out. We lived in a nice community with a gym and a little lake to walk around. Our condo was a cute three-bedroom with a fireplace that made it feel cozy. We wanted to make sure the boys were thriving before we took them up to our mountain home at an altitude of nine thousand feet.

Now, finally, after living in the hospital for seven weeks, Jamie was able to come home. He did well for the first few days. He was calm and quiet and slept fine. Things didn't seem right without Jack, but he was released three days later, and at long last our family was together.

I had become really close with the staff. Before leaving, we took pictures with them, exchanged hugs, and said our good-byes. It felt a little uncomfortable leaving the place that had the ability to meet the boys' every need. I had grown accustomed to entering their room each day and finding out immediately their heart rates, the level of their oxygen saturation, and every detail of their other bodily functions. But it was time for me to take over, and we were ready to find some normalcy with our children.

Once the boys were strapped into their car seats, it was surprising to see how small they really were. At birth, Jack weighed five pounds one ounce and Jamie was just under five pounds. By the time we headed home, they weighed eight or nine pounds, but they were still tiny bundles, wrapped up for the Colorado winter with thick layers, and swimming in the extra space of their seats.

Each night, both boys were hooked up to oxygen as a precautionary measure. From the start, nighttime was rough. Getting twins to sleep through the night at the same time seemed impossible. *But there must be people out there who are managing it,* I thought. I needed to find a book on the topic as soon as I had the time. I slept lightly, waking up when the boys did, and then again to check on them, and again to pump breast milk. Between the excitement and worry, there were three or four nights when I hardly slept at all.

With my mother-in-law visiting, I could get more sleep because she stepped in to help. One night, I peeked in on the three of them, wide-awake at three in the morning. They were all on the bed, and she had them both laughing. I had to laugh, too, when I saw how much fun they were having in the middle of the night, at a time when everyone was supposed to be sound asleep.

The sleeping problem was one I couldn't seem to solve. I wondered when things were going to become more consistent. The situation became so uncontrollable that I tried to create a completely silent environment for the boys to sleep in. However, on one occasion, when James's parents and brother came over to watch the Super Bowl, we all got wild and crazy, cheering and yelling loudly while the boys were napping. The Denver Broncos and John Elway were battling for victory, and we were all seriously invested in the outcome. That was unusual for me, a person who normally couldn't be less interested in football, but I got caught up in the excitement of the local team playing their hearts out.

I realized how loud we were being, but each time I went in to check on the boys I found them fast asleep. Even with all that noise, they didn't wake up. James's theory was that they would sleep better with more background sounds rather than with the level of quiet I had been trying to create. It turned out that more noise didn't solve the problem, but at least I stopped wasting my energy trying to keep everything silent.

After a little over a month in the Denver condo, the time came to take the boys home to Summit County. We had their room set up with new cribs and cute baby-boy decor. During the drive up, we could barely contain our enthusiasm; it was hard to believe this moment had finally arrived. Being at our home for the first time together was wonderful.

As time went on, we continued to adjust. I began looking for pediatricians closer to home who could follow up on the boys' health and progress. I had been asking around about vaccinations, doing my own research, wanting to be prepared to make a decision before the boys' next doctor visit. I visited the library, bought books from different stores, and talked to my father-in-law—an osteopath—in an attempt to make a more educated choice.

For the boys' first checkup in Denver, we had seen a pediatrician who brought up the recommended timing for newborn vaccinations. Still hesitant, I questioned her about it. She explained that although it wasn't the normal route to take, I could choose to wait on the shots or I could even waive them altogether by signing off on the back of the immunization card. Getting a doctor's affirmation that I truly had choices in the matter, and that other options existed, eased a few of my concerns.

During a follow-up visit in Summit County, another pediatrician brought up the familiar topic. I couldn't help but wonder if these doctors were working from the same script. "It looks like the boys are due for all their vaccinations."

I expressed my concerns. "I'm leery of vaccinating. I was wondering if you have ever seen any problems from it."

"Only one time. I gave a baby girl the DPT vaccine, and she had a reaction to it that caused severe brain damage. It was a unfortunate situation. Sadly, she was kept alive in a vegetative state, but ended up dying at four years old. That was an extreme case, though, and an occurrence like that is very, very rare."

I was shocked at the story and sat stunned for a moment, trying to understand how it could happen to anyone. The doctor noticed my reaction and continued, "They were using the live pertussis to vaccinate back then, until they discovered the potential dangers it posed. Don't worry, the live virus is no longer used."

My stomach was still churning. Knowing they had changed to a safer vaccine settled my nerves a little, but I still had questions. "Okay, what about the other vaccines, like polio? Why is it given when there are no cases of it in North America?" There hadn't been an answer for this in any of my research.

She apparently didn't have an answer either, because she simply replied, "We can skip that one if you want."

It seemed to me she wasn't completely convinced that the rigid vaccine schedule was necessary. I held off again on the round of shots because my reluctance was only growing stronger.

A friend with twin girls occasionally hung out with the boys and me. My friend and I had a lot in common and spent some time skiing, shopping, or having lunch together. One day I brought up vaccinating to see how she felt about it.

"Have you gone ahead with the regular vaccinations for the girls?"

"They've actually only received a few of the regular shots," she told me. "It doesn't seem right to me that they get such powerful injections all at the same time, especially into their little bodies. I'm trying to be selective, and space out the shots I feel are necessary."

"It is nice to hear that someone else has questioned the 'regular' system of vaccinating. I don't feel right about giving them to the boys yet. Besides, I've read about some negative side effects, and I've heard some seriously upsetting stories."

Her eyes widened and she nodded. "Well, I hate to bring this up, but I have another terrible story to add to the bunch. Last week, my good friend took her son in for a checkup where he received all the regular vaccines on one day. That night, he died of SIDS."

The situation was unimaginable. Were the vaccine and the boy's death on the same day a coincidence—or not? The possibilities brought a lot of weight to our conversation. Later, one of the books I read gave the pros and cons of vaccinating. A group of children who had died of SIDS had been studied. It was found that they were completely lacking vitamin C in their systems. It was suggested that this lack of vitamin C was caused by the overload to the body of so many vaccines at once. My quandary deepened.

Meanwhile, our daily family life grew more and more hectic. With the ongoing lack of sleep, I felt like I wasn't able to give my all to the things that were important to me, especially the boys. So we decided to hire Carla, a woman who could help with Jack and Jamie as well as with some cleaning and cooking. She was wonderful and it was such a relief to have another source of energy to back me up.

Around this time, in part due to my lack of rest, I stopped producing enough breast milk and was forced to rely on formula. Soon afterward, Jack developed eczema and Jamie's breathing sounds also changed, becoming more guttural. He started to sound like he had asthma or a frog in his throat. On top of these reactions, they both began having terrible intestinal problems, including chronic constipation.

I asked around about different formulas because I thought their stomach issues might be increasing their sleep problems. I received various pediatrician recommendations and tried them all, including adding apple juice, lots of water, prune juice, and even corn syrup in their formula to help their constipation. It seemed crazy to put corn syrup, which was not only pure sugar but also purely addictive, into a baby's bottle. I had confidence in my own knowledge about nutrition, but I didn't know about babies' digestion specifically, so I forced myself to follow the doctors' advice.

The things they suggested worked sometimes, but never for more than a few days at a time. I even tried a prescription formula, one last-ditch attempt. Not only was it expensive but it also tasted horrible. The boys wouldn't drink it. In fact, I wouldn't drink it even if I had to. It had a strong, awful smell, and the texture and color made it even less appealing. After a lot of frustration, I ended up going back to the first milk-based formula I had used, because that was all the boys would drink.

I traveled around, from Denver to Vail, visiting different pediatricians, looking for someone who could solve the mystery, but I wasn't getting anywhere. It occurred to me that I needed an alternative doctor who was knowledgeable about diet and nutrition. I wanted to find an open-minded practitioner who worked "outside the box." I tracked down Jay Wilson, DC, ND, working out of Boulder. I heard he practiced skin and muscle testing, a form of Applied Kinesiology (the use of manual muscle-strength testing for medical diagnosis), and that he could help determine the sources of different allergy problems.

Dr. Wilson used a wide array of foods and environmental sources to test the boys for sensitivities. What he discovered was that the boys had negative reactions to most of the main ingredients of over-the-counter formulas, including dairy, soy, and corn. He put the boys on supplements and suggested I try goat milk.

In the summer of 1998, goat milk was not exactly a product you'd find on most grocery store shelves. What I could find for sale didn't taste good, and had been pasteurized, so the nutrients were compromised. Somehow, I managed to track down a farmer who could provide a direct supply for me. We arranged a meeting spot north of Boulder, and my friend Mari said she'd come along.

The farmer arrived in a beaten-up pickup truck. When she got out, I was amused to see her wearing dirty overalls and an old straw hat. It was as if she'd stepped out of the small-town setting of some classic novel.

Mari turned to me and said, "Are you sure about this?"

I answered honestly, "No, I'm not."

But the goat milk was as fresh as could be, delivered from the hands that collected it. I was pleased at my discovery and the authenticity of its source. If only the boys had liked the taste. I couldn't blame them, because even I winced when I drank it, with its odd, grassy flavor.

Another recommendation directed me to Helios Integrated Medicine in Boulder to see Pierre Brunschwig, MD, a holistic pediatrician. In addition to being an MD, Dr. Brunschwig was also a naturopath. I liked the idea of having both a naturopath and a mainstream medical doctor for the boys. On one of my trips to see Dr. Brunschwig, I wandered to a corner of his office building—where the practice sold high-powered supplements, shakes, and bars—and began to browse around. I noticed a Metagenics protein product on the shelves called Ultracare for Kids. I read the label and asked some questions about it. It was a rice protein powder with docosahexaneoic acid (DHA), vitamins, and minerals. I needed something just like it to use as a formula for the boys. However, it specifically stated on the label that it was not nutritionally complete enough to be used as a baby's formula. Why couldn't I just make my own formula?

I began asking around to find acquaintances who knew about nutrition. It was a little intimidating to take on the responsibility of such an important component of the boys' health, but I had a feeling I would help more than I could hurt. I spoke with several people: Pat Frasier, a nurse practitioner from Helios; Dr. Wilson; and Janet Berlin, my good friend and a craniosacral therapist with knowledge of nutrition. I learned about all the nutritional necessities of a baby's healthy development. According to my gathered information, I could use the Ultracare for a base, with its DHA for brain and eye development; adding cashew milk for fat; and almond milk for protein, calcium, and magnesium. I added other vitamins as needed.

I began to stay up late, like a mad scientist, working on my creation. I would spend hours hunched over the workspace I had made on the washing machine in the laundry room. I chose that area because I was afraid that working in the kitchen would be too loud for my sleeping boys. I had a long sheet of paper with all my calculations on it: 32 ounces a day . . . X amount of calories . . . so many ounces of flax oil . . .

After the organic cashews and almonds were boiled, they were more easily liquefied and the jackets could be popped off the almonds. With the addition of filtered water, I blended them to make milk, but it required numerous pushes through the strainer to get a nice, smooth texture. I also added organic brown rice syrup to it in order to provide a complex carbohydrate as well as a sweetener. I used the information from the cans of the regular, store-bought formulas to mirror the ratio of ingredients in my formula. James had to step in and help out with the calculations at times because it was very involved with ounces and calories, and math had never been my forte.

When the concoction was complete, I thought it tasted pretty good. I enlarged the hole of a bottle's nipple so the formula could pass through it. Then I tried it out on the boys. They wouldn't drink it. Not giving in to my discouragement, I strained it a bit more and tried again. This time they sipped on it for a while, but they still didn't love it. What would fix the taste and texture? Maybe cutting back on the protein powder and adding a bit more syrup would do the trick. I tried this variation, ran it through the strainer again, and then gave it to the boys for a third time. I waited with anticipation . . . and they both loved the taste and drank the entire bottle! Hallelujah!

By the next day, the new formula had cleared up the boys' constipation problems, and it wasn't only a temporary fix. Just like clockwork, they had regular bowel movements every day from this change in their main food source. Of all the formulas I had tried, there hadn't been one that resonated with their bodies like it should have. Over the next month, Jack's eczema even went away. Earlier, I had tried cortisone on his skin but his scratchy patches had subsided only temporarily. My homemade formula healed his skin from the inside out, and—along with some Egyptian Magic, an olive oil salve applied directly to his skin—cured his eczema completely. It never returned.

Each night I went down to my lab to mix a batch of formula because it was good for only twenty-four hours at a time. I wanted to make sure the boys had fresh, live food in their bodies every day rather than nutrients from a can. I was able to modify my formula even more by adding powdered green vegetables and antioxidants as well as Body Bio Oil, which has a 4:1 ratio of omega-3, -6, and -9 essential fatty acids.

Me with the boys in the cute but heavy stroller

Rachel and Jamie hanging out enjoying the sun

The formula was working wonders with the boys' health. I had taken on their food allergies and my hard work had paid off. Unfortunately, even though the formula was a solution for their intestinal and skin problems, Jamie's breathing had not improved.

With the progress the boys had made, we decided a little getaway from the cold weather would be the perfect way to celebrate, and I owed my mom a visit anyway. My sister-in-law Rachel, with whom I had become close in the previous couple of years, was spending time with us during the summer and helping me with the babies. She and I planned a visit to my mom's home in Indian Wells, California, near Palm Springs. Afterward, we would travel to Santa Barbara to meet up with James.

Driving off I-10 and toward my mom's house was like approaching an oasis. We left the brown desert behind us, and our surroundings soon became thick walls of bougainvillea, green foliage, snapdragons, and petunias galore. The pungent scent of orange blossoms in the air was delightful. We rolled down our windows so that we could take it all in. The beautiful environment made me feel happy and put a big smile on my face.

Our visit with my mom was refreshing, and she was delighted to spend time with her new grandchildren. I brought a double stroller for the boys, another one of my many impractical purchases. Instead of the sleek, aerodynamic, lightweight strollers most babies travel in, mine was antique-style metal and super heavy. It took a lot of effort to push it, but the main reason I bought it was because it *looked*

Eyes wide open

Happy

good! It made for a more strenuous workout as Rachel and I pushed the boys around the complex on our frequent outdoor jaunts. We also enjoyed being outside at the pool, and taking the boys for their first swim. It was the perfect place, with its warm and dry climate.

I thought the lower elevation would surely help Jamie's breathing. But it didn't improve; instead, it was worsening. His breathing sounded more and more scratchy and labored. Obviously I would have to pursue a solution more aggressively when we got back from our trip.

We traveled on to Santa Barbara, the place where I had grown up. We visited friends and walked on the beach. Carla, our nanny, joined us there, so James and I took the opportunity to go out to nice dinners and spend some time alone, which we hadn't done for a while. It turned out to be an enjoyable and much-needed break.

When we got back home, I scheduled a visit with Dr. Allen. I'd found him during my Denver search, through a recommendation from a friend. Although he was an MD, he used herbs and homeopathics in his practice. He also understood that I was undecided about vaccinating and never pressured me about it. We talked in depth about Jamie's harsh, noisy breathing, which he called stridor. Dr. Allen explained that stridor occurs when there is an obstruction in the air passages. He strongly recommended that Jamie have a commonly used procedure called a bronchoscopy in order to identify the cause of the problem. I hated the idea of another procedure, especially after such a long stay in the NICU. I just wasn't ready to commit to this extreme measure yet.

During a family dinner a short time later, Jamie choked on some mashed potatoes. After we got through the choking, his breathing was noticeably worse and it stayed that way. I kept waiting for it to improve, at least to what it had been before, but it never did. I called Dr. Allen. We decided to go ahead with the bronchoscopy. I got exact details of what would happen in order to educate and prepare myself. I was really dreading it, and was disappointed that we actually had to go through with it.

Being back at the hospital made me extremely nervous. They gave Jamie a heavy sedative and he seemed fine; the only effect was that he got sleepy and relaxed, which was good for him in that situation. (Maybe I needed some, too!) They took him into the surgery room and I couldn't bear to watch, so James went with him. Initially, they had to abort the procedure because his oxygen saturation dropped the first time they went down into his esophagus. They quickly got the level back up again and were able to complete the task. It was quite a scare for James. I was thankful I hadn't gone along because I would not have handled the situation well.

The bronchoscopy revealed that seven-month-old Jamie had "Tracheo/Laryngomalacia with significant acid reflux." This condition was producing swelling in his throat, making it hard for him to breathe and causing the awful sound of stridor, which I was hearing every day.

Jamie began taking a drug called Zantac to combat the acid reflux and swelling of his throat. He took the drug for two weeks but it seemed to me that he was experiencing bad side effects. He often woke up screaming during the night. He cried every time that I gave him the medicine, so I took him off it. I talked to Dr. Allen and he told me to stop for only a little while, until he could get going on the medicine again. But I never went back, hopeful that I could simply find a replacement. Time went by and things got busy during the holiday season. I thought Jamie was doing okay without any medicine, but I was wrong.

CHAPTER

3

The Sickness

Around the boys' one-year birthday at Christmas, all thirty-six members of my husband's family paid a visit to Colorado. More than half the family were sick with colds, and James's dad had bronchitis. I kept the boys hidden in our room because I was afraid that they would catch something. Nobody else seemed concerned about being contagious, which really upset me. Even though we had rented a house next door for most of the family members, my father-in-law stayed with us, and as I feared, the boys also came down with colds.

Jamie and Jack began to cough. Jamie's breathing and stridor worsened. I called Dr. Allen and explained that both boys seemed sick, but Jamie was definitely worse. I felt that something was very off. Dr. Allen told me to bring Jamie down as soon as I could get there so he could evaluate his condition.

Since we were going to Denver, James's parents wanted to tag along. They were hoping to see a bit of the city. Also, James's brother Paul joined us. But my only intention was to get Jamie to the doctor. We loaded up the car and started to head down the mountain. Jack stayed behind with Carla and the rest of the family. As the day wore on, I wasn't certain how sick Jamie was, but I couldn't shake the uneasiness I was feeling.

As we drove around Denver, everyone began to make arguments for why Jamie didn't need to be seen. They worked to convince me that nothing could be done for him anyway because he just had a virus and it would work its way out of his body. My intuition told me differently. I felt so extremely pressured as we drove around, everyone teaming up for the opposition, that I insisted we pull over somewhere so that James and I could get out of the car and talk privately.

James asked, "Why can't we just get home and see how he does tonight?"

"Dr. Allen specifically told me to have Jamie come in so he could be looked at."

"My dad is right. What could they possibly do for him? Come on, he seems fine overall. It's probably just a virus and he'll get over it on his own."

"He's not fine. I can tell there's something going on." I was getting really frustrated.

Pointing through the car window, James said, "Look at him. He's fine."

I turned to look at him right then and he did seem content.

James continued, "They're just going to give him antibiotics again. Why would you want that?"

"But James, we don't know for sure. You're just guessing."

I had run out of arguments. Reluctantly, I gave in to the pressure, and we just didn't show up. If only I had listened to my gut feelings and taken him to the doctor that day, we might never have had to go through the tragic days that followed.

Two hours after going to bed, Jamie woke up, agitated and fussy. I took him out of his crib and into the living room. I laid him on my chest, where he fell asleep. He slept for a few minutes and then woke up with a gasp. I comforted him and he fell back to sleep again, repeating the same abrupt awakening. I tried giving him the oxygen I still had from the hospital, but he wouldn't have anything to do with it. About every fifteen minutes, he drifted off, only to wake right up again. I couldn't quite pinpoint what was wrong. It turned into the most sleepless night we'd had yet. I was bitterly angry that he was suffering when he could have been treated earlier in the day. I was up with him, dealing with the stress, when everyone else who had talked me out of taking him to the doctor continued to sleep. I was seething.

First thing in the morning, I called Dr. Allen's office. After explaining the night's events, he reprimanded me for not bringing him in the day before. I began to cry and handed the phone over to James so he could deal with it. I thought that he should take responsibility for the decision. He listened to Dr. Allen and then apologized. After he put the phone down, we hurried to get Jamie into the car.

When we got to the office in Denver, Dr. Allen took one look at Jamie's throat and told us to go to the hospital immediately. They checked us in at once. Our room had a bed and a crib in it. Right away they started Jamie on a nebulizer, a machine that dispenses medicine through a mist so it can be inhaled. The idea was to do this every three or four hours to keep the swelling in his throat down, but something about the air blowing in his face made him afraid and hysterical. He flailed his arms around, swung his body back and forth, and tried to swat the mouthpiece away. They had to call in a few extra nurses to help hold him down as they worked. James had to help while I left the room. This was a choice we made together, knowing that Jamie would still trust me if he saw that I wasn't involved. I peeked around the corner, though it was difficult to watch my son being restrained by so many people. I was horrified at the sight, even though I knew that the restraint was necessary. Once the treatment kicked in, he calmed down.

Since Jamie appeared to be stabilized, we decided it was a good time for James to go back home to Summit County quickly to get Jack and Carla. He turned right around once he got them and came back down the mountain. He got a hotel room in Denver near the hospital, so they could be close and get some sleep. It wasn't long before Jamie needed another dose of medicine, and the time between each dose became shorter and shorter. After each treatment, Jamie would be calm and eventually fall asleep in my arms. I would lay him down in the crib carefully, trying not to wake him, but after about thirty seconds, he would begin to scream, which would make his breathing worse. I would pick him up again and again because the only place he would stay calm was in my arms. I held him for hours. Finally, at about four in the morning, I was so terribly exhausted that I called James for help.

"James, I need you to come to the hospital. I haven't slept at all and this is the second night in a row. Jamie won't let me put him down, and he can't stay calm for more than five minutes."

"Are you serious? Why? What's going on?"

"I don't know. I think the medicine is losing its effectiveness. Jamie just keeps waking up in a panic."

"I can't believe it. I can't believe he isn't getting better. I'll come as soon as I can."

When James got there, he took Jamie from my arms. I lay down on the hospital bed for what seemed like five minutes but turned out to be an hour. I went into a light dream state that wasn't a deep sleep, but was still refreshing. James had to wake me up because Jamie kept crying for me.

At about six in the morning, James returned to the hotel to be with Jack. I continued to hold Jamie until the sunlight shone strongly through the windows. Jamie woke up, and his condition seemed to be even worse. The doctors decided to transfer him to Presbyterian/St. Luke's Medical Center, another hospital with a Pediatric Intensive Care Unit (PICU), considered to be better prepared for his necessary treatment. This was the hospital where the boys had been born, and I had every confidence in it.

I held Jamie close, my heart pounding, as we traveled in the ambulance. When we arrived at the hospital, they flung open the heavy back door, and in an instant, ten people surrounded us, ready and waiting to tend to my son. His stridor was so heavy that they wanted to intubate him right then and there. I tried to convince the pediatric intensivist that we had been through this for the past twenty-four hours and if they could only give him the medicine in the nebulizer. I begged them just to try it, and they gave in to my plea.

Over the next three days, I rarely put Jamie down. My muscles were tight, my arms stuck in 90-degree angles from holding him for hours, but I was willing to do anything to help or comfort him. I understood his desire to be held, as he was suffocating and panicked, desperately needing to be soothed. For three of the most physically challenging days of Jamie's and my life, I held on through each grueling hour that passed.

My mother was with me during this ordeal, which brought me some comfort. She had arrived at the hospital during the first couple of days; she had been on her way moments after I called to share what was happening. I had already grown to count on this kind of support from her whenever I needed her, and she never disappointed me.

Once again, the nurses requested that someone become "the bad guy" who would help the medical staff administer Jamie's treatment.

I immediately said, "James, I need to be the one to hold Jamie. He cries every time anyone else tries to hold him, so you'll have to be the one who takes on this role."

He hesitated, but knew he had no choice. "Okay. I'll do whatever I have to."

When it was time for the treatment, with the help of two nurses James was able to hold Jamie still so he could receive the medicine. He put my son in my arms immediately afterward. He was calm again, thank goodness. I could rest my weary mind for just a while longer. After about an hour or so, I asked James if he could hold Jamie so I could take a quick shower. I used the bathroom in Jamie's room because I didn't want to go far. When I was in the shower, James lay Jamie down on the bed very carefully so as not to wake him. As I came out of the bathroom I saw him lying there, and I snuggled next to him in the bed so I could rest my body. Jamie was content for only a few minutes and then got fussy. As drugged up as he was, he still knew my smell and touch, and needed me to hold him. James had to leave to check on Jack and also to check in at work. He was planning on returning later that night.

That evening, on our fourth day in the hospital, James came back from work at around two in the morning. He could see that I was completely exhausted, and he insisted that I get some sleep while he held Jamie. I was so, so tired. I agreed, on the condition that he wake me in no later than one hour—or sooner, if anything changed. He promised he would. I went upstairs to a vacant hospital room to sleep.

A short time later, Jamie's condition worsened. As James held him, Jamie stopped breathing and became limp in his arms. The medical staff had to be called to resuscitate him and the room quickly filled with intensivists. Jamie's throat had become so swollen that he couldn't even be intubated. The doctor explained afterward that his throat was so obstructed that a newborn tube had to be used because it was the smallest size they had. It was astounding that Jamie held on for that long and made it through. That early morning in December, Jamie really showed his strength and will to live.

At about six in the morning, James came into the room where I was sleeping. I woke up and my heart dropped in an instant. I looked at the clock: three hours had passed. I felt sick to my stomach. James looked like he was in shock. A hundred thoughts flashed through my mind. Had Jamie died? Why else would he have left his side? He had promised not to leave him. Why had he left me sleeping for so long?

James was broken down and distraught. He told me the entire story, and I fell to pieces as he relived the fear along with me. My heart sank and I shook, giving way to heavy sobs. It took a while before I could absorb the news that he was breathing better with the help of a ventilator. I was incredibly relieved to know Jamie was alive, and I pulled myself back together. James and I held each other tightly, and then we went to see.

We learned that they had added sedatives and other medications to the steroids and antibiotics he was already taking. He had IVs coming out of his wrists and feet. His arms were tied down to keep him from pulling at the tube. It was excruciating for me to see my one-year-old on the ventilator, and I was overcome with feelings of helplessness. On the other hand, I was relieved in a way, not knowing how much longer I could have held him, and certain at least that he was relaxed and comfortable.

The nurse came in and told me that James's mother, Marian, was on the phone. She was calling to check on us because they had left as scheduled, right before Jamie was admitted to the hospital. She was totally unaware of Jamie's condition and the fact that he had had to be hospitalized.

I couldn't believe that James hadn't called her to tell her about the situation. When I hung up, I was furious with him. Through Jamie's sickness, I had already begun to resent James and his parents for not only bringing an illness into the house but also making light of Jamie's need to be treated. I shouldn't have blamed James for his father's nonchalant attitude around the boys, which I'm sure came from the experience of raising ten kids, but I couldn't control my anger over what Jamie was going through.

The appearance of Jamie's small body quickly changed. A couple of days after being on the machine, he became swollen from head to toe. Even his eyes bulged from the drugs he was on.

I asked the doctor, "What's happening to him?"

"That's what happens when you're on a ventilator for that long while lying down," he answered. "We're going to give him medicine for it, though."

After Jamie received the new medicine, his appearance improved. But he was so drugged that his eyes became heavy and he hardly ever opened them. I was very aware that yet another medication was being put into his small body. All the drugs were obviously helping to keep him alive, but I thought about what possible side effects might come later. He was being treated for so many things at once. He was given antibiotics for his bacterial infection and antivirus medication for any viruses. Intravenous steroids had been added to the mix to bring down the inflammation in his throat and help open his airway. The effort it must have taken for such a little body to process so many substances! The hospital was constantly taking his blood to try to figure out what they needed to do next.

After five days on the ventilator, Jamie's throat was not cooperating. It was still not opening up. The doctors decided that exploratory surgery was necessary to reveal if Jamie needed a cricoid split (the cutting of the bones in the throat to help air pass through more easily), a cyst removed, or both. I was bombarded with one piece of serious news after another.

The time I spent in the hospital was very spiritual for me. I was deeply affected by Jamie's illness, but I was also aware of the other sick children around us. There was one boy, about Jamie's age, who was in the room next to us. His name was Brian and he was so, so cute. As I walked by his room, our eyes would meet and he would smile my way. Each time I passed, I made a point to look in his direction, because for a brief moment, seeing his shining face really touched me. Sadly, his condition was extremely serious and he had been chronically ill, in and out of the hospital, most of his young life. He was also hooked up to numerous machines and several IVs. He was rarely alone. Usually, he was accompanied by at least one family member. As sick as he was, he was a bright spot on our floor.

The day before Jamie's scheduled surgery, there was a dark cloud hanging over the PICU. I asked the nurse what was going on, but she was vague and didn't really tell me anything. There was such a detectable sadness in the hospital and I really wanted to understand why. I saw a group of doctors gathered in Brian's room and after they left one of the nurses finally told me that he was in the hospital for the last time; his condition had worsened and he would not recover this time. The machines were keeping him alive. It had been decided that it was time to turn them off so his suffering could end.

Understanding this situation was extremely painful. I didn't want to accept that the boy with the sweet smile was dying. I tried to tell myself that maybe deep down he had known what was coming all along and that he had already made his peace with it. Various family members filed through the hospital halls to say their good-byes to him. Watching it wounded me to the heart. The reality of losing a child was right in front of me. I related so completely to the impending loss that I took on this family's pain as my own. My grief was so deep that simply breathing in and out became a chore. I was having a breakdown and I couldn't get myself under control.

In the hallway there was a phone next to the nurses' station. I had slipped into a mindless daze, but somehow managed to work my way to it. I dialed the number of my friend Janet. When she picked up, I desperately blurted out my need for help.

She advised me, "Krista, you need to remove yourself from the situation right away. You cannot take on this loss right now. Go into Jamie's room, close the door, and pull the curtains. Put all your energy into Jamie. Get on your knees and pray, pray for light. Focus on bringing light to Jamie. Touch him and visualize it."

I knew she was right, so I did exactly as she said. Instead of praying every couple of hours as she had advised, I did it constantly and with every ounce of faith I had. I did this for hours and, little by little, I found more and more peace. My insides were still weak, but I was redirecting my energies in a more positive way.

That evening, I found the courage to venture out of Jamie's room. I walked by Brian's room and he was lying there by himself. There were no cords, no wires, no machines. It was obvious that he had passed away; his spirit was gone and his little body was like an empty house. Seeing him was torturous and it even made me a little angry. I asked a nurse why he had been left in the room all alone. She said he would be taken out in just a few moments. I couldn't stand the thought of him like that. The sadness was crushing, and I felt raw, grounded in the awful reality of a small child's death.

Sometimes it is hard to accept our lack of control in life. And at these moments, when we are forced to carry on whether we like it or not, life seems unfair. After this torrential chain of traumatic events, I had to find a way to prepare myself for Jamie's surgery the next day.

I remembered an article I had read called "The Power of Prayer"; it had depicted amazing stories of recovery and healing. It discussed how powerful prayer can be, especially when large groups pray for an individual. I decided I was going to call everyone I knew to tell them to pray at 6 P.M., when Jamie's surgery was scheduled.

With the help of James's mom, who I knew felt awful about everything that had happened, I called James's relatives, all of whom have a strong faith in God. Then I called my family members, who have diverse spiritual beliefs. I knew that each person, in his or her own way, would send Jamie what he needed. I was committed to doing anything that might benefit Jamie. Everyone I spoke to was completely supportive and eager to put him in their thoughts, each in his or her own way. I was overwhelmed with gratitude.

I returned to Jamie's room and I continued to focus on bringing the light to him. I did this every fifteen minutes for the next couple of hours. This action made me feel that strength was replacing my fear and the dark cloud was moving away.

As they wheeled him into surgery, James and I walked next to him as far as we were permitted to go. I spoke with the surgeon right before they took Jamie in and asked if there were any other possibilities besides the cricoid split and the cyst removal. I was extremely worried because if Jamie needed that surgical procedure, he wouldn't be able to move at all and would be drugged and on a ventilator for another seven to ten days. The surgeon couldn't tell me for sure. Then I asked him if everything was going to be okay, hoping for one little morsel of optimism to cling to.

He responded in a cocky tone, "I haven't lost one yet."

That wasn't exactly what I had been looking for, but his confidence was slightly comforting. As we walked alongside Jamie toward the heavy surgery doors, I held his hand tightly. I felt my breathing become faster and faster, and I started to sweat as I looked ahead and read what was on the doors in big red letters: "STOP: NO ENTRY." Just as they were taking Jamie away, he opened his eyes and looked at me with a little bit of coherency. Trying to hold myself together, I gave him a kiss, and told him I loved him. My hands slipped away from his as they wheeled him through the doors. We stood there for a moment as the doors closed in front of us, making sure this wasn't a dream, that this was actually happening. Maybe they would turn around and bring him back out.

There was silence.

James and I knew it would be at least two hours before we would know anything, so we went to the hospital basement, where they had given us rooms to rest. We walked the underground halls, hand in hand, and talked about the boys and how great they were and how thankful we were to have them in our lives.

We stopped for a while in the waiting room. There we met the parents of a newborn girl who was, at that moment, undergoing open-heart surgery. They talked to us about their situation and listened compassionately to our story. It was encouraging to talk to them, because they had an unbelievably positive outlook. They truly believed their baby was going to be okay, recognizing that she had already proven herself to be a resilient child. It comforted us to recognize that Jamie had done the same. We clung to their energy and the room lost its heaviness as the four of us passed through time and worry with conversation.

Eventually, the surgeons emerged from the operating room, lighthearted and smiling. They were much different coming out than they had been going in. We were uneasy and concerned.

We hurried over and asked, "How is Jamie?"

They looked at one another and then at us. One of the surgeons turned to me with a smile and said, "Well, you won't believe this. We began the surgery after checking for airflow

Recovering from the hospital

In deep thought with James

through the stethoscope, but there hadn't been a change from our previous checks. We continued with the extubation, and noticed that his throat was very red, rough, and irritated, but yet, through these steps, his throat somehow opened up."

I said, "I don't understand. After two hours of this procedure, there was nothing else going on in his throat? His throat just opened on its own?"

"Well . . . yeah."

We were equally surprised and my heart was so full, I couldn't hold back the tears. They told us it was okay to see him, so we rushed to his room. From the doorway, we saw him lying there. He was receiving a small amount of oxygen through a nasal cannula, but he looked content. His oxygen saturation level was over 90 percent and he was sleeping peacefully. It was an incredible moment and a beautiful sight for our tired eyes. The doctors had said there was no medical explanation for the change. He was simply their "miracle child" of the year. As for what had really happened . . . there wasn't doubt in my mind.

CHAPTER

4

A Difficult Year

After Jamie's ten-day stay in the ICU, we couldn't return home right away. I felt we should be closer to the hospital in case he required more medical attention, and also because we knew the high altitude could further tax his sensitive condition. Jack and Carla were still at the extended-stay hotel near the hospital. We joined them there for the next three or four days, until we knew that Jack and Jamie were well enough and we could head back home.

Although Jamie was getting better, Jack was still really sick. His eyes were completely bloodshot, redder than I had ever seen anyone's eyes. I felt as if I had abandoned him while Jamie was in the hospital, even though James, Carla, or my mom had been constantly by his side. I hadn't recognized how sick Jack had gotten. I felt guilty for not focusing on him earlier, but I had been completely overwhelmed with fear for Jamie's life and the fear had taken over all my thoughts. When we got back to the hotel, I called the doctor who had treated Jamie and she didn't hesitate to give me a prescription for

Jack starting to recover from his sickness. Not so happy with his painfully red eyes

antibiotics over the phone for Jack. I was surprised that she was willing to prescribe the medicine that quickly, without seeing him first, but he was so sick that I was just glad to have it. After the length of the illness, I knew he needed antibiotics. Three or four days later, I saw that he was on his way to getting well. This was a good example of how effective antibiotics can be, especially when they are used at the right time for the right illness.

Upon Jamie's release, he was prescribed handfuls of medications. After ten days of having his system filled with anesthesia, antibiotics, steroids, and more, the plan was to continue him on antibiotics, along with some methadone and Ativan for the short term. I laid all the bottles out on the counter and it was a bit overwhelming. The bottle of methadone prompted me to call the doctor again for clarification.

He explained, "Jamie has been given methadone in order to wean him off the other medications he has been taking."

I was shocked. "*Wean him off?* Are you serious?"

I knew his system had been loaded up, but I hadn't realized that ten days was enough to cause addiction in a one-year-old. I was astonished that Jamie had developed a dependency on drugs.

My concern added to the anxiety that already consumed me, draining every bit of energy left in my body. During Jamie's hospital stay, I had been so wound up and emotionally distracted that I managed to eat only a very little bit. Somehow I had sustained myself with black coffee and vitamin C tablets. Now, even though we weren't in the hospital every day, I didn't feel well and I still had no appetite. I had barely slept the entire time that Jamie was in intensive care. I had thought that I might catch up afterward. But now Jamie wasn't sleeping well; he slept in only thirty-minute intervals. That meant I was sleeping for only thirty minutes at a time, too. Just when I would finally settle my nerves from the previous awakening and get to a point where I could drift off, he would wake up again. After a while I couldn't even rest, because I knew that his next wake-up scream would be coming shortly.

It occurred to me that Einstein had rarely slept through the night and yet his brain still operated at maximum efficiency. It may have worked for Einstein, but the opposite was true for me. I was like the walking dead. But as torturous as it was for me, I knew that Jamie was suffering even more. Luckily, my adrenaline kept kicking in, enabling me to function, and allowing me to rush to his side each time he needed me. I would do whatever I could to try to comfort him—rubbing his back, stroking his hair, or holding him, just so he knew that I was there. Knowing how he needed me, I just kept hanging on, waiting for the reprieve when we both could sleep soundly through the night.

I had given Jamie the methadone only a couple of times to start the weaning process. This particular medicine caused a reaction that completely shook me up. He literally began to try to climb the walls, attempting to dig his fingers into the paint as he tried to pull himself up off his bed. The whole time he would smile and laugh because he was so high. My one-year-old really was a drug addict! Was this from the methadone, I wondered? He hadn't acted like this before I gave it to him. He had definitely gotten worse. I couldn't bear it. I put my brain to work and searched out some alternatives. I knew more natural methods existed; I just had to find them.

My quest for healthier living, even prior to Jamie's health problems, had always led me to the health food store. I went back there and talked to Willow, a young woman who was knowledgeable about whole foods and herbal supplements. I told her about Jamie's current issues and she reminded me about valerian root. I had used this herb before as a mild sedative, so I went home to research valerian's possible side effects when used with children. I found out that there was a dose considered safe for children and after getting the okay from Dr. Wilson, our naturopathic doctor from Boulder, the only thing left to do was to make the decision. My options were to either watch him go mad with the methadone or try a mild herb with a strong effect. I decided to go with the herb.

It was always scary making choices where the boys' health was concerned, but I was starting to get used to owning the responsibility. At times, I felt like I was the doctor "practicing medicine." I hoped that my "practice" would be closer to success than to failure.

I started Jamie on a small dose of valerian root, and it didn't have any negative effect on him. I increased the dosage and noticed that, in the following day or two, he became more relaxed and calm. His crazy behavior lessened considerably and the rapid improvement really eased my mind. I felt better knowing that he felt better. I was grateful we were able to catch up on a few hours of some much-needed sleep.

On top of the other medications we had left the hospital with, Jamie had prescriptions for Prilosec and Propulsid for ongoing use. Jamie was supposed to remain on these for up to a year to help his moderate reflux. The Prilosec would decrease the amount of acid produced in his stomach, and it was also used to treat ulcers, gastroesophageal reflux disease (GERD, commonly referred to as heartburn), and other conditions involving excessive stomach acid production. The other medication—Propulsid—would increase the rate at which his esophagus, stomach, and intestines moved during digestion, and the rate at which his stomach's contents emptied into his intestines.

Jamie's reflux caused acid to come up into his esophagus and throat, which caused his throat to swell. This, in combination with his Tracheo/Laryngomalacia, half-closed his throat. His trachea and larynx were considered "floppy," and they were not the shape they should have been.

To me, it just didn't seem healthy to rush the food through the stomach. However, the doctors reassured me that the medications were safe, and I was desperately afraid of going through another episode at the hospital so I did as I was told, administering each and every dose to make sure he got it all. The liquid drugs for Jamie's reflux tasted as sweet as candy to him at first, and he took them easily and happily. His condition improved, but he just wasn't the same boy he had been before. His behavior had definitely changed; the talkative little boy who had been developing at a quicker-than-average pace now seemed occasionally distant and distracted.

Shortly after our return to Summit County, the owner of our leased home told us that his marriage was ending and he needed the house for himself. As much as we pleaded the case for our two recovering children, he was unable to help, giving us only two weeks to find a new place to live. The ultimatum brought us to the conclusion that Denver would be a better place for us anyway because of the lower altitude, warmer weather, and sunnier skies. I started to look for a new home in the city.

In the interim, I found a new condo where we moved for a month or so. Our friends helped us pack up and move when our two weeks were up, which eased a little of the stress. However, even with our trauma behind us, my unsettled nerves refused to calm. A feeling that all was not well hovered over me.

We had been planning to travel to Tucson for a business meeting and decided to go ahead with the trip, hoping it would lighten our mood. Since we were headed west anyway, I decided to visit California, knowing that I could find solace in the familiarity of home. We packed up the family and headed southwest to decompress.

After our short stop in Arizona, we spent the next couple of weeks in California. The ocean was peaceful and the moist air helped the physical state of the boys, who both kept healthy for the entire trip. While staying in a cottage in

Montecito, James and I continued to work with Jamie on his walking skills, which had really regressed since his hospitalization. James would stand on one side and I would stand on the other as we steadied him on his feet. He struggled to keep the momentum of putting one foot in front of the other. The practice turned into a daily family event and was a wonderful excuse to play in the green grass, enjoying the shade of the mature trees. Jamie's walking ability improved.

The relaxation of our trip didn't tide us over for long, though, because upon our return to Colorado, both Jamie and Jack came down with high fevers. This sent me once again into panic mode, anxious to learn what this illness might mean for the boys. Fortunately, it was only the roseola virus, which, after causing a red rash, ran its course and was quickly gone. But they continued waking up throughout the night, and my fatigue drove me closer and closer to the edge. In the middle of one particular night, after being woken up yet one more time, I had a complete meltdown. I started screaming frantically with uncontrollable agitation and worry. I was sure that I couldn't take any more.

Carla came out of her room when she heard me. She offered to take Jamie and stay with him so I could go back to sleep. Even in my irrational state I didn't feel right about letting someone else handle him; I declined her offer. She tried to convince me that she was not at all inconvenienced, because she didn't sleep much anyway, but I just couldn't do it. Then James stepped in, demanding that I let Carla take care of Jamie. He insisted that I get some sleep because my condition was not helping anyone. He grabbed Jamie and handed him to Carla, and the door closed silently behind them. The peace and quiet brought sleep to everyone in the house.

This change started a new wave for me because Carla would often take over the night shift and allow me to sleep. I was tremendously appreciative. My body must have been shocked at getting to sleep through the night, because instead of feeling better, I felt worse. At times, I felt like concrete was curing in my veins. The months without sleep had caught up with me.

Regardless of how I felt, I had to get motivated to search for our new home. I found a house in Evergreen on an amazing piece of mountain property. This area, only twenty minutes from Denver, seemed like a good compromise between the mountains and the city. I told the owner I wanted it, but when I called to make lease arrangements, he informed me that someone had beaten me to it. I was terribly disappointed! We had set our sights on living there, and I dreaded starting my search all over again. Shortly after we lost the mountain house, I stumbled onto a brand new home being built in a golf course community in a pleasant Lakewood neighborhood. It wasn't finished yet, but upon completion, it would be a beautiful home. We decided to buy it. From then on, I spent a lot of time driving down to the city to pick out carpet and other furnishings. That was a fun and enjoyable distraction for me. At that point, I would take all the little happy moments I could get.

When the house was ready, we moved as soon as we were able. Living in Denver was a welcome surprise. The weather was better and the temperature much warmer. In the mountains, the boys had always stood banging against the window of our condo, pleading with their body language to go outside. But even after bundling them up in the warmest clothes, I rarely felt like it was a good choice to allow them out in the cold, wet mountain weather when I was working so hard to keep them healthy. As it turned out, had we gotten the home in Evergreen, the climate there wouldn't have been any different than Summit County's. It felt good to know that things had turned out for the better. With that outlook and springtime in the air, I felt more optimistic. In the new neighborhood, the boys could play outdoors all the time. To the twins, the grassy backyard and shiny new swing set were Disneyland.

Four months went by as Jamie continued to take his medications faithfully. Then one day, without warning, he absolutely refused to take any more. It was as difficult as trying to force-feed him cod liver oil, because he was completely resistant. I called the doctors and explained his determination, but they reminded me of the terrible consequences he might face without the drugs and so, again, fear motivated me to continue forcing the medicine down. Then another troubling change occurred—his hair started falling out in clumps.

I called the pulmonary doctor with whom we had been working. He assured me the hair loss had not been caused by any of the drugs he was taking, and as for the change in my son's personality, he couldn't explain it. I also called our gastroenterologist, and he, too, assured me that the hair loss had nothing to do with the drugs. I let it go for about a week as the clumps of fine, blond hair continued to appear around our house, day after day, until Jamie barely had any hair left at all.

Frustrated, I called both doctors again and explained, "I have twin boys. They eat the same food, live in the same environment, and breathe the same air. The only thing different is that Jamie is on Prilosec, Propulsid, and antibiotics and his hair is almost gone."

They still insisted that the hair loss couldn't be from the drugs. They pressured me again to continue giving him the medications, even with the possible side effects.

I called Dr. Wilson and told him the situation. He looked up both Prilosec and Propulsid in the *Physician's Desk Reference (PDR)*. The information about Prilosec jumped out at him. He called me back the same day, eager to read to me what it said: Prilosec "could cause hair loss in adults." I was enraged. These doctors who were supposed to be the best in their fields hadn't even looked up the drug in the *PDR*!

Dr. Wilson, Dr. Allen, and I discussed taking Jamie off the drugs immediately. We talked about the *PDR* warning and how Jamie was no longer cooperative. I felt that he was trying to tell us he didn't need the drugs anymore and that we should stop them right away. The doctors agreed.

I called the gastroenterologist and told him what I'd learned from the *PDR*. I didn't even try to hide the fact that I was livid and much of my anger was directed toward him. He had me bring Jamie in right away for a twenty-four-hour pH probe to see if he still had reflux. I shuddered at the word "probe," and while driving to the office I thought about Jamie getting a tube inserted into his nose and down his throat. I couldn't grasp how terrible it was going to be for him. But at the same time, I told myself, *We have to do this. It is going to move us forward*. I could almost feel a new layer forming on my coat of armor. I was getting tougher on the outside and more determined, because I had to in order to survive.

We arrived in record time at the gastroenterologist's office. I was still so angry I could barely speak to any of the office employees. It wasn't directly their fault that Jamie had to endure this, and I didn't want to blame them for the doctor's oversight, but I was really struggling with my emotions.

They took Jamie in immediately. The doctor was shamelessly nice, but never took any responsibility for not checking the *PDR* or continually ignoring my concerns. He began the procedure, managing to insert the tube into Jamie's belly without any anesthesia or any drama. Sadly, instead of being content that Jamie didn't resist the procedure, I saw it as another sign of the drastic changes he was displaying. He was increasingly passive and increasingly detached from a surprising number of things, both socially and emotionally. It was heartbreaking to recognize that his personality had changed so much since he had been hospitalized.

After twenty-four hours of walking around and sleeping with a computer and wires attached to his body, Jamie's test was complete. The results wouldn't be ready for a couple of days. It was during an appointment with Dr. Wilson in Boulder that I got the call with the results. I stepped outside so I could give the call my complete attention. Jamie's pH was perfect. He didn't need the medication anymore. I hung up the phone and yelled out loud. I couldn't wait to call James with the news. I took the boys outside and kissed their faces over and over again. "You were right, Jamie. You were right!"

Before hair loss

I felt redeemed in questioning all the doctors until a solution was found. The process had given me a completely new perspective. I regretted not listening more seriously to Jamie as he tried to communicate his body's needs to us. Also, I was upset that the medicine, once no longer necessary, had continued to cause side effects and further weaken his system.

A couple of days later, on a Saturday afternoon, the gastroenterologist called me on my cell phone. He seemed excited to tell me that Jamie was going to be famous. His side effect was going to be included on the warning label for Prilosec as "may cause hair loss in children." Needless to say, I didn't share his enthusiasm.

On December 31, 1999, the United States Food and Drug Administration (FDA) announced that the use of cisapride, or Propulsid, had been associated with 341 reports

Jamie after sudden hair loss

Jack helping Jamie pose to get a picture of his thinning hair

Jamie starts to get more distant.

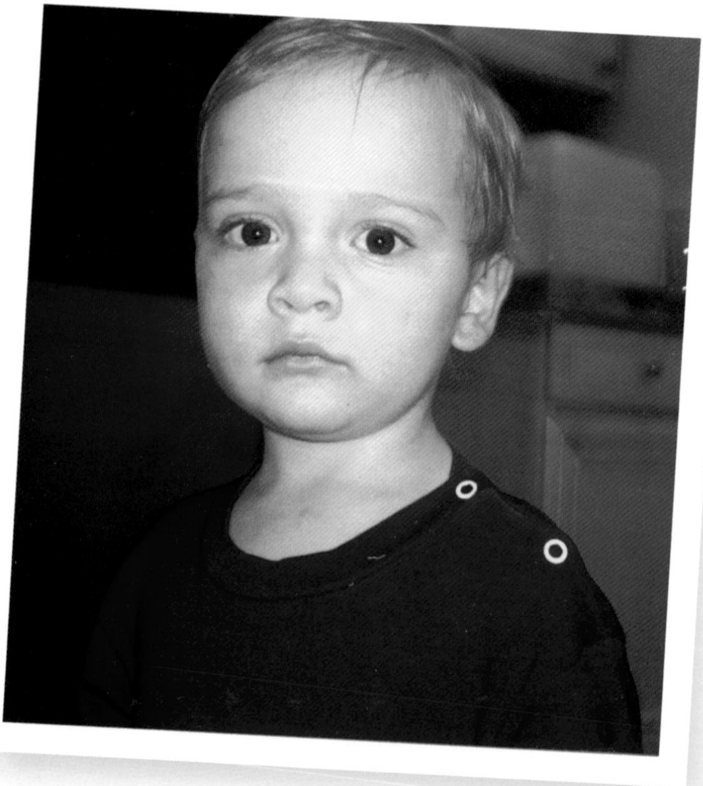

of heart rhythm abnormalities and 80 deaths. The drug was taken off the shelves not long after Jamie stopped taking it.

In a few months, Jamie's hair returned to normal but Jamie didn't. I kept waiting—waiting and watching for signs of the boy I knew—but he never surfaced. I tried repeatedly to get answers about his changed behavior, something to explain the cavernous distance between us, but I was told he was probably still recovering from his illness. In time, he would be back to his old self.

My subsequent goal became very simple: Return our lives to "normal." I just wanted to get back to raising healthy and happy boys, and to put these misfortunes behind us. What I learned instead was never to ask, "Can things get any worse?" because I wouldn't like the answer.

CHAPTER

5

Jamie Disappears

Joy and happiness completely eluded Jamie. At night the walls of our house rattled with the sounds of his crying. During the day, he was like a whirlwind that never stopped.

Before being hospitalized, Jamie had seemed surprisingly strong and was developing quickly for his age. At only seven months, he could pull himself up to a standing position and had already learned to crawl. James and I were shocked that he was getting ready to walk so early. We had a lot of fun fantasizing about what a talented athlete he would be, faking arguments about whether he would be a Super Bowl quarterback or the next champion of the U.S. Open.

Jack hadn't started to crawl yet. We would prop him up on all fours, prompting him by planting his arms in front of him, one step at a time, so his legs would follow. He would rock back and forth, trying to steady himself, his head hanging straight down between his arms. With a slight raise of his head, he could lift his eyes just enough to look forward. It was so cute; we would crack up over it. We noticed the difference

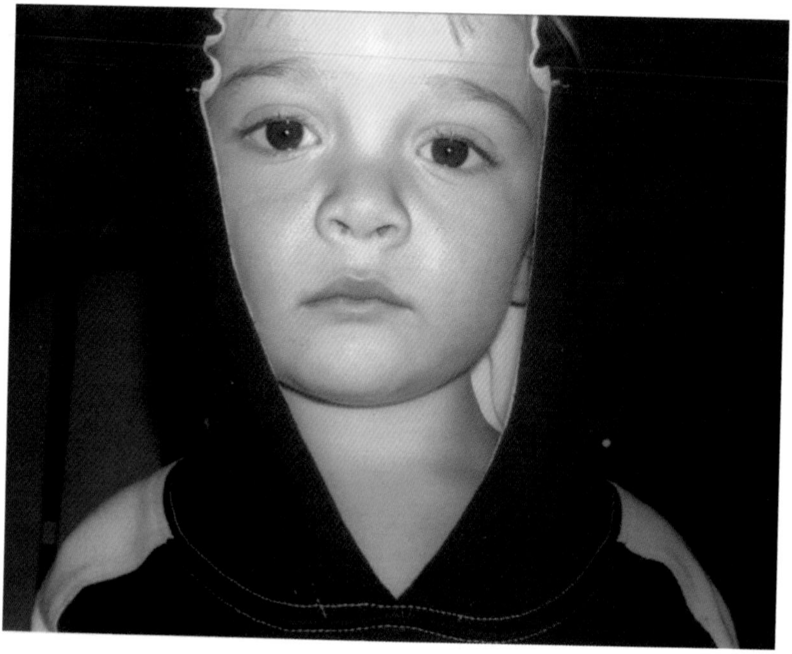

between Jamie's and Jack's development, and wondered what you did with twins when one was developing at a slower pace than the other.

Yet, ironically, at sixteen months, Jamie began to show signs of *decreased* coordination. His personality and behavior continued to change after the hospitalization. Also, over time, he lost all of his words.

September is always a beautiful time of year. That was when I decided to drive to Santa Barbara with the boys for a friend's wedding. James was planning to fly out and meet us there. I took a lot of opportunities to travel because I enjoyed getting away, and I loved taking the boys with me. We would often hop in the car on a whim for a road trip. For the boys' entertainment, I relied on small TVs with built-in video players. All I had to do was pop *Aladdin* in the VCR, and they would be happy for miles.

We made a quick stop in Las Vegas to visit James's parents overnight before hitting the last leg of the drive to California. At about ten o'clock that evening, Jamie started up with a croupy-sounding cough. His breathing was just bad enough to cause me worry and to elevate my stress level; it was so reminiscent of the problems he'd had only months earlier during our lengthy hospital stay. I decided that this time I would get on it right away, before it got worse, and take him to the hospital immediately. My mother-in-law came along for support and to show us the way to the hospital.

I was surprised at how dark and eerie the building was. This mood was only emphasized when we encountered the night shift. Most of the staff could have doubled as extras in *Night of the Living Dead*. With pale skin and dark circles under their eyes, they moved sluggishly around the halls. Their personalities fit their appearances; they lacked warmth and seemed emotionally absent. I wouldn't have given this too much importance if I'd felt Jamie got the attention he needed, but everyone wandered around, directionless, while we sat waiting for help for what seemed like an eternity.

Finally, they called Jamie's name and led us into another room, where we waited even longer for a doctor to come in. A pulmonary assistant entered, and after barely acknowledging our presence, began giving Jamie a breathing treatment. I asked what he was administering and the assistant told me it was Albuterol for his lungs. I hadn't heard the name before, but I knew it definitely wasn't anything he had been given in the past. Almost instantly, Jamie's breathing became about 50 percent worse. He was wheezing intensely and gasping for air.

I started to panic. "What did you give him? He's having an allergic reaction! Oh, my God! Where's the doctor? We need the doctor right now!"

"He's upstairs visiting patients."

I couldn't believe it. "What? The emergency room doctor is upstairs? We need him . . . *right now*."

A nurse went to call for him and in moments he was in our room. After quickly looking Jamie over, he said, "He needs to be intubated."

I thought, *Oh no, you don't!* I was completely panicked. Jamie had been in better condition when we brought him in. In my opinion, the Albuterol had seemed to worsen his condition. He'd had only mild croupy symptoms, and now the doctor wanted to stick an oxygen tube down his throat after looking at him for sixty seconds. He hadn't even asked any questions about his medical history.

I decided to speak up. "Maybe you should give him racemic epinephrine." This medicine was a powerful steroid. "I know that it opens up the throat and takes down any inflammation in it very quickly. His earlier breathing episode was caused by problems with his throat closing up. There hasn't been a problem with his lungs before, so I don't understand why you're giving him Albuterol." The doctor was irritated that I had questioned his medical assessment. He spoke sharply, arguing that intubation would help Jamie breathe, regardless of his history, but obviously I was not convinced. I had been through this once before, and I felt that his decision was rash. I made a frantic call to Dr. Allen. He recommended we find a pediatric hospital where doctors would be more familiar with how to handle Jamie's condition. I realized maybe this ER doctor wasn't experienced enough with children and especially not with this kind of health issue. Jamie was still struggling to breathe and I was losing my patience. I asked one more time for the racemic epi.

After a couple of annoyed sighs, the doctor surrendered to my demands. Within seconds, Jamie was breathing much more smoothly. My breathing mirrored his, coming more easily as I saw his struggle ease. I welcomed the end of the battle, and felt myself calm down as the minutes passed. My mother-in-law was astonished at what she had witnessed: Jamie's breathing attack and the fight with the doctor. There was obvious tension between the doctor and me, and I was thinking I could not get us out of there soon enough.

"Is there a children's hospital around here?" I asked him curtly. "I want to be transferred to it right now. I think he needs attention from a pediatric intensivist."

I knew that the ER doctor wasn't happy about my request, but he made arrangements for us to be transferred by ambulance.

On the way out the door, I couldn't keep myself from remarking angrily, "He needs to be intubated, huh?" Wow, had that just come out of my mouth? It hit me how much better I had become at speaking up for what we needed. I had come a long way from the girl who was too shy to talk.

We arrived at Sunrise Children's Hospital after a twenty-minute ride. The paramedics wheeled Jamie inside, and we were taken straight to a room. He would need to be watched for six to eight hours after receiving the racemic epi. Two doctors and an assistant entered the room immediately. The difference between the two hospitals was like the difference between daylight and total darkness. This staff had already been thoroughly briefed on Jamie's situation. The doctor explained to me, in detail, that when children like Jamie have a history of croupy breathing, the most important thing to do is to keep them calm, because the more they cry, the more upset they become, and the more the problem is exacerbated. She also told me that he shouldn't ever receive Albuterol again because he had experienced such a negative reaction to it. However, she administered dexamethasone to him to help reduce the swelling in his throat and felt that the medication worked well for him. It seemed that the doctor completely understood Jamie's condition, and she affirmed that the racemic epi had been the best choice to help him.

We spent the night in the hospital, and although Jamie was much better I barely slept. I was filled with anxiety because the breathing problem had recurred. Jamie hadn't needed another treatment for the rest of the night because he hadn't experienced a "rebound" from the racemic epi, so they let us go home at seven in the morning. I was elated, even without my sleep, that we were leaving the hospital after only a one-night stay.

A couple of days later, Jamie was still doing fine. It seemed safe to continue on with our trip to Santa Barbara. I was torn between my feelings of worry and optimism. California didn't disappoint us, and after a relaxing visit we returned to Colorado with hope that Jamie was through having any major breathing problems.

With Jamie's breathing problems but also with his recent hair loss and continual night terrors, I just wanted him to get healthy and stay healthy. Weeks passed while I waited and watched him, doing everything I could to help secure his welfare. I didn't want to let my guard down by focusing on anything else for fear I would miss something going on with him. Because I was wrapped in knots, emotionally and physically, I figured that for the sake of my family and myself I had to find a way to relax. Unfortunately, and to James's frustration, all my ideas cost a lot of money. But I pursued a few distractions anyhow, hoping they would lighten my mood.

We had moved to our new house only recently and I hadn't spent much time getting us settled into it. I decided that this would be the perfect project. The first thing I wanted to do was have the interior painted. The entire neighborhood was filled with houses decorated the same way, in neutral and earth tones. I wanted our house to reflect my individual taste, and I knew that adding a little color to brighten the environment would provide the distinctive touch I needed.

Once the home-improvement ball began rolling, I focused on other areas of the house that also needed my attention. An avid reader of health and nutrition publications, I had recently come across an article about the illnesses caused by living in a "sick home." The article documented investigations into a variety of household environments and their influence on different kinds of illness. I wanted to encourage Jamie's healthy breathing, so I made it a point to incorporate my new awareness of air quality and natural materials into my home improvements. For example, I considered the impact of new paint, doing some research before settling on a water-based brand that would not emit any toxic fumes.

It was interesting to me how even mainstream or everyday items could have truly negative effects on our bodies. I was reminded of this every time I saw a commercial or magazine advertisement for Prilosec, the medication that I believe made Jamie's hair fall out. Though the ads represented it as helpful, Prilosec seemed to be quite harmful to Jamie. It was important to me to avoid ever again being the uneducated consumer.

Having clean, fresh air in the house was a top priority. Knowing that our new carpet might off-gas chemical fumes, I was determined to counteract this. I could have replaced every inch of carpet at that time, but there were other options. I had already purchased some large plants for our home in the mountains before the boys were born because, being from California, I was used to having a lot of green foliage around. Plants help to improve the level of oxygen in a house, too, so there were many good reasons to fill this home with an abundance of greenery.

After discovering the benefits of ozone, I learned that it could be produced in the home environment with new types of air purifiers. I bought several Living Air brand ozonators (called Fresh Air), which I began to use around the house. The ozonator was designed to kill airborne mold, bacteria, and viruses. I didn't notice a change in Jamie, but I felt better because I could smell the difference in the air. Since then, more choices and more efficient brands of ozonators, HEPA air cleaners, and negative ionizers have come to market that help to reduce off-gassing, air pollutants, and dust. Newer models take into account recent concerns that excessive ozone can cause lung problems.

Along with the other enhancements, I switched all our household products from commercial mainstream brands to eco-friendly organic and natural products. This included all our body, dish, and laundry soaps, deodorants, and other cleaners. Making an effort to control the chemicals in our environment was obviously a sensible step. I was learning so much and, with all the new information, I wanted to put everything into place right away. Yet I had to prioritize and spread these changes out over time in order to be money conscious.

Another of my projects was planting several glorious flower gardens around the outside of the house. This was for emotional nourishment. It was springtime and I enjoyed the fun of picking out the various colors and types of flowers I loved. The sights and smells of vibrant, spring-colored flowers in bloom brightened my day and contributed to the stamina I needed to maintain my pace. Bringing the greenery and the scent of the flowers into my daily life made me feel at home.

Every trip to the nursery was a special event. The beautiful surroundings fed my good spirits. I often bought fresh flowers for inside the house, too, because I loved the scents and colors they added to a room. Arranging the different types of blossoms and leaves was an art that nourished me. It was the perfect outlet.

One day, after a big haul from the nursery, I couldn't wait to get started with my planting. Since I would be spending the afternoon outside, I took the boys with me so they could enjoy the sunshine, too. Jamie was standing near me when a car came driving down the street. Its engine wasn't loud and it wasn't traveling fast, but as soon as he heard it coming, he began to scream. Covering his ears, he ran back and forth and then fled into the house. It was obvious the car had startled him for some reason, and like some of his other recent behaviors, I didn't know what to make of his reaction. I followed him into the house and tried to comfort him, explaining that it was simply a car driving down the street. My efforts were fruitless. He continued to panic and show distress until, finally, he became distracted by a toy and forgot about the car.

That spring, my mom came out to Colorado from California because I wanted her help picking out some colors and furnishings for the house. We had a really nice visit and, as usual, she really enjoyed her time with the boys. She noticed how they had grown taller, and how they were similar in some ways and different in others.

Jack had begun asking questions about anything and everything. He wanted to know the names of all the objects around him. He would point and ask, "What?" and I would say, "Banana." Again he would ask, "What?" and I would answer, "Shoe." His curiosity was never-ending. That was one of the obvious differences between the boys; while Jack's verbal inquiries were increasing, Jamie was speaking less and less.

It was also worrisome to observe how Jamie was misdirecting his attention. One time, a plane was flying overhead and James and I were excited to point it out to the boys, giving them a chance to watch the white plume the jet left as it raced across the blue sky. Jack observed excitedly and pointed at it, following it with his finger as it moved over the horizon. We tried to get Jamie interested, too, but he just flashed a glance up toward the sky and then turned away without any interest or awareness.

Jamie was now sixteen months old and falling deeper and deeper into a seemingly isolated world. He usually played alone with the few specific things that captured his interest. He would sit on the floor of the bedroom and line up all his Matchbox cars in a perfect row. He would jump from one bed to another, and then return to his cars to examine them. He would examine the cars from every angle, from left to right and from front to back. Then he would return to jumping from one bed to another before he came right back to the cars to look them over in the very same way. This repetitious behavior was bewildering. On one occasion I took a car out of the line, not only to be playful but because I was curious about what he would do. His reaction was a long-winded, bloodcurdling scream. I gave back the car and he returned to his systematic sequence as if nothing had interrupted it.

I had my mother pay close attention to him to see what she thought about his behaviors. I had already asked some of my friends to do the same, but they were quick to tell me what I wanted to hear—that he just had a few silly quirks. "Don't worry. Jamie will grow out of it eventually," they kept saying. But as my mother observed him playing out one of his many routines, she could see what I was trying to describe. He would throw a toy airplane into the ball pit, run to get it out, and then ritualistically repeat the action the same way again. I must have seen him do this at least a hundred times. Then there were the red balls: Jamie was completely obsessed with them. He would go into the pit and pick out every red ball from the multicolored pile. He would play with them or simply line them up in one of his rows. And he was usually carrying one or two around with him wherever he went. After seeing it all for herself, my mom shared my concerns.

Worrying was a constant thing for me, and although I was trying hard to lessen the time I spent doing it, I developed a tendency to return to it over and over. I had to push myself to put my energies into more positive places once again. Working out was one of those places for me. I loved going on a good long run to clear my mind. It didn't matter how hard I worked out, because I always felt better afterward. Endorphins were my drug. They helped my mind and body, leaving me more energized, despite the fact that my sleep was constantly interrupted by Jamie's ongoing sleep problems. Carla would take over the night shift for several days in a row. But there were times when she was away. And when she was there, sometimes Jamie would start crying and Carla would take him to her room, but then later put him back in his room. Once he was back in his room, he might wake up again and begin to cry. His second round of crying would drag me into full alertness, and I wouldn't be able to get back to sleep.

After my workouts, I got into the habit of making a protein smoothie. I enjoyed experimenting with different ingredients and I would make drinks for James and the boys, too. Using the blender, I would throw in fresh fruit or vegetables, along with protein, vitamins, and antioxidants. I might forget about Jamie's sensitivity to noise, and turn on the blender when he was nearby. Each time I pressed the power button, he would absolutely lose it. He would grab his ears and close his eyes while screaming at the top of his lungs. I didn't know what to do. It got so bad that I had to take him upstairs to a far-removed bedroom and close the door before I could come back down to use the blender.

There were other problems with loud noises. One of the hardest to control was Jamie's reaction to the flush of a toilet. If he even suspected flushing from anywhere in the house, he would become completely petrified. I would see the sheer panic on his face as he froze with alarm. He refused to go anywhere near a bathroom. Public bathrooms were the worst for Jamie, because they were filled with other people and the noise of pumping soap dispensers and electric hand dryers. If we were out and I needed to go to the restroom, I would have to pry his fingers off the handle of the door because he would be dead set on keeping us from entering.

Accepting these changes in Jamie was difficult, but watching his response to physical touch change was the most heartbreaking. I would go to him and give him a big hug, but it was as if he didn't even feel it, as if his skin weren't connected to his feelings. He hated anyone else touching him at all. If another familiar adult patted his head or touched his shoulder, he would shrug or move away so he could avoid their touch. When a neighbor kid would see him and say hello, he would walk away or act like he couldn't hear a word. If someone would put his hand up, giving the signal for the high five, Jamie would just stand there with no reaction. Eventually, he wouldn't let even James hold him or pick him up. I was the only one he would let get physically close to him, but I could not describe our relationship as emotionally close.

Then Jamie began a unique ritual with his father. James would walk in the door and set his keys and work bag down on the table. Before he finished loosening his tie, both the boys would come running. Jack would welcome James home with a hug and a kiss and then run off, returning to his toys. When Jamie came near his father, he would begin tugging at his shirt. He would pull and pull on it, and then try to lift it up.

At first, James was confused and didn't know how to play along, but he soon figured out the game. He would lie down on the floor so Jamie could reach his shirt. Then Jamie would untuck James's shirt and pull it all the way up in order to expose the skin on James's stomach. Jamie would then pull his own shirt all the way up, crawl on top of his father, and just lie there, their bellies touching. He would stay for a few seconds and then get up and lie back down, crossways. Like many of his other tasks, he was repetitive and methodical.

James and Jamie did this every day for weeks. We laughed at first about how odd it was, but then we found the action very endearing. Jamie seemed to be trying to bond with James, repairing the connection they had lost in the hospital when

James had to be the "bad guy" who held his son down for his breathing treatments. We were moved by the sentiment and realized that Jamie was reaching out to his father from the deep, inaccessible place where he stayed most of the time.

Unlike me, James preferred not to make a big deal out of what was happening with Jamie. He didn't share my level of concern, and this was frustrating for me. He thought that I was overreacting, that things weren't as bad as I was making them out to be. James is the most optimistic person I know, and I absolutely love this trait in him. But I felt that he needed to see his son more realistically.

James relies on his spirituality when life gets hard. He uses his faith for answers and help. This probably accounts for his laid-back attitude and his ability to be relaxed most of the time. I, on the other hand, tend to take action when things get out of control. I believe in taking advantage of every opportunity and harnessing my motivation to make life all it can be. I am constantly brainstorming, or I am in a problem-solving mode. I don't know which way is better or healthier . . . maybe his way? If we could just put our minds together, we might form the perfect person! Over the years together, our different traits have balanced out, but during that time with Jamie, these differences started causing a lot of friction between us.

During the next visit to James's family in Las Vegas, I had an important realization about how I was feeling—a lot of anger toward James was surfacing in me. I also got angry and irritated every time I was near his father. It was as if I had just started dealing with all the emotions I had experienced when Jamie had first gotten sick. The sequence of events and interactions among James, his father, and me played over and over again in my mind. I knew it was eating away at me, but I couldn't seem to shake it. I just wasn't at a place where I could forgive. All the tension came out during James's and my interactions with each other. For the first time, I recognized a serious strain in our marriage.

Looking back on our relationship, I remember how, from the beginning, James and I had been so in love. For us, it truly was love at first sight. From there, we instantly discovered a strong connection that drew us together, despite all the obstacles that stood between us. We met when I took a spontaneous ski trip to Park City, Utah, to see my brother, Dana. I had been longing for an escape from my life after the recent death of his best friend, who was also a close friend of mine. I thought it would be good to get away and take in a change of scenery, but I had no idea I was in for such a dramatic and permanent life change.

When I met James, I was still married to Steve, a man much older than I, well established in his career and his life. I was settled and was well taken care of. Mine was the type of exciting life that I'd always thought I wanted: working as an actress, mingling with celebrities, living in the lap of luxury. Steve was incredibly kind and did everything he could to make me happy. I wasn't aware that I was lacking for anything at all—until James came along.

James was a college student who worked at a ski shop and, of course, spent most of his free time on the slopes when he wasn't in class at Brigham Young University. His life was

grounded in the Mormon Church, and it entailed a lifestyle that was the polar opposite of the one I had been living in L.A. The vision he held onto was marriage and family according to the guidelines of the church, and from the start I was supposed to be the wrong one for him.

But our passion and love for each other couldn't be denied. As time wore on, we uncovered more and more commonalities. I realize now that the course we traveled in order to unite served the purpose of making us a stronger couple, something we would desperately need to be as parents.

One afternoon I was sitting in the family room watching Jamie. He was playing with an airplane, making it go around and around.

I tried to get his attention. "Jamie?"

No response.

"Jamie!"

Still no response. He was lost, focused only on the plane.

His reaction scared me. I called to him again. "Jamie, can you hear me?"

Walking over to him, I got down on my knees. I spoke his name, but he showed no reaction. I put my hands underneath his shoulders and pulled him onto my knees so I could look directly into his eyes. There was an emptiness that hadn't been there before. When he looked back at me, it was as if he didn't know who I was. He looked right through me. I knew at that moment that Jamie was no longer the same child I had brought into this world nineteen months earlier.

My adrenaline kicked into high gear. Something was seriously wrong and I needed to find help. My son was living in a world I could not enter, and I needed help getting in. I turned to Dr. Allen.

It was the next visit that brought the word *autism* into our world. It was that day that forever changed the direction of my life.

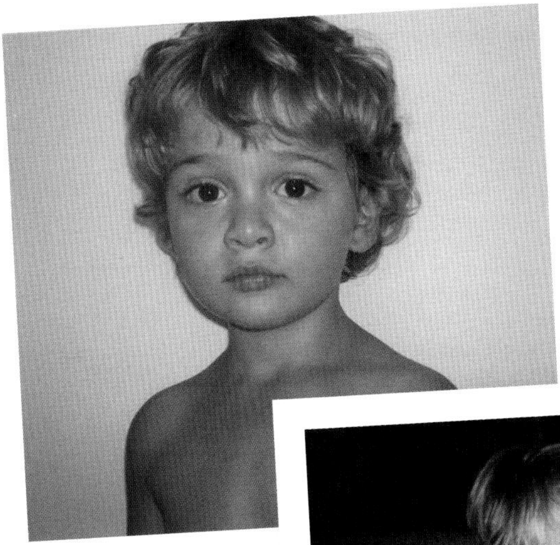

Jamie's hair grew back, but the Jamie I knew never returned.

CHAPTER

6

Finding My Own Answers

> Autism is a syndrome characterized by impairments in social relatedness, language and communication, a need for routine and sameness, abnormal movements, and sensory dysfunction.
>
> —Sallie Bernard et al., "Autism: A Unique Type of Mercury Poisoning"

There wasn't a definition of *autism* that could hold much value for me. I understood that there was a problem and I already knew the symptoms. I had three doctors tell me that I should accept the diagnosis and move forward, because there was no cure. Everything I had read so far confirmed what they were saying. But I didn't want to hear it, and I didn't want to read it. I needed someone to tell me how I could make it go away.

Was I supposed to sit forever with my sadness, tasting my tears? This beautiful boy, my gorgeous child—I couldn't let him go through his life without living it fully. I wanted him to experience every emotion—to love deeply, to feel great joy and happiness, and even to feel the pain and regret that comes with growing older and wiser. I couldn't accept any other way for him to be. Every possible thought ran through my mind. Could I help him? Could I find a way to make everything right? Was I in complete denial? Was there truly nothing that could be done? I had heard that sometimes people tuck their children away in a special facility or home where someone else can care for them. Was this what would be best for him? No. Hell, no! But should I just accept that I have a child with problems? Should I just live with it? Would I have the strength to handle it?

I'd had Jamie and he was *mine*. But he had been taken away. I grabbed and grabbed, trying to reach and pull him back, but he didn't know how to hold onto me. I knew what I wanted, but I didn't know how to get it. I had no grasp, no guide, no real direction. I filled the cavern of despair inside me by sitting with my son and dreaming—dreaming about the way he used to be and the way he was going to be again. That's what kept me going. I would have to pave my own way. I was reminded of something I had once read.

The Road Not Taken

By Robert Frost

Two roads diverged in a yellow wood,
And sorry I could not travel both
And be one traveler, long I stood
And looked down one as far as I could
To where it bent in the undergrowth;

Then took the other, as just as fair,
And having perhaps the better claim,
Because it was grassy and wanted wear;
Though as for that the passing there
Had worn them really about the same,

And both that morning equally lay
In leaves no step had trodden black.
Oh, I kept the first for another day!
Yet knowing how way leads on to way,
I doubted if I should ever come back.

I shall be telling this with a sigh
Somewhere ages and ages hence:
Two roads diverged in a wood, and I—
I took the one less traveled by,
And that has made all the difference.[1]

Where should I start? How will I know if I took the right road? It felt better to take some control in this situation rather than to stand still, feeling helpless.

I recalled everything I knew about health, nutrition, and the connection of the body to the mind. My life experiences had opened my own mind about both mainstream and alternative treatments. My mother had raised us a little differently, keeping up with the newest discoveries and treatments to promote wellness, and that included a diet different from what all my friends were eating. My parents were both fit and athletic, and they took good care of themselves, inside and out.

Growing up, we would wake twice a week to home deliveries of different dairy products: raw milk, eggs, cheese, and butter. My mother was of the opinion that because raw dairy products are neither homogenized nor pasteurized, more of the nutritional value remains. "Raw milk," she would say, "is full of healthy enzymes and beneficial bacteria, and its protein, fat, carbohydrates, vitamins, and minerals are in their perfect state." My mother's opinion about raw milk wasn't conventional. But after an early rebellion against her rules, I came to appreciate her beliefs. And over the years her wisdom reminded me that pasteurizing alters and diminishes most of the many good things in milk. So it made sense to me to try to keep as much food as possible in its original state. I think of cooking food at high temperatures as burning it, killing most of the vitamins. By the same token, I'm pretty sure that, as crazy as it might sound, heating breast milk to 150 degrees would destroy all the benefits.

Thirty years ago in California, buying raw dairy was unusual, but these days it seems that people are downright afraid of raw, unpasteurized milk products. Some theorize that pasteurizing contributes to the development of allergies in a lot of people. I realize this is just another one of the ongoing controversies about the pasteurization process versus the raw process. I had read that raw milk was actually good for autistic children. But raw milk in Colorado was nowhere to be found. I started to remind myself daily to continue learning about whole foods and incorporate them more and more each day.

My mom never allowed my sister, my brothers, or me to have any white sugar—except on Halloween—because she was acutely aware of its harmful properties and lack of nutritional value. I remember one Halloween when I was a young girl; my mom told my brothers, sister, and me we could eat as much candy as we wanted for that night only, and then in the morning, anything left over would be thrown out. Naturally I ate as much as I possibly could because we had been given the green light which happened only once a year. When we got home, I walked in the front door and immediately noticed the Spanish tiles on the floor, how the light was dancing off the oranges, blues, and yellows. The light glistened; my senses were overloaded. I felt warm inside, and the next moment the light and colors from the tiles were gone, covered by a beautiful array of half-digested Halloween candy. I'll never forget that moment or how too much sugar made me feel—and my mom wasn't happy about it either.

Most days my mother made us brown-bag lunches for school with only the healthiest contents, like an apple or a pear and a sandwich made with two slices of twenty-grain whole-wheat bread. (Well, it might have been closer to a nine-grain, but it tasted like twenty-grain.) After I drooled over the baloney, American cheese, and mayo sandwich on white, spongy Wonder Bread that the kid next to me was eating, my healthy lunch usually ended up uneaten—thrown in the trash on my way to the nearest market, where I opted for a dozen doughnuts instead.

In my case, the benefit of a childhood filled with healthy food was clearly not a complete commitment to healthy eating but rather a consciousness about the impact of nutrition. Thanks to my mother, I later learned how to be consistently aware of everything I put into my body.

With this kind of thinking ingrained in me, I knew I had to be open to more than the existing treatment for Jamie's illness, because accepting the status quo meant that there would be little chance of bringing Jamie back. Mainstream medicine had already thrown in the towel, with little endurance for the fight. I knew I couldn't let him go through life with autism and I was willing to do anything to get him well, even if it meant taking a journey on the road "less traveled."

I started calling, reading, researching anywhere I could. I learned that trauma could be a possible cause of children slipping into autism. Clearly, all the breathing problems Jamie had experienced, along with the intense medications he had ingested, had taken their toll on him.

I began discussions with the people closest to me, one of whom was my father-in-law, Robert Vance, DO. He listened to the feedback I had gotten from Dr. Allen about Jamie and said he'd look into some options for us. I had developed a kind of love–hate relationship (which he was unaware of) with my father-in-law over the years, especially after carrying such bad feelings toward him about what happened to Jamie. That said, Dr. Vance has been a constant support in our lives.

Dr. Vance was a doctor of osteopathy who had practiced for over forty years. He did everything from stitch wounds to treat a cold or flu, but was also the pioneer of chelation therapy in the state of Utah. It was initially used in the form of EDTA (ethylenediaminetetraacetic acid) to detoxify people with lead poisoning. Since its onset, many different kinds of chelating agents have been used, and the treatment has evolved to remove a variety of heavy metals.

When I lived in L.A., I had overheard people discuss their chelation treatment. It seemed to be a popular alternative health practice in the entertainment industry, probably because, generally speaking, this group of people has a less conventional lifestyle in terms of medicine, religion, and politics. Even back then, the little rumblings I had picked up about chelation had captured my interest.

I experienced Dr. Vance's knowledge firsthand in my earlier days with James, before I had the boys. James and I had been working hard at our jobs, putting in twelve- to sixteen-hour days. I wasn't an early-to-bed person and certainly not an early riser, but I had been getting up at three in the morning to shower and get to work. After several months of this, my body was really run down. On a trip to Las Vegas to visit James's family, I had the chance to visit Dr. Vance's clinic. He gave me something new: a vitamin C IV drip. It was a mix of vitamins, including B12, calcium, magnesium, and folic acid. I had taken these orally in the past, so I figured why not receive them directly into the vein? After receiving the drip, I noticed I felt better and my body felt stronger.

During these treatments, I spent time around the office and I began to understand better what Dr. Vance did and what his practice was all about. His patients shared impressive stories with me about how their health had improved because of Dr. Vance's work. They described how receiving chelation had helped them, and in some cases even saved their lives. How can you deny a method's effectiveness when the evidence comes straight from the mouth of someone who has benefited from it?

Dr. Vance came to the rescue more than once. I had just had my wisdom teeth pulled prior to another trip out to Las Vegas, this time for business. I was in so much pain—not only from the procedure but also from a massive headache and terrible nausea. Days went by in Las Vegas, and I only felt more and more horrible, unable to eat or sleep. I woke up in the middle of the night just to order cornflakes and milk from hotel room service. It seemed like the only thing that would calm my upset stomach.

During a quick trip to see Dr. Vance, he found the cause of my problem: the contaminated gauze had infected my mouth. (Oops, I guess I was supposed to take it out.) He removed the gauze and thoroughly syringed my incisions with hydrogen peroxide and then again with some homeopathic solutions. He went on to adjust my neck and back. After that, he sent me to see Janet Berlin, the craniosacral therapist who worked in his office. (I could not know when I first met her that she would have such a big impact on Jamie's life and mine in the coming years.)

She treated me with craniosacral therapy, a treatment I had never received before. Craniosacral therapy is described on the Upledger Institute International website: "CST is a gentle, hands-on method of evaluating and enhancing the functioning of a physiological body system called the craniosacral system—comprised of the membranes and cerebrospinal fluid that surround and protect the brain and spinal cord. Using a soft touch generally no greater than 5 grams, or about the weight of a nickel, practitioners release restrictions in the craniosacral system to improve the functioning of the central nervous system."[2]

I didn't know what to expect but was pleasantly surprised to find how quickly I recovered. I felt wonderful and was headache-free soon after the visit. I could even eat food other than cornflakes! Dr. Vance had definitely gained my respect, and I was impressed with the work he was doing. Later, I knew that he would be a good source for help with Jamie.

One of my first appointments for Jamie was with Diane Osaki, a specialist referred by Dr. Allen. Diane worked at JFK Partners at the University of Colorado Health Services. (She worked there for several years and then went on to open the Alta Vista Center for Autism. Later, she opened the Aspen

Center, now called Firefly Autism House. She helped to develop the Denver Model, an internationally renowned program for preschool children with autism.) Diane evaluated Jamie over several different visits. When her evaluation was complete, she confirmed his condition as autism. I skipped the next step, which was to see a psychologist to have another evaluation.

We had already gone through Child Find and received an evaluation by their team of psychologists, occupational therapists, and speech therapists. Jamie didn't need any more labeling. Diane had already made me aware that because autism was not considered to be curable, once diagnosed, children carried the label with them their entire lives, through every classroom and even beyond school. From then on, I refused to ever label him this way or, more importantly, to believe he would never get better. I remembered the story of Wilma Rudolph. She was the "fastest woman in the world," winning three gold medals at the 1960 Olympics. It is astonishing to imagine that, as a child, Wilma was forced to wear metal braces on her legs because they could not carry her on their own.

She once said, "My doctor told me I would never walk again. My mother told me I would. I believed my mother."[3]

I wanted to be the kind of mother to Jamie that Wilma Rudolph's had been. I couldn't allow him to be identified by the label of autism, and I wouldn't believe the people who told us that there was nothing to be done. I would be the one who told him he *would* get better.

Our insurance company documented his diagnosis as autism to cover the few benefits we had for his condition.

However, with this categorization we received only one hour a week each of speech and occupational therapy. It was not nearly sufficient and hardly worth the stigma of their label in order to receive the paltry services. Every other claim I filed was rejected with the excuse that ASD (Autistic Spectrum Disorder) was "too broad" a condition. I later learned how to be creative with insurance claims, sometimes filing a claim for just the test that was conducted and the symptoms it tested. It never required dishonesty, just a different delivery. For example, part of Jamie's condition included overgrowth of yeast in his intestinal tract, so the insurance paid some of the cost of the treatment.

Diane had written a full report on Jamie and created an individualized treatment plan for us. I continued working with her over the next year to fine-tune our home therapy program. The plan included working with a speech language pathologist and an occupational therapist at our house. I was excited to have this option because it was more convenient and I thought Jamie's treatment could be better managed from home. Diane helped us find just the right professionals to work with Jamie, and she updated them on his profile while training them about the requirements of his new curriculum.

Around the same time, Dr. Vance phoned with information about an out-of-state facility called the New Hope Clinic. It dealt mostly with cancer patients, but specialized in analyzing the meridians of the body to determine the core of an illness. This type of testing was obviously unconventional, but it was the kind of option I wanted to explore with an open mind. According to traditional Chinese medicine, twelve meridians, or rivers of energy, flow through the body, specifically through the kidney, large intestine, bladder, stomach, heart, governing vessel, pericardium, gallbladder, small intestine, lung, liver, and conception vessel. I knew it sounded a little crazy, but the cost was minimal, and I thought the testing might give me more information or at least identify something more specific that could better direct us.

We drove from Denver to California to see what we could find out about the clinic. Deanna Jarvis, one of the clinicians, worked intensively with us for one week. Over that period, James, Jamie, and I drove back and forth to the clinic every day from my family's vacation home in San Clemente.

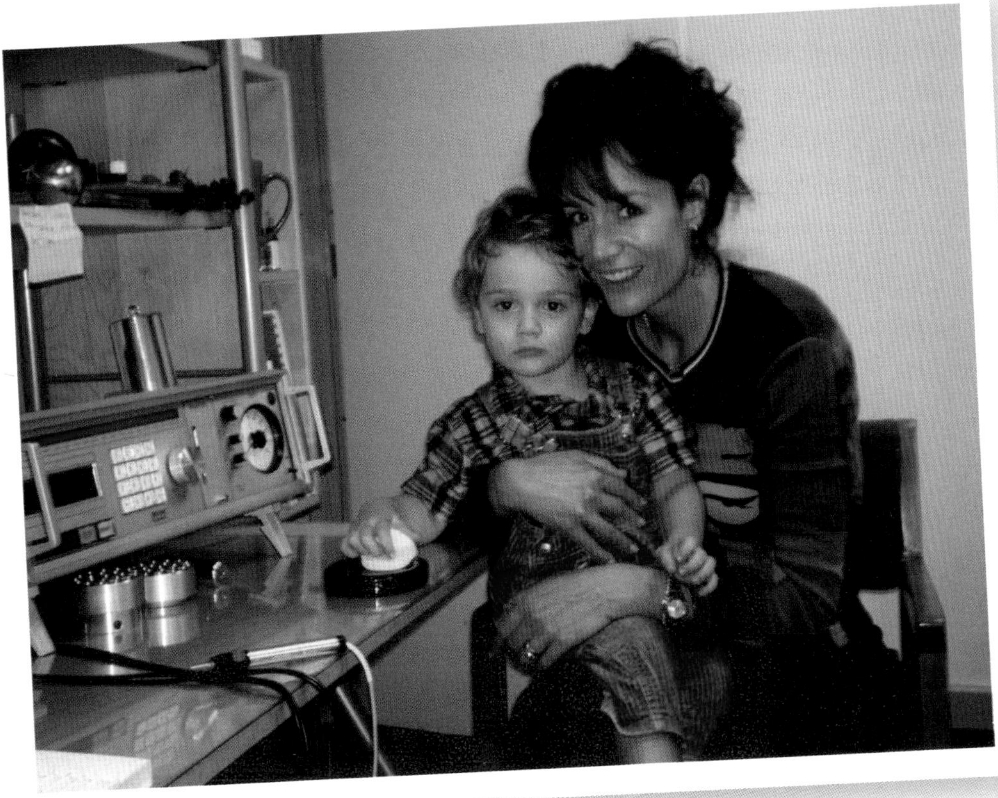

With Jamie
at the clinic

I had many conversations with Deanna. I told her about Jamie's red ball fixation and how he spent hours at a time moving back and forth on the swing in our backyard. She interpreted this as good news; Jamie *wanted* to get better. The things he was doing were calming and healing to his brain. He was giving himself the sensory input his body wanted and needed. Her feedback was encouraging. The idea that Jamie was signaling to us that he wanted to get better motivated me even more. I was thrilled at the possible meaning behind these behaviors.

Meanwhile, new tests showed that he had weaknesses in his intestinal tract, brain, and liver. Deanna recommended being more conscious of his diet. She recommended physical therapy and Brain Gym® exercises to stimulate his brain activity. This was just the beginning of the information I obtained in the early phases of my search, but things were starting to click. I took stock of the progress we'd made and returned to Denver to pursue additional avenues.

Red ball

Deanna was a terrific health care practitioner and a very special person. I was saddened to hear, a few years later, that she had passed away. I'll never forget her or how she helped Jamie advance on his path to wholeness.

Before making the trip to California, I realized that Jamie needed further-reaching attention than he was receiving. Dr. Jay Wilson, whom we had seen from the beginning in Boulder, had been a blessing, and had directed us down the right path. But it was time to search for different and more advanced therapies. At that time, I came across the name Bill Cunningham from White Dove Healing Arts in Boulder. We visited him for an analysis technique similar to the one at New Hope, but with quicker and more accurate results.

He used an energetic medicine device, a machine that worked as both a diagnostic tool and a treatment. It provided an overwhelming amount of information. The first issue the machine listed was autism, but it was also specific in identifying deficiencies in Jamie's body. From there, I could use certain homeopathic and supplemental remedies to address his needs. Bill worked with Jamie for about three months. We drove to Boulder twice a week to get homeopathic and energetic medicine treatment. Shortly following our work there, Jamie began repeating after me when I modeled the letters of the alphabet. At the time, it was a notable achievement because at least he was making a few sounds again. We also noticed that his eye contact had increased ever so slightly.

Bill had a strong impact on me and my quest for information, and he was always full of optimism. I continued to work with him because he seemed to truly believe that Jamie could get better. He helped Jamie gain some momentum, but once his progress reached a plateau, I knew that I needed to step up the pace, working to uncover more powerful treatments.

I found a comprehensive article on autism in *Mothering* magazine, which listed a vast range of available treatments. I delved into the article, absorbing every detail. I was excited to see that, in addition to the traditional speech and occupational therapy, there were many alternative treatments. Those listed in the magazine included the Floor Time approach from Stanley Greenspan, MD; The Lovaas Method, or ABA (applied behavioral analysis); music therapy; listening programs; nutritional changes, including gluten-free and casein-free diets; and The Option Institute's The Son-Rise Program®, created by a family who had actually healed their autistic son. To me, reading the list was like Christmas morning. I had been given a special gift of options that fed my hope, and I vowed to try each one.

My goal became for us to surround ourselves with people who could focus on the etiology (cause of) and solution to the problem, not on gathering evidence to label it. Once I knew the cause, I could find the solution. I knew Jamie had been fine before the trauma with his breathing, and deep down I just knew that he could be healed.

I voraciously gathered up every bit of new information I could find about autism. Networking with friends and family also kept the resources coming in. I picked up the latest *Mothering* magazine. I will never forget the intriguing cover, which pictured an ominous view of an eerie-looking, liquid-dripping needle. A large portion of the magazine was about vaccines and what the magazine saw as their dangers. The pros and cons of the administration of vaccines to children were discussed. One article, an interview with Stephanie Cave, MD, detailed what she believed was the detrimental role of the preservative thimerosal, which, at the time of the interview (2002), was loaded into more immunizations than it is today. Dr. Cave said that this preservative makes children retain mercury in the body and that this metal has been shown to impair brain function. The article also discussed "pulling" metals from the body (chelation therapy).[4]

Chelation and its benefits continually resurfaced in my research. I made a resolution to learn more about it. What I found intrigued me. According to one source, "For the most common forms of heavy metal intoxication—those involving lead, arsenic or mercury—the standard of care in the United States dictates the use of dimercaptosuccinic acid (DMSA)."[5]

In "Chelation of Mercury for the Treatment of Autism," Amy S. Holmes, MD, says this about DMSA, the antidote to heavy metal toxicity: "DMSA is an excellent chelator of most heavy metals including mercury. When used appropriately, it is safe and effective. DMSA has survived the testing necessary for FDA approval for use in children. This means it has been tested *in children* and was found to be both safe and effective. Despite the FDA's poor record in testing and approving vaccines, the procedures for testing and approval of drugs are quite rigorous."[6]

I felt that the information I uncovered about chelating opened up another world of opportunity for Jamie's treatment. It was a valuable discovery, but I wasn't sure I was on the right path until I reread the interview with Stephanie Cave in *Mothering* magazine. Dr. Cave said that in one study, more than 53 percent of the mothers of autistic children were Rh-negative; these mothers had received an immunoglobulin preserved with thimerosal while they were pregnant. (By contrast, only 3 percent of the mothers of nonautistic children were Rh-negative.)[7] Mothers with Rh-negative blood typically get RhoGAM (immunoglobulin injection) shots while they are pregnant. RhoGAM, also known as HypRho-D, is used to reduce problems that can arise when an Rh-negative woman becomes pregnant.

Until April 2001, RhoGAM shots contained thimerosal, which has been used in some vaccines since the 1930s, when Eli Lilly and Company first introduced it. It is 49.6 percent mercury by weight and is metabolized or degraded into ethyl mercury and thiosalicylate. A mother receiving an average dose of RhoGAM would take in about 10.5 micrograms of mercury. The Environmental Protection Agency (EPA) says that the "safe limit" for mercury exposure is .1 microgram per kilogram of body weight per day.[8] Mothers who hemorrhaged early in pregnancy would receive multiple doses and a much larger mercury intake. High levels of mercury can permanently damage the brain and kidneys, resulting in tremors and memory and vision problems. Mercury in a mother's body can be passed to her fetus. A *New York Times* article says "the umbilical cord can have an average mercury concentration 1.7 times as great as the concentration in the mother's blood."[9]

Since 2002, when the interview with Stephanie Cave appeared in *Mothering* magazine, the question of whether a mother with Rh-negative blood is more likely to have an autistic child than a mother with Rh-positive blood has been controversial. I recalled that after each of my six miscarriages, before I became pregnant with Jack and Jamie, I had received a RhoGAM shot.

So Beautiful, so lost

And there was more. When I had been pregnant with the twins, everything seemed to be going along smoothly. Then, during the fourth month of my pregnancy, I was working outside, gardening and planting. It was springtime, the weather was warming up, and I was in great spirits, excited to get out in the sunshine after a long winter. I thought maybe the activity had been too much for me, because I noticed that I had begun spotting a small amount of fresh, red blood. I was panicked, suddenly haunted by my history of lost pregnancies. I couldn't help but think that I might be losing these babies, too. One of my miscarriages had begun with four days of spotting and ended with dangerous hemorrhaging, so I constantly carried the trauma of that event in my mind.

Missing my sweet Jamie

I walked carefully inside the house to call the doctor. They told me to come in right away for a checkup. I felt the urge to get down on my knees, so I kneeled beside my bed, praying hard with all my faith that I not lose my babies. I sensed the heartbreak I would feel if I were to sustain another loss. By the time I got to the doctor's office, the spotting had slowed and almost stopped. They checked me and found that the babies were perfectly fine. It had merely been ordinary spotting. I was happy and reassured, but from that point on I was cautious with all my activities. Before I left, I received my seventh RhoGAM shot.

Two months after the spotting incident, I experienced a problem with heart palpitations. I returned to the hospital, where I was put on oxygen and given an order of bed rest. Again, the boys were fine, but my nerves were a little rattled.

The final visit to the doctors came after my water broke at thirty-three weeks. The boys were delivered without too many glitches, but during the delivery I was losing so much blood that the doctors gave me yet one more RhoGAM shot. That made a total of eight RhoGAM injections.

Now, my mind sparked as I acknowledged the connections: my own B-negative (Rh-negative) blood, the large amount of thimerosal in my body, and my son with autism.

I had been overexposed to mercury! The light had not only clicked on, it was blazing like the sun! It was the most significant piece of information I had uncovered yet. It tied all the factors together. I knew this was an important link to my son and would be an integral step toward his recovery.

Of all the potential treatments I had put my finger on over the past months, the treatment for metals would continue to weigh heavy on my mind. (No pun intended.) I knew I needed to increase my knowledge about how to remove the metals from Jamie's little body. The problem was the only chelation or metal detoxification I had heard about was for adults. But there was no denying that this avenue was wide open as a route for one of Jamie's treatments. But I didn't want to stop there. I felt like there was even more to do, including making a connection with the family who had cured their son of autism and founded The Son-Rise Program®.

I carried on relentlessly, driven by my dreams for Jamie and my belief that he would return. Never before had I been simultaneously so energized and so exhausted. Apparently, I hadn't gotten the memo that it was going to be this hard.

CHAPTER

7

The Road to Massachusetts

James and I were struggling. We both had our individual stressors. James was working all the time, and I was working, too. But I was spending most of my time with Jamie. We had just furnished our new home, as well as work got busier and busier. I wanted to invest money in healing possibilities for Jamie, while James was concerned with how we were going to support our business and pay our personal bills. He was frustrated with all the money I was spending. I knew I was being excessive, but I felt willing to do anything, even if it meant taking out a loan. To me, money was going to come and go, but if we might be on the path that would take us to recovery for Jamie, it would be the investment of a lifetime.

I had only a small window of time. I had learned the importance of timing in early childhood growth, and knew that although it is not impossible to go back and "reprogram" a child's development after the age of five, it is much more difficult. But on this issue, James and I were just too divided, living in our separate worlds, distracted by our own priorities. It was crazy how life had seemed so easy for us before we had a business of our own and had become parents.

Back when James and I were first together, he had been in college at Brigham Young. I had moved to Utah from L.A. so we could be together. I found acting and modeling jobs in Salt Lake City and kept myself busy while James took classes. I was shocked when I first arrived, because it was a whole other world. I thought I might have arrived on another planet—one where no bars or coffeehouses existed. Where was the coffee, anyway? The only place in Provo that had it was a 7–11. But

aside from my involuntary coffee sacrifice, there was no place I would have rather been than wherever James was. I loved him more than anything and he was in my every thought. I stepped right into his life, and it was a refreshing and uncomplicated change. At times, I felt like I was watching my life on a big screen, seeing the actions and feeling the emotions of a completely different person.

James brought the outdoors back into my life. We exercised, mountain biked, and hiked—all activities that kept us outside and moving. We had so much fun together: eating dinner out, going to movies, or just staying up late and talking about anything and everything. We uncovered the many things we had in common and became more and more attached to each other. Life was so entertaining, relaxing, and stress-free that we rarely found anything to argue about. It was a simple life, one I was unfamiliar with.

We could never have foreseen that, years later, as finances became tight and we were each pulled in different directions, our entire foundation would be rocked. We had added twin boys to our lives—one of whom struggled with autism and breathing problems. How in those early years could we possibly have prepared our relationship or ourselves for what lay ahead? When the time came, we acknowledged our problems but we didn't know how to repair them.

I was undeterred in my efforts to maintain momentum in Jamie's healing. I felt I was on the right track and had learned and gathered a great deal of information, but the question was, *What next?* I constantly thought about The Son-Rise Program®. I just knew that if they had actually cured their son, it would be worth looking into. I contacted them and they suggested the first thing I should do was read their book *Son Rise: The Miracle Continues*, written by the boy's father, Barry Neil Kaufman.

In no time, I had the book in hand and was reading it every night before I went to bed. It moved me to tears. The story of what this family had experienced was unfathomable, and the account of how they had developed their own treatment program was inspiring. Oftentimes, I read different sections of the book to James so he could get an understanding of what they had done and what they had accomplished. He was incredibly interested and impressed.

I hoped he would feel as strongly as I did about making a trip to Sheffield, Massachusetts, where we could get a closer look at the program. But he just didn't feel like we had the money to spare, especially if there were no guarantees that it would help. My gut feeling was so strong that I couldn't let it go. He finally relented, deciding that we could turn the trip into an adventure by renting an RV and driving across the United States, visiting historical sites along the way. I rolled my eyes at the idea of traveling by RV, as I definitely prefer an airplane and a comfortable hotel, but I knew we would all be better served if I took the compromise.

The day of our departure, we planned to pick up the RV and drive until we reached Kansas, where we would stop for the night. James had rushed that morning to get the vehicle, and somehow managed to talk his way out of watching the instructional video because he was in such a hurry. He made it back home with the RV in record time, but it took us all day to load it. We stocked the RV with a big supply of snack foods—natural chips, fruit, PowerBars—and water, and every cabinet was packed full. Our nanny, Carla, came along to help with the boys and to stay with them while we attended the program.

James had pushed the RV idea because of the freedom it offered for moving around inside while traveling. It seemed like a good idea at first, and our trip began with excitement. We were all upbeat, singing to the radio, laughing, and playing in the RV as James drove. The boys and I were having fun playing games, lying on the bed, and running all around. It was less enjoyable when, after an hour on the road, I remembered my susceptibility to motion sickness. But the fun mood ended altogether when James hit the brakes on the highway after a semi abruptly pulled in front of us, and we were all slammed across the inside of the RV. The rest of our time on the road, the boys and I remained firmly strapped down with seatbelts.

As we drove through the night, it was getting cooler outside and the moisture in the air was changing. I noticed that Jamie seemed a bit "off." He didn't have any noticeable

Boys in the RV

symptoms of sickness, but I could tell that something wasn't right. I thought about the smell of the air in the RV, wondering if the plastic cabinets had any off-gassing effects or if there might be any other unseen factors that were causing him problems, like an allergic reaction.

I lay down with him in the back while Jack slept behind the curtains, above the cab. Jamie was sleeping comfortably at first, but then he became feverish. Before long, I could hear his breath, because he was starting to struggle with each inhale. I let him be but sat by him, just to be near in case something changed. He slept on for a while until suddenly he woke up and began a mild, barky cough. I felt fear creep up on me. We were about to experience the third breathing episode and I knew it. James and I locked eyes, sharing a look of understanding. Jamie went back to sleep, but we knew we were just biding our time until things escalated. We were in the middle of nowhere and had no emergency plan.

An hour later, Jamie was startled when we stopped to refuel and woke up again. This time, the labored breathing was much more audible. There was panic in his eyes. The distress only caused his breathing to worsen. In moments, he was in a bad way, gasping and choking for air. I yelled for James to call 911. I looked out the window and saw only complete darkness off the road. I thought to myself, *There's no way there's a hospital nearby.* James grabbed his cell phone and pleaded with the operator for information about the nearest hospital. The gas station attendant overheard the call and noticed the concern in James's voice.

He interrupted, saying, "Excuse me, sir. I live around here and I can tell you there's a hospital right down this road."

Thank God!

James pulled out the gas nozzle, threw it to the ground, and jumped back in the driver's seat. He drove as fast as he could. I bundled Jamie up in a blanket and stood in the doorway of the RV with him in my arms, ready to jump out upon arrival. As I stood there, I turned to look over my shoulder and was horrified to see Jack crying in fear, "What? What's happening?" Everything had turned to chaos, food and dishes falling out of the cupboards as the cabinet doors swung open and slammed shut. I closed my eyes as the tears ran down my face; I turned my head away because I was unable to answer him. Luckily, Carla was there to hold him. All I could do was focus on holding Jamie and keeping my balance as we raced to the hospital.

We arrived in minutes. The instant James stopped the RV at the emergency entrance, I swung the door open and sprinted inside, screaming for help. No one was around. I started searching in a rush, looking up and down every hallway. It felt strange being in a completely empty emergency room. As in a scene from some movie thriller, I began running through the empty halls yelling for help. There was a phone on the wall that read "For Emergencies." James came through the doors and went straight to it. The operator came on the line and he told her our son wasn't breathing well and we needed help immediately.

She said, "Go to the emergency room!"

He yelled, "We *are* in the emergency room! We're here and there's no one around!"

Just at that moment, two nurses came hurrying toward me. I pleaded with them to give Jamie racemic epinephrine. The nurse said she needed a doctor's orders to do that.

I demanded, "Just get it. He needs it now!"

She replied, "There's no doctor here, but I'll get him on the phone." I couldn't believe it. We were in a hospital without a doctor!

I told her I knew that the racemic epi was what he needed and to make sure to tell the doctor we'd been through this before. She returned in seconds with a shot. She gave it to him and instantly his breathing got better. She also administered epinephrine through a nebulizer, followed by a shot of dexamethasone in the leg. Jamie's airway appeared to open fully. After about an hour, when his breathing was temporarily stabilized, we were sent to a pediatric hospital thirty minutes away.

We drove to the hospital and parked the RV right in front of the emergency room entrance. Jamie was sleeping peacefully and his breathing sounded good. I told James I didn't want to wake him up because I wanted him to rest for a while instead of being dragged into the cold, sterile examination room at two in the morning to be poked and prodded again by another doctor. In my mind, I knew he needed as much rest as he could get so his body could heal. James went in to tell the staff our plan, and they were adamant that we bring Jamie inside right then. I was confident about my choice to override their suggestion, so we stayed in the RV. About four hours later, Jamie woke again with labored breathing—a typical response to the drug wearing off.

We took him inside and the staff was very aware of who we were and the fact that we had waited outside instead of listening to their directions. They reprimanded us, giving us looks of disapproval, even as I tried to explain that he had been fine and sleeping comfortably the whole time.

Things only got worse when the doctor came into the conversation. He was especially rude and spoke angrily to us.

"Obviously, your son has been in need of medical attention."

"His breathing was fine until a few minutes ago, when he woke up," I responded. "We were right outside the doors in our RV."

"Yes, I'm aware of that."

Jamie's stridor was worsening as we talked, so I said, "What Jamie needs is some racemic epinephrine to ease his breathing."

I could tell by the look on the doctor's face that I had said the wrong thing in the wrong way. He was visibly irritated.

"I can't possibly give him something based on a suggestion you make. I need to examine him before I can make a treatment plan."

The medical staff had already attempted to insert a nasal cannula in order to give Jamie oxygen, but he hadn't allowed them to do it. He had become completely frantic as they tried to force it on him, making his condition even worse. I told the staff, in the most diplomatic way I could, that he had sensory issues, which was why he should just be given the shot. He was working harder and harder to breathe. I resented the way we were being treated and was beginning to lose patience.

I tried to reason with the doctor, explaining that Jamie had been successfully treated with racemic epinephrine in the past. I tried to persuade him that I knew this was what my son needed. The doctor, further annoyed by my nerve in telling him Jamie's medical needs, said, "This is not the best way to help him."

That was the doctor's way of putting me in my place and it infuriated me. We began to argue. We were going back and forth, each of us questioning the other's knowledge and intention. I got so desperate to be heard that I forced myself to regain my composure.

I started over, this time speaking calmly. "I'm not trying to tell you how to do your job," I reassured him. "It's just that we've been through this before. I've learned that Jamie needs to stay calm so his breathing doesn't worsen. The more he struggles, the more he panics, and as you can see his breathing is definitely getting worse. Please, if you could just give him the racemic epinephrine."

His response did not change. "Yes, you've said that already. However, I'm still assessing the situation. And you know, I should report you to Social Services for not bringing your son in here immediately. It's borderline child neglect."

I couldn't believe how helpless we were. Jamie was ill, waiting in discomfort, and I was unable to help get him what he needed.

At this point, James broke his silence. "Listen, we care about our son. I don't understand why you feel justified in the way you're treating us. He just needs an epinephrine treatment. Come on, just help us out here."

The doctor looked at James and then turned around, mumbling something as he walked away. We never saw that particular doctor again. However, he must have ordered the medication, because an assistant came in shortly after he left to give Jamie the racemic epinephrine and a dose of dexamethasone. As we expected, his breathing improved.

Following the shot, he was admitted to the hospital and moved to a room upstairs. By this time, it was early morning. Shortly after getting settled in the new room, we were greeted by a pediatric doctor, a nurse, and another visiting doctor. The pediatric doctor was warm and friendly and we told her about the earlier events. She was aware of all that had happened, but explained that the emergency room doctor probably lacked experience with this particular breathing condition. She apologized for the way we had been treated.

Jamie was doing better, but all we could do was wait and see how long he could go between treatments. The first time, four hours went by before he needed another one. After the second treatment, he lasted six hours, followed by eight hours the next day. On the second evening, he lasted through the night: eleven hours. On the third day, he didn't need any breathing treatment.

I couldn't sleep the first night in the hospital because I was just waiting for Jamie to relapse. I was watching the clock, exhaling a little deeper as each hour went by. The most consecutive sleep I was able to get was on the last night; I slept for three or four straight hours, which felt really good.

After three nights, Jamie was ready to be released. None of us had taken a shower for days. Finally, on the last morning there, I used the guest shower in the hallway of the pediatric ward. That probably goes down in history as my best shower ever. James, Jack, and Carla had been sleeping in the RV the whole time. Right after me, they snuck in for much-welcomed showers, too. Of course, the RV shower had been out of commission from the beginning.

Our pediatric doctor had taken exceptional care of Jamie. He received antibiotics for his infection, and the doctor closely monitored every bit of his progress. She was knowledgeable, and we appreciated her attentiveness. Upon Jamie's release, I told her about my worry that he would have a problem before our trip was over and that next time we might not be close to a hospital. She completely understood. She decided to send us on our way with a prescription for a nebulizer and some racemic epinephrine. At that

time, it was highly unusual for anyone but a doctor to be allowed to manage that kind of powerful drug. In fact, we had to go from one pharmacy to the next before we could find one that had it in stock. We ended up waiting an hour for the drug in its liquid form. Having it in hand comforted me; it was more valuable than gold.

Once we were back in the RV, I focused on relaxing. I tried hard to enjoy the feeling of being on the open road with my family. Jamie's throat was raspy but I could tell his health was improving. The mood was still heavy, but it had just begun to lighten when James and I noticed an unpleasant smell. As it turned out, the RV's "gray water" bathroom waste had begun to back up, coming up through the shower drain. We had purposely not used the bathroom so we wouldn't have to bother emptying it. We were confused at first, but then had the unfortunate realization that the waste we were privy to (pun intended) had been left there by the people who rented the RV before us. Yuck.

We laughed at first and dared not ask ourselves what could possibly happen next, because we were already sure we were on "A Trip from Hell." To add to the craziness of the situation, James admitted he didn't know how to hook up or empty the waste because he hadn't watched the instructional video before we had left. Great.

We drove on for what seemed like forever with the horrid smell. We searched for a location to empty the RV and finally stumbled on a place that looked like it could accommodate us. We were able to get help from a man who worked there. He rattled off a to-do list to James, who listened quickly to the directions, assuming he could basically figure it out once he got started. Anxiously, he began the task, and we were on our way as soon as he was done.

Only a few miles later, we realized the stinky problem had not been solved. James really thought he had gotten it figured out, but I guess he hadn't. Traveling across Kansas accompanied by that horrendous and increasingly rancid smell, all the while looking for another RV facility, we debated what to do. At one point, we noticed the road we were driving on was clearly deserted. James and I looked at each other with wonder, and when we saw people walking across it he said in a tone reminiscent of Dorothy in Oz, "Toto, I've a feeling we're not on the interstate anymore."

He had taken a wrong turn in the middle of nowhere. By now, the stench had completely filled the small compartment of the RV. It was so bad that we were all fairly nauseated by it. We couldn't pull over to take a break because we were in such a rush to empty the tank before it got even more unbearable.

It was as if we had entered a maze. We couldn't find our way back to the main road. We tried turning around, and then turning around again, but we couldn't get where we needed to go. We began to question if we would ever get out of Kansas. The boys could no longer stand the putrid smell, so they squeezed up to the front to sit on our laps as we continued driving. We must have been a sight to see.

By a stroke of luck, we finally found our way back to the highway. Hundreds of miles later, we found another RV facility. James tried again to empty the tank without any success, and this time there was no one on hand to help. We had no choice but to get back on the road. We drove on with the windows wide open, trying to breathe in as much fresh air as we could. We even threw appearances to the wind as we took turns hanging our heads out the open windows, inhaling the clean country air.

At the end of our overextended and aesthetically unpleasing tour of the countryside, it was obvious that a nice roomy hotel with comfortable beds, a clean bathroom, and room service was in order. We chuckled at the view of the RV, empty and alone, parked in the hotel lot. We decided then and there that the RV was not our friend, and we needed to part ways as soon as possible.

Jack in front of the infamous RV

We had planned to visit James's brother Robbie, who was living in Pennsylvania with his family while completing his medical residency. Once on our way, we came to a city that was bigger than anything we had seen in a long while. We marveled at the sight of a Starbucks and even a Panera Bread Company; these signs of civilization seemed like a welcome mirage after our expedition. It's amazing how a latte can make everything so much better.

After a few more hours on the road in a vehicle that smelled worse with each passing moment, we arrived at Robbie's house. Surprisingly, he was the one who figured out how to empty the tanks. We were inexpressibly grateful as we made the remainder of the drive to Massachusetts.

At long last, we arrived at the Option Institute™. It was about 10 P.M. when we checked Carla and the boys into a funky-style bed and breakfast just down the street, and they fell asleep quickly. The B & B was charming and warm, decorated with antique phones, old bottles, and other rustic decor. James and I didn't want to leave that cozy place, but earlier in the evening we had decided that we didn't want to wait another day to get rid of the RV, so we had made some calls and found a place to drop it off right away. We were exhausted from the long drive, but the idea of being free of the albatross motivated us to get back on the road.

After a two-hour drive we got to the Hartford Connecticut Airport, where we exchanged the RV for a Ford Excursion. Laughing about the misery the RV had caused us was cathartic. We went even further by taking pictures of ourselves mocking it before we left it behind. Being in the new SUV was a dreamlike ride in the lap of luxury compared with the traveling we had done during the past week. The "new-car smell" was welcome to our wounded nostrils. James was completely energized after we made the change, and had a newfound endurance to drive the long distance back. We returned to Sheffield and fell into bed at three in the morning, crashing into unconsciousness the moment our heads hit the pillows.

The next morning, we soaked up the beauty of the sunlit landscape. There was a pretty little stream that ran alongside the property. I went for a run down one of the many country roads in the area. Acres and acres of thick trees were growing

Jamie checking out the view
at The Option Institute

across the hills and valleys. The views were breathtaking. The boys were content to stay in one place, where they could roam and explore the surrounding property.

James and I were off to an early start. I was happy to be arriving at the Option Institute™ after months of reading about it and days of traveling to it. As it came into sight, it looked exactly as I had expected. The compound was built around a large white Victorian mansion. Off to the side of the main building were newly built guestrooms for parents. The entire complex was set quietly in the middle of a serene, wooded forest on more than eighty acres. It sat at the top of a hill overlooking a green valley of mature trees, thick greenery, and beautiful pathways and bridges. The chirping birds and a trickling, curvy creek made the only audible sounds. I found the perfect spot looking out across the vast hillside. I sat down, taking it all in. I let the cool air in through my nose and let go of the built-up stress, little by little, with each exhale.

Along with the learning program for parents, the Institute offered all the amenities and comforts of home. The kitchen and café served only natural and healthy organic meals to the guests. Everything was fresh and delicious-tasting, without a dessert or sugar-added food in sight. There was even a full workout facility, set up in resortlike style. We might have felt guilty about enjoying our surroundings so much, but quickly learned that an important component of being a successful parent is finding ways to take care of yourself so you can better take care of your child.

The Son-Rise Program® is geared toward teaching parents how to manage a home program that will help lead their child out of autism. After their training, parents put the program in place back home, and have the choice of returning with their child so that he or she can work individually with a treatment group. The Kaufman family, who founded the program, had an autistic son named Raun. They helped him to fully recover from autism by the age of four, using the philosophy they developed. They established the Institute with the intention of educating other parents and sharing their discovery of how to improve daily lives affected by the disorder.

Raun was an adult at the time of our visit. He had recently become a counselor at the Option Institute™ after moving back to the area from California, where he had been running a children's learning center. We were excited when we learned that he was our counselor the first day. He was bright and witty, and had me giggling throughout our session. We began our visit by walking with him on one of the pathways that stretched along the beautiful creek. I remember watching a few leaves floating on top of the water as I took in the serene environment. It was almost fall. The temperature had started getting brisk, but the air was cool and refreshing.

Our discussion began with Raun asking, "So how is your relationship going?"

We were both caught off guard. I laughed nervously, a little starstruck because I was actually talking to the boy I had read about. I stuttered, "We-We're doing okay. We have some conflicts, of course, mostly caused by the stress of all the things we have going on."

"What does that conflict look like?" Raun continued.

I felt a bit uncomfortable delving into our relationship, but I knew why he was directing us there. Parents of autistic children often end their marriages because the relationship absorbs a lot of the frustration and tension the parents experience around the child's struggles. I glanced quickly at James. I knew that I had to just go with the conversation, so I opened up: "Well, James says things that make me feel bad."

"I see. Can you explain a little more about that? Maybe put into words why you feel bad?"

Again, I laughed nervously. My discomfort must have been obvious. "I just do. It hurts my feelings."

"What do you mean when you say it hurts your feelings?" Raun said, trying to dig deeper.

"It hurts me. I don't know. I just feel bad when he says mean things to me."

"Why are you calling what James says 'mean'?" he persisted.

We continued back and forth. I got confused at one point, wondering why he kept asking the same things. But after a few minutes, Raun managed to point out that I felt bad because I had made a choice to feel bad. His lesson to me was that you shouldn't give other people control of your happiness. Happiness is a choice you make for yourself.

The philosophy makes all the sense in the world, but even to this day, I have a hard time applying it in my own life. I have gotten better at it over the years though. When James and I have a conflict that is hard to resolve, I take some time and space and go do something that I know will make me happy. That improves my attitude and better prepares me to return and try to resolve the problem.

Those first few hours with Raun were spent in discussion about James and me, both as individuals and as a couple. It seemed odd at first that we didn't talk about Jamie at all. But this was all preparation for the in-depth events we were about to experience.

The people we met at the Option Institute™ were incredible. We all shared a common bond—our children. We spoke about them each day. Our teachers included Bryn Hogan, the daughter of Barry and Samahria Kaufman; William Hogan, Bryn's husband; and Barry "Bears" Neil Kaufman himself. What an outstanding team! They made us laugh and cry and feel like we weren't alone. The leaders' motivational presentations, often presented through comedy, were really enjoyable to see. Bryn's way of teaching and the stories she told had me laughing so hard that I often had to catch my breath.

The entire group of parents initially convened in a warm, wood-paneled room in front of a beautiful glass window that had the image of a sky and a star etched into it. It was obviously a symbol for the mission of the program, and it helped add to the environment, which already felt conducive to growth and self-discovery.

Each couple was instructed to stand up and tell something about their child. Various parents stood up, saying, "My child is Jeremy, he has autistic spectrum disorder" or "My child has autistic spectrum disorder with pervasive developmental disorder" or "My child has autism with ADHD" or "My child has Asperger's."

I had become so sensitive to all the labels. Jamie had been diagnosed with autistic spectrum disorder (ASD), but I just couldn't bring myself to describe him with those words, even though it was relevant to why we were there. I felt like there were so many other things to say about who he really was.

My turn came and I walked to the front of the group, as everyone else had. I began, "My son is Jamie. He's two years old." Taking a deep breath, I continued, "I really don't want him to be what he has, because I believe that he's going to get better and that's why I'm here. Jamie is a beautiful child with curly blond hair and a sweet smile. He's an amazing kid. He loves red balls and airplanes. He makes me laugh—and cry. He's actually here in Sheffield, down the street with his twin brother, Jack. I love them both so much."

By the time I said the last few words, a sizable lump had formed in my throat because I was touched and proud to be talking about both our sons to the other parents I had met that day.

Each day, the parents gathered together and then broke off into groups to work on various exercises with one another. We practiced role-playing and worked on our communication skills. Along with these kinds of learning activities, we watched a movie about what it is like to be an autistic guest at a birthday party. It was a horrible thing to experience. The visuals showed complete overstimulation, with excessive movement and really loud noises. There were faces and bodies pushing all boundaries of personal space as the viewer searched frantically for a quiet and peaceful place to go—a place that he or she could find.

During breaks, we went for walks outside and indulged ourselves in the gorgeous views of green grass and trees in all directions. We were invited to take a closer look at the swing set for adults, built on a little hill off in the distance. The swing set boasted six adult-size swings, the likes of which I had never before seen. They hung down from tall pine posts and swung in the air about thirty feet high. Just as Jamie had found sensory comfort from swinging, the Institute knew

Jamie feeling the same way, overwhelmed

their visiting adults would do the same. Obviously, we were being shown a form of moving meditation that would help ease our stress.

James and I visited the swing set every day. We are never ones to pass up an opportunity to play outside or act like little kids. We even brought the boys back up to the grounds so they could see the swing set and take turns sitting on the swings, too.

The visit was pleasant from the start, and we couldn't believe how much we had learned. Many different kinds of affirmation exercises taught us how to make positive changes

Option Institute swing sets

in all areas of our lives, even through seemingly small actions.

The Option Institute™ was so successful at helping children that it had developed other programs for adults. A variety of guests came to receive help or support in anything from better business operation to recovering from the loss of a loved one. A person might stay for a few days, or he or she might stay on for six weeks. The facility was a haven of positive energy and a source of empowerment that met the diverse needs of its visitors.

We continued to meet with and talk to the most amazing couples, some of whom had traveled across continents to be there. There was one Argentinean couple with whom we connected particularly well. We would tell each other stories, eat together, and spend time sharing about ourselves. Talking about what we had done for our kids gave each of us a wealth of new ideas and information.

Most of the parents had stories about how their children had changed after being vaccinated. They had observed drastic changes in them either right away or over a period of time. One of the fathers, a cheerful man who was visiting the Institute by himself, had a daughter who was in bad shape. She was back home, being cared for by her mother. This girl had received the MMR (measles, mumps, and rubella) vaccine and had to go to the hospital immediately afterward because she had a terrible reaction to it. She began vomiting and then suffered some drastic damage to her digestive system and esophagus. Surviving with the help of a feeding tube, she needed a full-time nurse. She'd had other vaccines prior to receiving the MMR vaccine; had this been the one to push her over the edge?

In 1998, a doctor named Andrew Wakefield published a controversial study in *The Lancet*, which suggested there were links between the MMR vaccine and a syndrome of autism and bowel disease. (Dr. Wakefield also published studies suggesting a link between the measles virus and Crohn's disease.) In February 2010, *The Lancet* retracted the 1998 paper.[1] Despite this significant step on the part of the journal, Dr. Wakefield continues to defend his study.[2] Both sides present compelling arguments. That said, I feel that Dr. Wakefield's research has been profoundly important. It has led to more awareness regarding the issues of the intestinal tract in children with pervasive developmental disorders.

After the vaccine, this father's poor daughter not only suffered physically but also slipped into autism. I couldn't even imagine dealing with that kind of tragedy. What could anyone say to her father? It was inspiring to me to meet a person who had remained so positive through it all.

Finally, our visit came to an end. Being at the Institute had given us an enormous dose of joy. We left the program with a better understanding of how to enter into Jamie's world instead of being frustrated that he wasn't in ours. We learned to celebrate the place he was in, rather than be discouraged by it. All the principles we had learned were centered on consistent and unconditional love and acceptance. I felt a dramatic shift in mindset, and acknowledged that the experience had definitely been life-altering.

We had decided that our next stop would be New York City, only two hours away by train. We planned to take the boys for some fun in the Big Apple. But time got away from us and before we knew it we were terribly late. Somehow, our serene and reflective departure from the Option Institute™ regressed into a mad dash to the train station.

Knowing we would be away from home for almost three weeks, we had packed a ton of things and ended up traveling with eleven bags among the five of us, including a stack of toys. We had packed the RV without concern for space, and now we found ourselves carrying all of it by hand. Trying to hurry out of Sheffield with two kids, a nanny, and more luggage than we could carry must have been hilarious to watch. We were so late that we were forced to leave our rental car in the parking lot of the train station with the keys inside. We even left an oversize chalkboard and a couple of basketballs behind. We made it onto the train in the nick of time, after somehow managing to load our abundance of baggage without any help. James and I were both sweating profusely by the time we made it to our seats. Relaxing eventually, we enjoyed a meal and made some fun out of our mini-adventure on the train.

We arrived on time at Penn Station in New York City. Then we were suddenly faced with the daunting question of

how we would navigate through the busy sidewalks with all of our bags. A station assistant stopped to help us, offering to load our luggage onto the cart he was pulling. Looking at the size of the cart, we scoffed at his offer, thinking that he would probably need at least two more carts to help us, but he assured us our bags could all fit. Sure enough, within minutes and with precision, he had every piece of luggage stacked neatly to the top of the cart and was ready to move us along through the bustling, crowded train station. We were awfully impressed.

We hailed a couple of taxis, thinking they could accommodate us, but our luggage wouldn't fit. We ended up taking a stretch limousine, squeezing most of our luggage into the trunk and the remainder in the aisles, between us on the seats, and at our feet. Mere minutes after we were finally traveling, I insisted on stopping at the sight of the first Starbucks. The limo driver agreed to double-park while James went in to get us all drinks, including one for the driver. We continued to find humor in our travel misadventures.

I had reservations at the Benjamin, a small boutique hotel around the corner from the Waldorf Astoria. It had just opened and was offering a good rate for New York City. When we arrived, we were excited to see that it was a European-style hotel, quaint and hip, with a cool bar and restaurant off the lobby. The rooms were charming, decorated with crushed red velvet and Italian chandeliers.

We checked in and got the boys settled with Carla, and then James and I ran out to catch the musical *Rent*. Drinks in hand, we found our seats. We were ecstatic to have this night out and felt great after our stay at the Option Institute™. It was the perfect release from all the drama, hardship, and spiritual highs and lows we had experienced since leaving home a few weeks earlier. It had been a long while since we'd had as much fun as we had that night. We looked at each other and were filled to the brim with contentment. We found ourselves exchanging smiles throughout the evening. The performance was fabulous, the best we had seen. We had dinner afterward and walked back, hand in hand, through the bustling city streets.

The next day, we took Jamie and Jack to Central Park. We walked and walked, pushing them in strollers down the curvy

Cruising at Rockefeller Center with the boys

paths, admiring the changing greens and golds of the tall, old trees. We stopped a few times so our boys could run around and jump on rocks in the large open spaces.

Jamie's breathing had stabilized and he seemed to be feeling well. Our plan was to see *Beauty and the Beast* that evening, and we decided to go ahead with it since everybody seemed healthy.

As we entered the theater, we were thrilled that the boys were about to see their first Broadway show. The show started with loud noises and banging drums, and all of a sudden it hit me that this was going to be hard for Jamie. At the first noisy sounds, he became squirmy and uncomfortable, crawling onto my chest, gripping me tightly, and burrowing his head into my shoulder. It seemed that he and I would probably need to leave. Then I remembered what I'd learned from the Option Institute™ about autistic children; Jamie's sense of hearing was magnified tenfold compared to everyone else's. I recalled how upset he became at certain noises, screaming anytime he heard the blender or the flushing of the toilet.

I thought about how I might possibly help him—maybe by blocking the noise so he could still watch the show? I hesitated to cover his ears because he hated anyone or anything touching his head, but I was desperate for a solution. I tried it and, amazingly, he let me hold my hands there. With the volume softened, he quickly sat up and turned around to watch the stage. He spent the first part of the show fascinated, while I tightly cupped his ears. I was elated that it was actually working! About halfway through, he fell asleep. We were on our way out of the theater afterward when he woke up. I expected him to be agitated and disoriented, forgetting where he was, but he acted rested and happy.

We flew home the next day, excited, tired, and glad to be getting back. Now it was time to put all our new knowledge to work. Part of what I had learned was that Jamie would benefit from interacting with people other than his usual caretakers. The Son-Rise Program® suggests that parents ask friends and acquaintances to volunteer their time to work with their

Jamie and me on the flight home

child. I was never one to ask for help without offering something in exchange, but the Option Institute™ teaches that when others help, they themselves benefit through giving. I had to work on accepting this idea, recognizing that the situation could be mutually beneficial.

I began asking everyone I knew if they could spend time with Jamie. I spoke with people from church, acquaintances from the health club, and other friends and family members. The response was completely positive! The process requires that parents teach others how to interact with their child at the child's house, in his or her own environment. In this way, caring adults support the child for most of the waking hours of the day, to bridge the gap between the child's world and our world. This might include conversation, playtime, or just sitting near the child during whatever activity she or he engages in. If the child sits and rocks quietly, the support person does the same in an effort to unite with the child.

I followed the program guidelines by designating a separate room in our house where Jamie could play. I had a two-way mirror installed, as the program suggested, so I could watch and learn from his interactions without his awareness. We had a group meeting with our volunteers, where I shared information from the Option Institute™. We worked out a schedule for everyone to come to the house, along with windows of time in which I would work with each volunteer.

One of the best volunteers I had was Dave, a firefighter whom I had met in a spinning class at the health club. I couldn't believe how wonderful he was with Jamie, gentle and loving. He really got into his role, and he and Jamie had a lot of fun together.

Changing our thinking about autistic behavior, we moved from having expectations to exorcising acceptance. We stopped expecting Jamie to act in a certain way as a "normal" or typical child, and instead began to accept him as he was in the moment. Once this transformation of perception, or paradigm shift, occurred, it was easier to understand him. This allowed us to connect with him in a way we had never before thought possible.

Jamie's way of communicating was to scream to get the things he wanted. Our new philosophy required patience to slow down the communication and de-escalate the situation, along with training for him on how to communicate to the best of his ability, without using words. This meant that I could no longer simply give him what he wanted, as I had grown accustomed to doing, just to get him to stop screaming. I learned that I needed to help him calm down first. I had to talk at half-speed in order to convey calmness. For example, if he wanted some almonds, he would motion in their direction and scream. I couldn't immediately give him almonds anymore. Instead, I would ask what he wanted by pointing to other things first, like an orange, and asking, "Orange?" Then I would point to an apple and ask, "Apple?" He would have to stop screaming and think about what he wanted. Once I finally pointed to the almonds, he would be more focused and calm, having listened to my slow, controlled voice. I could discern an immediate difference in Jamie's thought processes the first time I tried this technique.

Our trip to Massachusetts had provided us with the perfect starting point, and we were on our way to building a solid foundation. I acknowledged that we were actually progressing. Each day I took another piece of the puzzle and found the place where it fit.

CHAPTER

8

Doctors, Doctors, Doctors

I related to the white-blossom snowflakes I watched twirl through the night sky; they were hopeful and promising, but with an unknown destiny. In moments of despair, I tend to look up at the sky, as if I might find the answers I need written in the clouds. For a long time now, I had been completely consumed with Jamie's well-being. From inside the shuttered window, against the snow-lit darkness, I imagined his face: his innocent, beautiful eyes looking back at me, the sound of his voice speaking words I wished to hear. The power of this emotion was more than my heart could hold. I had searched and cried and screamed and prayed. All I wanted was some certainty that he was going to be all right, but there was no certainty when it came to Jamie's future. If he was going to get well, it was up to me.

The only thing I was certain of was my profound love for him. That kept me going, pursuing further knowledge, no matter what anyone said about his condition. I wanted to know what he was thinking and how he felt. Was he afraid?

Did he know how much I loved him? Could he hear me? *One day*, I told myself, *I will know my son, sense his love, and know he feels mine, and I will watch him as his thoughts grow and take shape.*

Sometimes hope is so elusive. . . . One afternoon, Jamie glanced at me out of the corner of his eye as I talked to him. Although it was just a quick glance, it was a connection—very real, very powerful. I wanted him to stay right there with me. In those split seconds, I knew we were making progress.

And then, seemingly infinite periods passed when he didn't look at me; it felt like he didn't even know I existed. The staggering burden of my plight turned to a heavy weight in my body.

I don't know why or how, but I have something inside me that has always helped me get through difficult stretches in my life. It's a mystery where it comes from, but I thank God I have it. I've found a way to keep happiness around me through simple moments of laughter. I love to laugh. It always makes me feel better. Maybe it's just a way to practice being happy, or a wonderful physical release, or a combination of both.

Growing up a fairly shy girl, I know I laughed a lot throughout the years. Perhaps it was because I wasn't confident or because I was nervous. I remember laughing even at times when I wanted to cry. James and I have had some serious laughing sessions. If anyone had the ability to get me going, it was James.

He and I still work hard to maintain an environment we can laugh in, and sometimes it is much harder than it sounds.

One of the valued weekly rituals we have always kept to help nurture this part of our marriage is a date night once a week, even if we don't feel like it at first.

One evening, with our plans already in place, James came home from work after a chaotic day. I'd had a tough day, too, and we were short with each other, disinterested, and impatient. We struck up the daily small talk, irritation seeping through each overarticulated word we exchanged.

"Are you going to be ready to go on time?" he asked, knowing I am usually running behind.

"Of course," I lied.

"Well, let's get going if we're going." We swapped glaring glances.

"Whatever."

I was a little on edge, which had become a consistent element of my personality in those days, and I was quick to display it on this particular evening, uncomfortable with having to leave the boys. They were extra clingy, which caused me to take even longer to get ready. James was in the car waiting, and the pressure was mounting. We were at least an hour late for our dinner date, and I was dreading the mood of the evening. I knew James didn't understand why I was so upset about leaving the boys when they were crying, but there was no other excuse for the huge delay.

He started in immediately. "Are we ever going to pick a time and keep it? I'm so tired of always being late. We're keeping our friends waiting. Are you even capable of being on time . . . ever?"

"James, I did my best. The boys were unsettled tonight because they knew we were leaving. Come on, is it really that big a deal for me to give them a little bit of extra time?"

We exchanged razor-sharp looks again.

"Come on, Krista. It's embarrassing to be late all the time. I'm really tired of it. And the boys are fine. They're young and more adaptable than you give them credit for. You know they're always fine five minutes after we leave. Don't use them as your excuse just because it's impossible for you to be on time."

After about a minute, we caught each other's eye again.

"You're crazy. I'm always on time," I said with a half grin.

We tried our best to hold that wall up, but it came crashing down as we burst out laughing. As has usually been the case with us, we find our common ground with a good laugh. We had a fun time that night and decided that the night out had been exactly what we needed—time alone and away together when we could just play. Our infallible philosophy kept us happier as individuals and as a couple.

Hanging in there was an art form. I had other ways to keep up with the outrageous pace of life, like getting away for an hour or two to go shopping in Denver. Shopping was my favorite distraction. I loved shopping at Fred Segal or Barneys when I was in Los Angeles, but outside California I had to find the best substitutes I could. Near downtown, there was a unusual bookstore called the Tattered Cover. After using up my clothes-shopping energy, I would hit that bookstore. I would go to the health and wellness section and look for the newest books on autism, although there was always a limited selection or no choices at all.

On one of these many occasions, I was searching through the few shelves that held the kinds of books I wanted, looking for something new. I picked up certain titles, glancing at their covers, putting them back when they didn't catch my interest. One of the books I moved sent another book falling forward, exposing the title of a book sitting behind it: *Biological Treatments for Autism and PDD* by William Shaw, PhD. It felt like I had stumbled upon the hidden control of some secret passageway. Reaching out, I scooped up the treasure.

I flipped through its pages and realized right then that I had struck gold. I couldn't wait to take the book home, and once I did I kept it by my side constantly. It was the first book I had found that really addressed the internal systems of autistic children. Dr. Shaw discussed the biochemical changes, and his insights brought everything together for me. I learned more from this book than I had from any other single source so far. It was my bible, my secret weapon. Several of the alternative health specialists we visited even adopted his plan after I shared Shaw's discoveries and philosophies with them. I pointed out to several doctors that The Great Plains Laboratory, Inc., founded by Dr. Shaw, was renowned for its diagnostic testing on patients with autism.

This book was extremely informative about which tests to request from the doctors we visited and which labs to send samples to for evaluation. My pediatrician had left me with little to go on after the initial diagnosis of Jamie's illness. There were many answers to be found by delving deeper. The mainstream labs had no process for or capability of handling the kind of investigation The Great Plains Laboratory could offer. After reading this book, I felt stronger. I knew I was armed with new, valuable knowledge to fight the mysterious disorder that had a hold on my son.

I started a more intense search for doctors, going from one to the next, looking for the right one—or for whoever might help Jamie improve. It seemed like I created a rhythm: Jamie and I went to a doctor and I sucked every drop of information from our visits. If I didn't see marked improvement within two or three months, we moved on to another one. Looking back, it reminds me of the movie *Speed*, where Sandra Bullock is driving the runaway speeding bus. She can't take her foot off the gas or the onboard bomb will detonate. Racing down the highway, she yells for directions at the exit, "*Stay on or get off? Stay on or get off?*" She makes the turn, keeping the bus in motion despite all obstacles.

Periodic calls to Dr. Allen were still a part of my routine. "Hey, I just wanted to check in to see if there's any new research you've come across lately."

"Well, I'm always keeping my eyes open for you, Krista, but there just isn't anything to report," he would reply. "I'm sorry. I'll be sure to call when I see anything of interest."

That was a typical phone conversation. Nonetheless, I continued to stay in touch with all my contacts, hoping that, through one of the calls or conversations, I would get a little closer to my goal. I never stopped being proactive.

Part of my research process always included a good once-over of the new month's *Mothering* magazine. It was the only periodical that had its finger on the pulse of autism. One of its many reliable issues led me to the Autism Research

Institute, founded by Bernard Rimland, PhD, in San Diego. I got in touch with the Institute and talked at length with the medical staff. They sent me a large amount of information that included recommendations for supplements being offered by Kirkman Labs. I was extremely excited to find this kind of research. From the beginning, I had wondered why every pediatrician wasn't looking at the causes of autism from inside the body, like Dr. Shaw and Dr. Rimland were. The fact that Dr. Rimland's group was recommending natural treatments for deficiencies in the bodies of autistic children had me completely invested in learning about everything they had discovered.

The supplements Kirkman Labs had available were being sold to those who were willing to test their effectiveness. Some of the supplements brought changes and some didn't; it depended on the individual. I had learned earlier that Dr. Rimland had an autistic son of his own whose condition had improved through treatments uncovered by Dr. Rimland's research. I began by following some of his recommended guidelines, first giving Jamie Super Nu-Thera P5P, a supplement high in vitamin B and zinc. It had the advantages of being hypoallergenic and gluten- and casein-free, and it was made especially for children in a liquid form. It also contained vitamin B6, which supported brain activity and focus.

I've always been open-minded and interested in trying new supplements and therapies, but I was a little apprehensive about giving Jamie this new supplement. I felt like a pioneer with no one to show me the way, no doctor to guide my every step. I had no idea how Super Nu-Thera would affect him or how he would respond. The first time Jamie took it, I gave it to him quickly by mouth via a syringe, and there was no negative reaction. *Phew!* The second time he took it, his swallow seemed a little more forced, and he grimaced. He looked up at me with his big, almond-shaped brown eyes, and I could only wonder what he was thinking.

After a while, I had to lure him into taking it with my sweetest voice, encouraging all his trust. "Jamie, sweetie, we have this yummy new supplement that's going to make you so strong. . . ."

I tasted it so he could see it wasn't that bad. But he had caught on to my tricks by this time, and he ran and hid.

"Come on, Jamie, it'll be fun. Look at the color! It's a pretty orange, and it even tastes like oranges. You love oranges."

He peeked out from behind the couch, still hesitant and unconvinced.

Plan B: Jack will help me. I whispered, "Jack, I'll give you a surprise if you take it first."

Jack was quick to accommodate me, opening up and swallowing down the colorful liquid with ease as Jamie looked on. Jack went first with most of the things I wanted the boys to try, which usually did the trick for Jamie. This time was no exception; thank goodness for Jack. I gave him his reward—chewing gum—and he was happy.

Another Kirkman Labs supplement called DMG (dimethylglycine) came to my attention. I learned from Dr. Shaw's book that Dr. Rimland's son was taking it. Its chemical makeup is basically water-soluble vitamins, mainly B15. Many parents who used this vitamin noticed significant improvements with

Jack always protecting Jamie. At the pool in Santa Barbara

speech, eye contact, social behavior, and attention span. So far, things seemed to be going well with the Super Nu-Thera, and what I had read about DMG sounded promising. I ordered it, although I didn't give it to him. Not right away, at least. I was still reluctant.

After a few weeks, the DMG was still sitting in the cabinet. Each time I opened the door and looked at it, it seemed to be looking back at me, reminding me that I needed to keep trying new things.

Like the dirty dishes in the sink or the laundry that needs folding, you can only look at a necessary chore so many times before you just have to do it. I had looked at the DMG so many times that, one day, I just had to go for it.

I remember clearly the first time I mixed the DMG with some rice milk and had Jamie drink it. Afterward, I put him in the ball pit, where he and Jack could play. Jamie began his usual repetitive routine with the balls while I ran upstairs for a minute. When I came downstairs, he had thrown all the balls out of the open sliding glass door. He was screaming and grabbing his head. He threw more toys at Jack and acted aggressively toward him. I couldn't believe what I was witnessing. He became a crazed little boy. I held him closely and tried to calm him down, but it was like he was possessed. I thought it might be the DMG. Eventually, hours later, Jamie was himself again.

Perhaps the DMG had had the opposite of the intended effect. This experience was unforgettable. Maybe it would take giving Jamie DMG over a longer period to see any positive effects, but I was not willing to see him endure it. I never gave it to him again.

Going through the trial-and-error process was difficult, especially in periods like this. I wondered if many parents felt the frustration and uncertainty I was feeling, trying different supplements and watching desperately for some sign they might be working. Even with the help and experience of a few doctors and therapists, it still felt like the current state of medicine left my child and me stranded on our own island.

I longed for a way to communicate with others who were doing what I was doing. If there was a way to share information, maybe we could help each other. Back then, the Internet wasn't what it is today. (Hello, Facebook and Twitter!) But I knew there must be someone out there somewhere with that missing piece of information I needed. Were they on another continent, or did they live down the street? The process was like searching for something in the dark without even knowing what you were looking for. Each passing day seemed like a week and each month a year. Time was moving so, so slowly. I continued trying to get the perfect blend of supplements, one that would render some obvious and measurable results. I realized that I could open up the capsules or grind up the pills on a granite stone and mix the powders into Jamie's bottle. I was still giving the boys my homemade recipe of almond and cashew milk formula. I had kept them both on the bottle for an extended period because it was a exceptional delivery system. Anytime I mixed in supplements, I taste-tested my concoction. Sometimes it made me gag, so I would add a little more milk or agave nectar to increase the sweetness. Jamie took it well most of the time, which really surprised me.

While my mindset was to be open to trying new things, I wasn't sure Jamie needed everything I was giving him. I desperately wanted some help in managing the important tools I was using. I didn't want to just throw the kitchen sink at him. Every day I battled whether to give him this or give him that. Was it too much? Would the combinations cancel one another out? I felt like pulling my hair out. Anxiety riddled my decision-making process. Once again, I turned to my father-in-law, Dr. Vance, for his knowledge about internal medicine. He had been the one to introduce me to the benefits of chelation, and although he did not specialize in working with autistic children, he had helped guide me to my next move. He had already suggested that Jamie take pure supplements such as B6, B12, and folic acid, instead of only the homeopathic versions.

It was obvious I needed to find a doctor who specialized in autism. I knew exactly the kind I was looking for. (Where were you then, MAPS doctors?) I knew the perfect profile to fit my mold. This doctor needed to be like James's dad, who was experienced with a wide variety of nutritional supplements and who also practiced chelation therapy. He or she must also have a superior understanding of how to detoxify the body. I didn't know the exact causes of Jamie's illness, but the information I had made me believe that something was causing Jamie's body to be out of balance. The RhoGAM shots I had been given and other vaccines contained thimerosal and other preservatives. In addition, Jamie had received massive amounts of antibiotics. There were myriad possible factors that could explain what was wrong.

The copious stories of parents whose children showed negative signs immediately after getting vaccinated continued to reach my ears. I think that a connection definitely exists between the high incidence of heavy metals in the body and developmental problems in children. Even today, the subject is constantly debated. (It is my belief that vaccinations somehow contribute to the occurrence of autism, although I don't believe this will be confirmed any time soon, due to the incredible power and influence of the drug companies.) Although I hadn't had Jamie vaccinated, both boys received the Synagis shot for premature babies to help protect their lungs against RSV (respiratory syncytial virus). This is not a vaccine, but I didn't know at the time what they preserved this shot with. (Now they have it in a preservative-free form.)

Whatever the other factors, I felt certain that heavy metals had some connection to Jamie's illness.

A friend of mine recommended I speak to a nutritionist, an acquaintance of hers, about Jamie. I felt knowledgeable about nutrition and believed I made good food choices, but I was willing to learn from anyone who could expand on what I already knew. I ended up getting together with her, and after our diet talk, we discussed my search for a Denver metro area doctor who treated autism. She knew of an MD who had been treating her friend's twenty-year-old daughter for a variety of conditions, including bipolar disorder and schizophrenia. She gave me a flyer about him. He practiced in Lakewood, and his name was Terry Grossman, MD. He sounded good and I made a mental note to look into his practice.

Before I had the opportunity to follow up on this lead, while shopping at the health food store I noticed the same flyer posted on a bulletin board. The flyer announced a seminar about heart disease and chelation therapy that Dr. Grossman was leading. Of course, I had been looking for someone who practiced chelation. It was one of those coincidences you can't just shrug off. The only question was whether or not he used chelation and detoxification modalities with small children. When it rains, it definitely pours.

The Autism Research Institute had offered to send me a list of local doctors who had the kind of ideal profile I was looking for. More choices—MDs, in fact! I was hopeful that these references would lead to another potentially valuable connection. I had requested the list weeks earlier but hadn't

Jamie, seemingly relaxed in the car before doctor's appointment

heard back, so I made a quick follow-up call, which set things in motion. While I was looking over the list of recommended doctors they faxed me, one of the names jumped off the page: Terry Grossman, MD. Being hit over the head would have been less subtle than the signs I was receiving. I knew this was the doctor who needed to be in our lives. I made the call and took the first available appointment. I was enormously happy to finally identify a doctor who worked with autism and even had an office close to my home. I couldn't believe it! I was literally dancing with excitement.

I counted the days until that first appointment. When the date rolled around, we made our way to his office, but Jamie, screaming and crying hysterically, refused to enter the unfamiliar building.

I pleaded with him, "Jamie, sweetie, Dr. Grossman is going to make you better. You'll like him. He's really, really kind."

I tried to persuade him to move through the front door by making a game out of it. I was going to do whatever it took to get inside. It was important to me to have found such a promising doctor, and I couldn't let us be deterred now.

After thirty minutes of pleading and negotiating, I finally got him inside. I was thinking, *Oh, God, please. Jamie, just hang in there. Please!* They showed me to the exam room and we didn't wait long before Dr. Grossman walked in with a cheerful "Hello." He brought an immediate presence and energy to the room that didn't escape my attention.

"Hi, Dr. Grossman. I'm Krista, and this is Jamie. I'm sorry for being so late." Jamie was hiding under the table as I spoke. "It took a long time to get him through the front door."

Dr. Grossman spoke warmly, which came as no surprise. "Well, I'm glad you made it in. You don't have to apologize, I understand. So . . . I had a chance to read your file and I know we can help Jamie. About 80 percent of the autistic children we've seen have shown improvement."

His words were a symphony to my ears. Had I actually heard right? Had a doctor just used the words, "We can help

Jamie"? I had traveled miles and spoken to dozens of specialists, but finally I had found the doctor I was looking for.

Dr. Grossman and I spoke about Jamie's history and all the things I had done with him so far. I shared the thoughts I had about how this had happened as well as my belief that we would overcome it. During this conversation, Jamie's behavior was almost uncontrollable. He was climbing the walls and he refused to let anyone touch him. Dr. Grossman was calm and had a complete understanding of what Jamie was experiencing. He was warm and nurturing rather than distant. As much as I had expected him to be just like this, he was still a pleasant surprise.

"We'll start by gathering the information we'll need to begin our treatment. This requires several different kinds of testing, including a test for the levels of various substances in Jamie's body."

Though excited to hear the doctor's immediate plan of action, I was a bit hesitant about proceeding. I voiced my concerns. "Because of everything he's been through already, I really don't want to force him too much. I really want the next time we see you to be easier."

"No problem. Don't worry about it. I understand. We'll get everything we need. My nurses are great. I'm also going to send a stool test home with you that I'll need you to bring back."

With our next steps mapped out, he started his physical examination.

Watching him interact with Jamie during his exam was interesting for me. I saw my son through the eyes of a stranger:

hiding behind his own opaque curtain, shielding his secrets. Would I ever know what was going on behind those eyes?

After observing and studying Jamie for a fair amount of time, Dr. Grossman had his staff come in to gather hair, urine, and blood for analysis. Jamie was not cooperating. I knew he needed the tests, but I hated to make him go through that ordeal. Every time the nurse got close to him, he ran from her, hysterical, dashing from one side of the office to the other, eventually hiding underneath a nearby table. With my help and the help of the other assistants, we were finally able to get him to sit down.

It was quite intense to watch the sweat dripping from Jamie's forehead as his blood was drawn. Three of us had to hold him steady as Dr. Grossman stuck a needle in his arm. Here I was, holding my son, tears streaming down both our faces as I tried to smile through it like everything was okay. I knew he felt like he was being assaulted and didn't understand why. It was a traumatic moment for both of us. Driving away from the office, I was exhausted and relieved that it was over. I wanted to go home, snuggle in bed with Jamie and Jack, and take a nice, long nap.

Thinking back over the day's events, I realized that Dr. Grossman had established an instant rapport with me. I looked forward to the follow-up call he had told me to expect. When any doctor called, I was careful not to speak about Jamie as "autistic" within Jamie's hearing. My longtime friend Marco had brought to my attention the fact that children pick up on things more than we think. They may not even understand the meaning of the terms we use, but they understand the tones of our voices and they know when we are talking about them. I believed this to be true. Somehow, in my mind, saying that Jamie was autistic would affirm that he wouldn't change or get better. I didn't want that negative affirmation for him or for me. Everything about our lives was geared toward Jamie getting well, right down to the way we spoke.

The call came as promised.

"Hello, Krista, it's Dr. Grossman. I wanted to follow up to share some feedback. I do believe Jamie's condition is Autistic Spectrum Disorder, or ASD. There are mild to severe cases, but Jamie is more of a 'classic' case, which is somewhere in the middle, because of his complete loss of language and eye contact, and his nonverbal pointing, repetitive behaviors, echolalia, and high sensory issues, especially with touch and noise intolerance."

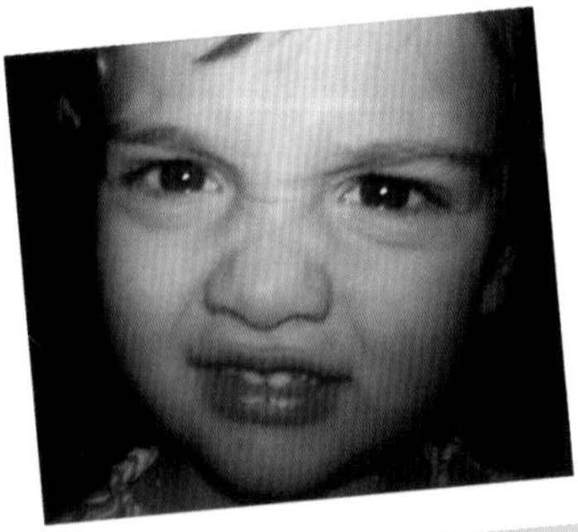

I appreciated the way he communicated with me, providing a lot of detail but never implying that we were at a dead end. I felt comfortable and happy to be working with him. But hearing the "A" word again caused that familiar response in me—that sickening hollowness in my belly, that all-too-familiar chill up my spine.

Pictures in
Santa Barbara

CHAPTER 9

Making Progress

Working with Dr. Grossman was like traveling on a speeding bus. I could tell that he was excited to work with us and that he and I were on the same page of the same game plan. He agreed I should continue to withhold dairy and wheat—which contain casein and gluten—from Jamie's diet. From my research, I learned that many autistic children don't have the enzymes they need to break down protein. I also read about opioid peptides, such as casomorphines in casein, and gluten exorphines and gliadorphin in gluten. These are chemically similar to opiates, and long-term exposure may be detrimental to brain activity, especially in autistic children.

I realized I needed to get even more serious about the foods I was giving Jamie. I had always bought organic foods whenever they were available. From that point on, I went out of my way to buy organic. My intention was to alleviate the extra load put on Jamie's body by the chemicals and pesticides so prevalent in typical grocery store food. I had to special-order many items from catalogs because there were few choices available at local health food markets at the time. It seemed like I was living at Vitamin Cottage and Wild Oats; I spent numerous hours each day making the drive out to their distant locations. (The effort this required has since been rendered obsolete by the increased availability and convenience of gluten-free, casein-free, and organic foods at natural foods stores and grocery stores. Over the years, Whole Foods has become our one-stop shop for everything we need, from delicious fresh organic and healthy foods to all our environmentally friendly products. It's probably my favorite shopping venue, and that is saying a lot! I continue to make sure we have all the right foods in the house.)

The detrimental effects of sugar had really become apparent to me. Too much sugar not only can cause you to feel sick but also, over a long period of time, can cause an overgrowth of yeast in the intestines, among other things. Reducing the level of yeast in Jamie's intestines was something I was trying to repair naturally. He loved ketchup on everything, and after acknowledging how much sugar it contained, I resolved to read the label of absolutely every product I bought. I decided to cut ketchup, as well as some other common foods, out of his diet completely. The decision forced me to find some creative substitutes, such as replacing ketchup with tomato sauce seasoned by Celtic sea salt. He watched me mix it and put it on his plate. He pushed it away and let out a scream that probably scared the neighbors.

"Come on, Jamie. This will be good. It's so much better for you. Try it." Why did I ever think the "good for you" argument was going to work with a toddler? He would have no part of it. I was disappointed because I thought I'd had such a good idea. But soon I figured out that he was associating the food he liked with the bottle it came in. I put my mixture together again, replacing the original ketchup inside the familiar bottle. Jamie never noticed a difference in taste. It worked like a charm.

I also used to give an organic cookie to the boys every once in a while. Before too long, I stopped doing that as well. A typical favorite for lunch would be organic turkey on brown rice bread. I thought this was mushy and funky tasting, but fortunately Jamie loved it. Every day after my workout, I always stopped at Starbucks for my own little sugar fix: a vanilla latte and a maple oat scone. It provided a great buzz and an additional few hours of extra energy, and it had become the daily indulgence that I really looked forward to. But I even scaled this back to a decaf soy latte and dropped the scone. I was walking the same walk as the boys.

Everyone was making sacrifices. Jack always went along with whatever we needed to do for Jamie. Just thinking about Jack illuminates my being. I was always grateful to have him by my side. He was (and still is!) a consistent, steady, positive force, with his beautiful curly blond hair and beaming disposition. Even though I knew he didn't always want the food we ate, he usually just went with the flow.

When he saw his friends eating orange-colored corn chips, he would ask, "Please, Mom, please, can I have some?"

"No, you know you can't. They're not good for your body. They have MSG, which is a neurotoxin, an endocrine-disrupting substance. It kills brain cells! This is not what we want."

He didn't know what all that meant, but it sounded bad, especially because of the tone of my voice.

"Mom, they're good. They're orange."

I responded, "Yes, and notice how your friends' hands are dyed that color. Listen, if you want some colorful food, I'll make you a special green smoothie when we get home."

He wasn't quite as entertained by my solution as I was. Was it a little harsh? Maybe for his age, but I wanted to make a point about how strict we were going to be with what we put in our bodies. (Oh, boy, was I turning into my mom?) He didn't like it at first, but with his sweet and altruistic nature, he didn't take it any further. We really were all in this together.

My sweet adorable Jack

I continued trying to hone the nutritional routine for all of us, and with that goal in mind I became more and more rigorous as each month went by. At the same time, Dr. Grossman had me keep Jamie on vitamins B6 and B12, selenium, magnesium, taurine, essential fatty acids like DHA, and vitamins A, D, and E. Even the brand name became truly important to me. I learned about the manufacturing process of each supplement company and how important that process was in understanding exactly what you were getting. I wanted to avoid products with any fillers to ensure they had just the right level of potency. Product packaging was also extremely important. If a product such as omega fish oil or cod liver oil came in a light-colored plastic bottle, it was possible the oil was already rancid. Oils need to be in dark-colored containers to keep light out. (Typically, the best doctors carry high-quality, high-potency supplements in their office, so they are a trustworthy source.)

Many autistic children show signs of improvement when these kinds of diet changes are made, but I had yet to see any profound change in Jamie. Even so, I kept up the strict diet because I knew it was a potential component of his recovery. It was also the best way for our family to stay healthy.

Health and happiness were two things I tried fervently to hold on to. As the days continued to get colder and the nights longer, I became terribly tired of the Rocky Mountain winter. I was a California girl from the inside out, with a love for warmer temperatures. I had definitely enjoyed the weather in Colorado my first few years there with James, when we took the time to soak up the mountain environment during all four seasons. Maybe the cold weather was a novelty that wore off, or maybe I just really needed more warmth. But it was also true that our lifestyle was different now that we had children, and the winter was more of a limitation to our activities than an opportunity. The weather kept us all under house arrest, stuck inside much more often than we wanted to be.

After moving down to Denver from our mountain home, I thought we would see warmer weather and the boys would stay healthier. I was also looking forward to shorter distances to the health food store, doctors, and shopping. But the climate disappointed me. July was nice and warm, and August was full of sunny mornings, but they often turned into stormy, cloudy afternoons. I longed for a full day of sunshine.

I felt that if I just had more sun, my days would be better and happier, and maybe make up for the long dark, sleepless nights. (I have since discovered that sunlight actually does keep you healthy. There are many recent studies showing that vitamin D, which the sun delivers, pumps up the immune system—not to mention it is obviously favorable to a person's emotional state. For this reason I have found it helpful to supplement with vitamin D during the winter months.)

The weather had a definite correlation with our health. When fall changed to winter, the frequency of Jamie's sicknesses and labored-breathing episodes increased. It had been twelve months since we left the Option Institute™, and Jamie had been to the hospital no fewer than fifteen times during that period. Each time he had been given medication for his illness, and his sleeping pattern had worsened, changing from waking up two or three times each night to waking up ten to fifteen times.

At one point, I remember being adamant with the emergency room doctor about giving him antibiotics because he almost always needed them when he was fighting an infection. Several times, Jamie's viral infection had turned into a bacterial infection. I carried the constant fear that he would get worse and be hospitalized again. I was dead set against overusing antibiotics with him because of the havoc they had already wreaked on his intestinal tract, and yet he needed them to get healthy again. I couldn't seem to find a way out of the catch-22.

Each time Jamie was sick, I showed better resolve to improve the antibiotics problem. I went from "Give them to him!" to "Wait a minute . . . " to "Are you sure he needs them?" to "Don't give him any!" I knew I had to take proactive steps to strengthen his immune system. Dr. Grossman began focusing on this concern by adding a supplement called Transfer Factor to Jamie's mix.

Even though he was doing his own lab testing, Dr. Grossman supported my desire to have further testing done through Dr. Shaw's Great Plains Laboratory. I was curious to see the latest results and how the Transfer Factor was affecting Jamie. That way, I could keep constant tabs on what was happening with his body. The Transfer Factor was helping strengthen his immune system; he showed a slight increase in energy level and it seemed like his colds were shorter in duration. The Great Plains tests revealed more extensive results for a wider variety of intestinal imbalances, and also allowed for a comparison between the two labs' results. This kind of information was priceless to me because I could see values and measurements of the different levels in his body, concrete evidence that his body chemistry was changing. I had also integrated the services of the Great Smokies Diagnostic Lab (now called Genova Diagnostics) and Metametrix, both renowned labs for advanced stool-sample testing. The test results showed elevated levels of yeast and bacteria in Jamie's gut. Aha! It was the finger that pointed out the culprit for Jamie's ongoing gastrointestinal problems. I wasn't surprised at his yeast levels after all the medications, antibiotics, and steroids he had taken over the last couple of years.

When I was thirteen, after the first time I took antibiotics, my mother gave me an abundance of yogurt to eat. It was curious to me, but I knew she always had a purpose for every food she chose for us. She explained that the yogurt contained lactobacillus acidophilus and that, since the antibiotics would be hard on my digestive system, this ingredient would aid in my body's natural repair process. My mom's awareness of health issues was definitely way ahead of her time.

A year later, at fourteen, I lost my biological father to colon cancer. Our relationship had been unconventional because of a difficult divorce. I had just recently reconnected with him after years of absence, so his loss was all the more devastating. Although my mother had remarried and my stepfather had been filling the role of father in my life, my father's death was very sudden and it impacted my life and my siblings' lives profoundly. This lit a fire in me to become more educated about not only the whole body but also, more specifically, the alimentary canal. By the time I had children, I had learned all about the impact of yeast and harmful bacteria on the body. I knew that the intestinal tract makes up about 85 percent of the immune system, and I understood how it functioned.

The newest test results led to many long conversations with Dr. Grossman about how I didn't want to give Jamie any more prescription medication. Somehow, despite my justified reasoning, he managed to convince me to give Jamie a drug called nystatin along with intestinal flora. Intestinal flora are beneficial bacteria that colonize the intestinal tract. In combination, the two components would help address Jamie's high levels of yeast. I liked the idea in theory, but it stirred up the nervousness I had felt in the past when I gave him other medications that had caused so many problems.

To my delight, after about one month, the nystatin helped bring undeniable progress. Jamie actually spoke four words. He said, "Hi." He also said, "No!" "Oh," and "Mom." He hadn't used any words for more than two years, so that was a radical, significant change. Also, he became much more aware of his surroundings. These improvements were absolutely astounding! We kept Jamie on the nystatin for only one month, because overusing it can potentially cause problems, such as an even higher level of recurring yeast than had developed originally. Secretly, I didn't want to stop because he was doing so well. When something is working, why not keep it going? But I guess it was just too much of a good thing. Dr. Grossman reined me in, keeping us on a cycle of one month at a time.

After Jamie stopped taking the nystatin, he continued using the intestinal flora. I also gave him other probiotics, such as Ortho Biotic Powder with several bacterial strains, including Saccharomyces boulardii, made by Ortho Molecular Products. In addition, I gave him another probiotic, Saccharomycin DF (Saccharomyces boulardii), made by Xymogen. Both these products can be obtained from health care practitioners. Florastor (Saccharomyces boulardii) from Biocodex is similar to Saccharomycin DF, and you can get Florastor over the counter at a pharmacy. In the beginning, I used Culturelle probiotic (Lactobacillus GG) and Primal Defense, which you can get over the counter at major pharmacies, supermarkets, and health food stores. I felt it was right to rotate probiotics to make sure Jamie got all the different strains of bacteria. I did this each month or two to keep his yeast levels low and create a positive domino effect. I didn't get this as a direction from any doctor. I saw the success of this rotation and was confident in the choice, even though I had gone out on my own, following my instincts and my own research. Thrilled at the outcome, I continually kept an eye out for new probiotics.

The initial test results from the hair samples revealed that Jamie also had high levels of many metals. My hunger to learn even more about their impact on health was ravenous, and I continually quizzed Dr. Grossman, prompting him to dig deeper to find the answers I was looking for. He really seemed to enjoy the challenge of fielding my many questions.

The levels of some metals in Jamie's body, such as tin and antimony, were so high that the graphs were literally printing off the end of the page! Where had all this metal come from? Questions like these circled in my mind constantly. The odd thing was that the mercury level was the only one that measured normal. I thought, *The mercury has got to be hiding in there!* We had already discussed the option of oral chelation therapy, and with the new results we knew it was a must.

Dr. Grossman had made a considerable impact on Jamie's health, and he never fell short of our expectations. Jamie's treatments were worth everything to me, albeit very expensive over time. The tests alone ran between four and eight hundred dollars each. I continued to battle with the insurance company for payment of at least some of the office visits and testing costs. Most of the time the company refused, and my inquiry calls received only the standard response:

"I'm sorry, but we don't have a code for autism."

I still couldn't understand the logic. "What do you mean, you don't have a code for autism? It's a major illness!"

"It's just too broad an illness."

"'Too broad'? People are either autistic or they're not." I couldn't believe what I heard time after time.

The fact that these expenses fell solely on our shoulders added stress and further frustration for James, who always had to tame the financial beast. As for me, I had grown up believing that money grows on trees. I refused to accept that the same tree wasn't still growing in my backyard. In my mind, if the insurance company wouldn't pay, we would. My attitude about Jamie's treatment being a top financial priority hadn't changed a bit over the past year. I still wouldn't allow any excuses because of a shortage of funds. If Jamie needed more blood tests or a stool test, I wasn't going to deny him.

James had yet to see things my way. Our money was being drained from every direction and we constantly fought about the costs of Jamie's treatment. I had tunnel vision and could see only the goal. I was desperate to get whatever our son might need, and I just knew we'd find a way to pay for it, some way, somehow.

I pressed on, determined to keep in motion. With Jamie's internal functions under the careful watch of Dr. Grossman, I continued the The Son-Rise Program™ techniques at home. Jamie also kept working with Diane Osaki, the specialist I had contacted months earlier through the JFK Partners at the University of Colorado Health Services, during periods of time when I was without The Son-Rise Program volunteers. When Diane was called away for a long time on family business, I reluctantly decided to look for a new practitioner. I just didn't know how to establish this kind of relationship. I decided to try the old-fashioned way, the Yellow Pages. Under "Speech Language Pathologists," I found a specialist by the name of Joan A. Eckert, MA, CCC-SLP. Her name leaped off the page when I noticed her ad, which cited her background with The Son-Rise Program. I called her right away. We spoke over the phone and set an appointment to meet.

My first impression of her was perfect: She was sweet and warm, a wavy-haired strawberry blonde whom we would come to expect to see wearing flowing skirts and dresses. She had a rare serenity about her, and over time it became apparent that she was amazingly gifted with kids.

At our first session, she spent twenty to thirty minutes in the main room trying to get Jamie down the hall to the therapy room. Walking down the closed-in hallway brought his sensory issues to the surface, and having only a few words at the time, he was unable to communicate his feelings. He just wouldn't go. Joan decided to begin in the main room instead. For the first four or five visits, she worked to get him down the hall, each time persuading him to move a few inches farther. After about seven sessions, she was able to get him all the way back to the therapy room. They began actually making progress in many areas, although slowly.

I was sold on the work Joan was doing, and ecstatic when she shared her plans to start a school for kids with autism in Denver. G.E.M.S. (Growing Experientially Multi-Disciplinary Service) would be a daily program incorporating everything preschool offered, but with unique care: three or four teachers for a special group of six to eight students. It would be a forty-five-minute drive daily across town, but I felt it would be worth it.

At this point, Jamie had progressed to four hours of specialty therapy each week, along with The Son-Rise Program. I incorporated daily techniques learned from the program into his life. It was amazing to see the spillover effects on the rest of my family. It brought a variety of daily relationship tools to all of us. The Son-Rise Program philosophy was exceptionally worthwhile for Jamie, and the fact that Joan was incorporating these principles into her curriculum was a strong selling point for the school.

I decided that beginning school would be a good move. I was ready to step it up, with music and daily speech and occupational therapies, so Jamie was receiving four to eight hours of combined therapy each day. As committed as I was to making changes from the inside out, I knew I also needed to step up the behavioral therapies so he could improve and grow from the outside in.

Jack and Jamie began attending school together at G.E.M.S. There were two students in the class who were not autistic—an employee's daughter and Jack. Even though the class was specifically designed for special-needs children, Jack had no problem jumping right in. The class had all the necessary learning for prekindergarten, but it would also allow Jack's awareness to grow, while enabling him to advocate for his brother. There were students with different levels of autism, some more severe and some less than Jamie's.

I took the boys to school every day and often stayed with them for the first half hour or so. I had such a hard time leaving because I wanted to make sure they were okay. One day, I remember standing back and watching them. "If That's What It Takes," a song performed by Celine Dion (of course, Celine!), came to mind as I took it all in, watching Jamie play, stuck in that place of his.

The lyrics were moving. A song is such a little thing in the scheme of the world, but sometimes the little things can be the most inspiring. There always seemed to be a particular new song's lyrics that coincided exactly with a stage we were going through. It was as if the path were laid out for us already. Any inspiration I found helped fuel my motivation to get Jamie better. He needed to heal, and it had to be soon. The urgency I felt had me working at a frantic pace, always in a hurry. It was like running a marathon, a race against the clock. There would be no rest, no surrender. I would keep searching until I found the answer—or until my body fell apart.

CHAPTER

10

Crumbling Down

My life was not my own. The marathon had started to wear my body down. More and more often, I began to notice I didn't feel well. I usually took such good care of myself, eating healthy foods and exercising hard, but I guess that sleep deprivation and stress were finally getting the better of me. One morning I woke up with pain in the left side of my neck. At first, I thought I might have slept on it wrong. The pain continued for a couple of days, and although I iced and massaged it, it didn't subside. I talked to a friend who had been seeing a chiropractor she really liked; she suggested I give him a try. I had gone to chiropractors in the past, and I thought an adjustment might be just what I needed. From experience, I knew that the body being in alignment helped to sustain wellness and keep energy flow high.

I made an appointment. During that visit, I showed the practitioner where the painful area was. He adjusted the other parts of my body first. I noticed he was rough at the beginning, and I was feeling anxious by the time he worked his way to my neck. Either he didn't notice or completely ignored that I was very tense, because he quickly, almost carelessly, did the adjustment. He checked with me about how it felt, and I reached up to massage the sore spot, but clearly it was still not right. He misread my actions and surprised me by placing his hands on my neck and forcefully adjusting it again. The pain shot straight into my head like a bullet, forcing me to sit upright, grasping my head in my hands. It hurt so much that I cried. The chiropractor saw how upset I was, so he rubbed some kind of gel on my neck while massaging it for a few seconds.

I told him the kind of pain I was feeling and he responded, "We'll have to wait for a couple of days. Call me to keep me updated on how you're feeling." I knew from the way it felt that whatever had happened, the problem was definitely worse.

When I woke up the next morning, I had my first experience with vertigo. It crippled me that day and ended up lasting for about a week. I was so angry. I called the office to complain, but they only recommended that I come back in. Oh no, there was no way I was going back to him. I regretted having gone the first time; I certainly wasn't going to put myself in his grip again. The problem was really the last thing I needed at that time in my life. It was a parade of complications, one after the next, after the next. I felt like I might go completely crazy.

After this experience, I was leery of seeing any new doctors for my own treatment. Bill Cunningham, whom I still kept in contact with, gave me a homeopathic remedy that

Road trip

helped relieve some of the effects of the vertigo. Because my friend Janet Berlin was such a skilled craniosacral therapist, and because I was desperate for help from someone I could trust, I put Jack and Jamie in the car and drove more than eight hours to Utah so she could treat me. I figured I could manage the drive with the help of the homeopathic remedy.

I continued to enjoy long road trips and the opportunity to allow the miles to pass behind me—along with the stress. It's a moving meditation that usually leaves me feeling relaxed and well. Other times, it's simply a perfect time to express my love of music, singing along as we drive. Celine Dion was always a must-have for my road trips back then. It was the only music I knew all the words to, and belting out the tunes with her was sure to keep me alert and awake.

We arrived at Janet's house safely, although this time the drive seemed much longer and more tiresome than normal. I was looking forward to her treatment, knowing that her hands would ease my pain. We spent the entire day there, which was great for Jack and Jamie. While I was getting Janet's treatment, the boys walked with her husband around their acreage to see all their fruit trees, picking and eating along the way. The boys loved the outdoors, where they were free to run and explore. This allowed me to be treated for over three hours, and my body soaked up every minute. Janet and I agreed that I needed to find someone locally who could continue this therapy.

Before we returned to Colorado, we made a stop in Las Vegas. It was another chance to be in the heat, and I was looking forward to a visit with James's family while we were there. Most of his family lived in Las Vegas: his parents, his siblings, and his siblings' families. The boys loved seeing their grandparents and cousins, and I was thrilled to be taking in some of the Nevada sun. All the cousins were loving with Jamie; they played together for hours.

Once we got back home, I contacted Keith Swan, DO, DABMA, who practiced out of Boulder. He was wonderful, and his osteopathic treatments were beneficial in many ways, but most importantly in further decreasing the occurrence of my vertigo.

After seeing Dr. Swan, it occurred to me that the treatment he provided could possibly benefit Jamie. I had read that it was used to complement other therapies for autism. Keith saw Jamie several times. I was surprised at how well Jamie did with him because he was required to lie on his back quietly for several minutes, which for Jamie was an eternity. At first, it was obvious he was haunted by bad memories of being held down on his back by doctors. Add to that the stress of having someone touch his head, and he was destined for sensory overload. But I thought ahead and found a way to make it work. I would have Jack go first and then Jamie would be willing to "copy" him, as he had in so many things over the years. In Keith's office, there was also a collection of world archaeological artifacts that worked to mesmerize both Jamie and Jack before and during their therapy.

On one of our visits, I watched, fascinated, as Dr. Swan laid Jamie down on the table. A gentle man, packaged in an oversize frame and with a dark, bushy beard, he placed his big hands on Jamie's small head. It was sweet to see this large man take such tender care as he worked. He had a certain mellow nature that Jamie must have picked up on, because his instinct was to trust Keith enough to allow the contact. We went to see him a couple of times a week, although there were no noticeable changes for Jamie. I knew that a lot of these activities contributed to the effects of the whole, and I knew that it helped me, so I continued going for a few months.

As we gained ground in one area, we occasionally lost it in another. It would be discouraging, but I would rebound, overcoming each discouragement with the gleam of each new possibility. Looking back, the overwhelming moments seemed to be influenced by Jamie's ongoing breathing attacks.

They continued to come in the middle of the night, catapulting me out of a deep sleep and abruptly sending me into a state of panic.

During these attacks, Jamie's adrenaline would usually elevate, causing excessive saliva and mucus to collect, eventually making him throw up. He labored very hard just to catch his breath. The situation would then intensify. I would see from the alarm in his eyes that his throat was closing on him. Breathing would become so difficult that we would end the night with an ambulance ride to the hospital, where he would receive his regular fix: racemic epi and dexamethasone. I struggled to appear calm on the outside, but on the inside I was likely to be more panicked than he was. Always, I tried to comfort him with a calm and controlled voice, "It's okay, Jamie. We're going to make it. Just breathe. Everything is going to be just fine." I must have uttered this mantra a hundred times during more than a dozen trips to the hospital.

On other nights, he would wake up crying from night terrors and then quickly fall back to sleep. However, I couldn't fall asleep again because my adrenaline would get pumping from the fear of an emergency room run, and my energized state would not abate until the next day. Ghosts and goblins lived under my bed, waiting to emerge during the night. I truly feared the dark because it symbolized the time when these crises occurred. During the "fall back" daylight savings time in autumn, the setting of the sun came even sooner and I had another reason to dislike Colorado. While the fall was a favorite season for many people, I could never appreciate it through my shroud of fear.

A cloud of doom and dread hovered over me. At times, I literally felt like I was dying. I was beyond exhausted, but my nervous system was constantly running. I must have been in a kind of fight-or-flight mode. I needed help, and I struggled to find the right doctor for me, just as I had struggled to find one for Jamie. I needed someone who knew how to help me, not just medicate me.

The floodgates had certainly been thrown open because, along with the physical issues and other stress-induced struggles I was experiencing, I couldn't help but reflect on the turn my life had taken. I would look at my face in the mirror and see new wrinkles forming seemingly before my eyes! I was far too young to carry that permanent stress line between my brows. A photograph taken at that time showed me watching the boys swimming, and instead of taking part in their joy, I appeared deeply stressed and unhappy. My internal state was starting to show on the outside.

Looking in the mirror at my changing face, I remembered what life had been like years earlier when I lived in L.A. On a regular basis, I was made beautiful by professional makeup artists and dressed by local designers. For one of the Emmy Awards shows, I had a red dress made for me by the designer Tony Chase. The process began with an appointment to take my measurements. I got to describe the dress I envisioned, its shape and style, right down to the silk material I had in mind. He took in all this information, nodded, and said, "I've got it!"

When the dress was finished, he personally delivered it to my house. It fit perfectly and I felt it was the most beautiful dress I had ever worn. After all, it had been made especially for me! I remember getting out of the limo feeling like Hollywood royalty. When we walked down the red carpet, I could barely see because of the flashing cameras. The photographers were taking pictures of my then-husband, Steve, and I overheard whispers questioning who I was. I wore my dark hair long and curly, and I was often stopped and asked if I were Kelly LeBrock, a popular actress at that time. Her best-known role was in *The Woman in Red*. Maybe on this night the paparazzi thought that because of the red dress I might be "the woman in red." Steve and I had a good laugh about the paparazzi's frenzy and how they must have been hoping to score another celebrity photo op.

But now the lights had all faded—on the inside as well as the outside. No more lights, camera, action. In my memory, all the glamour had been only yesterday, but in reality it had been several years since I had lived that kind of life. I went into my closet and pulled out the same red dress. I stared at it, still just as beautiful as I remembered, and decided to put it on. It was a little tighter in the waist, even though I had lost the seventy-five pounds I gained carrying my twin babies. I looked in the mirror and the dress reflected back a painful reminder of life's hard lessons. I fell to my knees and broke down crying; I cried in self-pity for at least an hour.

Finally, my pity party ended and I was ready to move on. Empty of tears, I took off the dress, hanging it carefully back in the closet. Crying has always been cathartic for me.

Living the Glam life in LA ▶

It tends to clear away the mess and allows me to rebuild my perspective.

I called Bill Cunningham and asked him if he could refer me to anyone who had a different treatment regimen I could try. Although we no longer visited him regularly, he was willing to help whenever I called. I was obviously moving quickly through doctors, but I wasn't ready to settle in until I felt better. My symptoms were vague and it was difficult to pinpoint what was happening with me, but I desperately wanted to feel right again. Bill said the only other person he knew who might be able to help was Gary Klepper, also out of Boulder. Okay, so there was someone else out there. That was good. I called to make an appointment, but he had a six-week waiting period. That was not good.

Dr. Klepper's profile looked exceptional to me. He is an ND, DC, CTN, and a practitioner of functional medicine, which is the practice of finding balance among the emotional, cognitive, and physical processes. He was working in the areas I was aiming to explore. I felt like I should also see an MD, just to get the conventional testing and blood work out of the way. I made an appointment to see a doctor of internal medicine while I waited to see Dr. Klepper. (What is it about our conditioning that makes us feel like MDs are better for more serious medical problems? Are they better at diagnosing or just prescribing medicine?)

I was seriously concerned about my health, convinced that I had some dire disease. I was thinking it might even be cancer. (*Don't even go there!* I scolded myself.) My nervous system also felt out of whack—or maybe my mind was playing tricks on me. All I knew was that I couldn't manage to calm myself. I was fine in some moments and felt terrible in others. I couldn't find any consistency. The doctor ran every possible test but all the results came back normal. I felt silly and embarrassed when he told me there was nothing wrong with me. That same doctor ordered an MRI to see if my chiropractic treatment had done some kind of permanent damage, but the results also came back negative. He said that even though the MRI didn't show anything, I still might have had some minute tears that were not visible. Either way, he couldn't do much for me. I was then referred to an endocrinologist. When in doubt, send me to another type of doctor. I guess that's why they call it the "practice" of medicine.

It occurred to me that I might be experiencing adrenal weakness for a second time. Dr. Vance had found this problem earlier, when we were living in Arizona. During that time, I had been running off little sleep each night, working fourteen to seventeen hours each day. I had spent all my waking hours on my feet. Working like that left me physically drained. At the time, Dr. Vance had given me a few IV drips with vitamin C and minerals, and it immediately helped get me back on track. He explained adrenal fatigue and made clear how it was affecting my body. I recognized the way I was feeling now as similar to the way I had felt then—but I was much worse this time.

I went to the endocrinologist, a specialist who deals with disorders of the glands and hormones in the endocrine system. She took a blood sample for an adrenal test. The results came back showing that my cortisol, a hormone that is produced by the adrenal glands—and that responds to stress—was in the normal range. Therefore, my adrenals were working as they should, based on what the doctor considered a reliable measurement. But because of the "normal range" gauge and how it was determined, I wasn't convinced the results were valid. It is common knowledge today that this test is not an accurate measurement of cortisol because of other variables like DHEA and the influence of female hormones. My blood had been taken in the morning, which was not the time of day when I felt the worst. I usually started my decline in the early afternoon.

I was frustrated. The endocrinologist didn't have any suggestions for helping me, but I continued asking her questions. "What else can you test?" "Is the morning test accurate enough?"

She turned our conversation around and began asking questions about my personal life. Once she uncovered that Jamie was frequently ill and had autism, it was obvious she had formed her conclusion. She decided I needed an antidepressant. I was surprised. I regretted sharing information about Jamie. To her, there was nothing left to consider. She was sure of what I needed.

Antidepressants? I thought to myself. I didn't feel depressed. I'd always thought of depression as a feeling that made you lack motivation or the ability to enjoy life, so you wanted to sleep all the time. I had motivation coming from every pore of my body! I still laughed, had friends over to visit, and ran around all day long. How could I be depressed? Anxious, yes, but not depressed. I felt like anything I said would have been considered mere defensiveness and quickly dismissed by the doctor anyway, so I didn't even try. I left her office convinced that most doctors weren't really concerned with helping me. They just followed the same protocol for everyone, the same old cookie-cutter approach every single time, and once again I had no real answers. Was it too much to ask for a conversation? Could a doctor look me in the eye and consider me an equal participant in a conversation, self-aware and capable of a valid discussion about my own health needs?

Coming up empty-handed again (except for a stack of prescriptions for antidepressants and Valium) really caused things to begin unraveling. I tried talking to James about what I was feeling. He didn't understand, let alone know what he could do to help. I knew he was working hard, but he had an hour here or there and he spent it relaxing or watching TV. This was "normal" behavior for most working men, but at the time it infuriated me. He could do some research, or at least sit down to talk with me. We continued to struggle with our relationship and we got into a lot of arguments because I didn't feel supported. On the other hand, I know he didn't feel supported by me either, but I just didn't have any more to give.

The frequency of our heated arguments increased. When James felt stressed out about finances and work, or was affected by the pressure of Jamie's health, his worst qualities came out through mean words. I had a lot of hurt that stewed, turning into rage. Every one of our interactions was peppered with his demeaning comments and showered with my fury.

My anger grew to such heights that I was often provoked to threaten divorce.

In the beginning, James and I shared a powerful love for each other. On many occasions, this love had helped get us through hard times. I loved so many things about him: his warmth and kindness, his enduringly positive outlook, and his incredible heart, plus his passion for life. But during this time, we were going around in circles, and James didn't know his role. He must have felt stuck, knowing he needed to be at work, but that I needed him at the same time. I see it much more clearly in hindsight, of course, but back then I was at my wit's end, and I felt that his actions didn't reflect the

same concern for or commitment to Jamie that I had and was expecting from him.

Winter was ending, and each day was devoted to fulfilling my to-do lists, one for work, and the other for my family. I spent my time driving around to get everything done. One of my stops was the boys' school, G.E.M.S. I could check off more than one thing from my list after I had dropped them off. For instance, I was able to work out right down the street, go grocery shopping, run errands, and then, of course, stop at a nearby Starbucks. When I came back to pick up the boys, I often spoke with their teacher, Joan. I was happy to hear her say that Jamie felt more and more comfortable with each passing week.

One day I accompanied Jack and Jamie on a field trip to a charming ranch. I remember sharing their excitement at being outside in the country air, breathing in the smell of hay among the expansive green fields. It felt exhilarating! I even wore my cowboy boots. We spent the day laughing, especially over the shared thrill of riding horses. I appreciated that the boys were having a such a good time while also receiving a special kind of sensory input therapy. On the drive home, I sat soaking up the joyful thoughts of the day. I often tried to indulge myself with these kinds of sweet moments. Summer was just around the corner and spring was in full force. I was looking forward to longer days of warmth and sunshine.

The next day was particularly beautiful because it was the day of my first appointment with Dr. Klepper. It took me forty-five minutes to drive along winding roads through foothills to reach his office in Boulder. I was excited to meet him.

Would he say the same thing to me as everyone else, or would he be the one who could actually help me?

He worked from a home office on beautiful acreage. After getting out of the car, I descended the hillside toward the building, down at least one hundred steps, passing by beautiful pottery that decorated the path along the way. As I got closer, I saw a glass tower in which an enormous indoor tree grew. It was apparently the home of the few exotic birds that sat on its branches. I relaxed in the serene waiting room, where I was offered water and herbal tea. Not a bad first impression.

After his initial examination and our discussion about my current regimen, he ordered various tests: an analysis of the condition of my hormones, DHEA, and thyroid. I knew that he was looking at the body as a whole, and I was impressed from the start. He gave me a take-home cortisol test to determine the levels in my saliva and urine. I was to test five times throughout the day: morning, late morning, early afternoon, evening, and night. Now, those sets of tests felt right to me.

I returned for my second appointment to discuss the results. I asked the doctor if he thought I was depressed or just losing my mind. He explained confidently that I was neither and showed me that overall, most of the levels in my blood test were lower than they should have been, with the level of cortisol being the most deficient. My body was extremely tired and burned out. Dr. Klepper confirmed what I had suspected—that I had adrenal fatigue (low cortisol levels) and was lacking in nutrients. After he told me, I cried. It wasn't all in my head! He suggested that we start slowly to restore my health by rebuilding my body from the cellular level through acupuncture, supplements, craniosacral therapy, and homeopathy. My supplements included a shot of vitamins B5, B12, and folic acid two or three times per week. He also included a natural adrenal supplement—first licorice root and then IsoCort. After several weeks, there was already a big difference; I felt better all the time and rarely experienced any vertigo.

I was immensely encouraged by my work with Dr. Klepper. Someone finally understood what I needed! I was overcome with appreciation for his approach. With just a touch to the stomach or back, or a close look at the tongue or into the eyes, he could identify certain kinds of malfunctions in the body. The MDs that I had seen so far hadn't worked that way. I think it is both amazing and believable that the body can communicate if you know how to listen to it. Most of us get brainwashed into taking everything that doctors give us instead of gathering more information about our options so we can think for ourselves.

Because his office wasn't near my home, Dr. Klepper gave me work to do at home each day, such as moxibustion, a Chinese version of self-administered acupuncture. He would draw points on my legs, calves, belly, chest, and head. I must have looked hilarious, painted with crosses and marks across my body, when I returned home. I would put the cone-shaped moxa on these spots and light it on fire. It would burn down, getting hot near the surface, thus stimulating the acupuncture point. I did this in my room, late at night, and James often came home to what smelled like marijuana. He would joke, "Hey, who's smoking pot up here?"

This treatment seemed a little "out there" at the time, but the other doctors weren't helping, and what did I have to lose? I had started to feel much better when I woke up, with only a rough patch of four or five hours in the afternoon. I was going through a process to improve my adrenal glands, working to get my cortisol levels back to normal in a natural way. I could have taken a pill and maybe felt better right away, but that would have been only a temporary fix or would have created a dependency, and I wanted a thorough repair. I knew that it had taken three years to damage my body this way and I accepted that it would take six to twelve months to get it legitimately better again.

Dr. Klepper recommended resting, relaxing, or even lying down for an hour during the day. I almost had to laugh out loud, ha! Was he kidding? He clearly didn't understand what my daily life was like or he would never have made that suggestion! Taking a nap never even occurred to me. This was something that, when I first met James, he had done regularly. We had such different lifestyles back then. I remember him suggesting, one afternoon, that we just kick back and curl up for a midafternoon snooze. I was taken aback at the time, but then again, James was Mr. Mellow, the middle kid, number five of ten children. He had grown up with that laid-back "no worries" attitude. I had grown up in a family that never rested like that. We were all about using up every minute of every day in some kind of activity. It probably wouldn't have hurt had I taken on a few of James's little habits back when we were a new couple. And it would obviously be good for me now that I was a harried mother. I tried Dr. Klepper's suggestion. In fact, I still try to nap, because it certainly is relaxing to set time aside for resting, but I just have a hard time giving myself permission to do it very often.

Summer was on the way and I got the itch to make a trip back home. I began planning to go to Santa Barbara. I called my best friend, Beth, and told her we were coming out. My family still had a home in Montecito, where we could stay. We planned to spend a couple of weeks there.

Whenever I was back home in California, I always got together with Beth. We loved to meet family or friends for dinner at our local favorites, Pane e Vino or Lucky's. We played with the boys at the beach against lovely ocean backdrops and beautiful, lush scenery. It was easy for us to spend hours at the pool, splashing around with the boys. Their favorite game was having us swing them high in the air by their arms and legs into the water. They would beg for us to do it over and over again. And of course, Beth and I loved to shop. If we were visiting our favorite shops, we stopped at the amazing farmer's market on State Street to pick up the freshest organic vegetables. No matter what we chose to do, we always had a fun time together.

Because Santa Barbara was home to me, I always found it comforting. I began thinking of ways that I could spend the entire winter there. We would need a place of our own because of the length of time I wanted to stay. What a brilliant idea! I started asking friends about how the weather had been over the past couple of years. They said it had been between 50 and 70 degrees with a little rain here and there. That sounded really good, especially compared to the low 30s, snow, and dry, cold air in Colorado.

Just thinking about going through another winter with the snow and return trips to Denver hospitals filled me with anxiety and dread. I wanted to live from a new viewpoint, in a different environment. The wheels of my mind were turning quickly and in an instant I had a vision of us renting a house in Santa Barbara for a long stay through the winter. I was flooded with reasons why this was such a good idea: The weather would be better for Jamie; James and I could have some kind of break from each other; and I could spend more time in one of my favorite places with my best friend. I was convinced. I just had to make it happen.

I met with a real estate agent, who showed me some different homes in Montecito. Most of what I saw was too small and high-priced or too big or odd and even higher-priced. I began to regularly pick up a copy of the local Santa Barbara paper, thumbing through it to see the short-term rentals that were available. I just wanted to try on the thought of finding a house, even though I hadn't shared my idea with James yet.

One house in particular caught my eye, and I called the owners to set up an appointment. It rested on the hillside in the north part of Santa Barbara, pretty on the inside and out, with a big kitchen and an unbelievable view of the ocean. As we toured the house, I struck up quite a conversation with the woman who planned to rent it out. We began talking about their upcoming stay in France, where she and her husband planned to immerse themselves in the culture for the school year as their children learned the language. While on the topic of our children, we discussed my current battle with Jamie's health. She told me about a speech language pathologist she knew named Rochelle I. Greenbaum, MA, CCC-SL, known to be outstanding in her field. Shelley (we call her fondly) had worked with their daughter, completely solving her speech problems. With all the many alternative health communities and different mindsets in California, I knew there must be a wealth of specialists in Santa Barbara who could continue Jamie's many treatments. Planning a winter stay added some much-needed excitement to my life. I began planting the seeds with James.

Meanwhile, I continued to give myself shots while we were on vacation in Santa Barbara. I slept better at night, and the gap of daily fatigue continued to close, even though Jamie still woke up frequently. Carla, our nanny, and I continued trading off nights getting up with him, so I could get a bigger dose of sleep.

Upon our return to Colorado, I found my second wind. I went on with my routine, but with a greater momentum. One day, James and I made a visit to an antique store in search of a chair for our house. While we were there, we happened to meet John and Cheryl, the owners of the store. After talking for a while, we realized we had made an immediate connection. We kept in touch and ended up getting together socially. They seemed to have the perfect relationship. I wondered if it was really as good as it appeared on the outside. In one conversation over lunch, it came up that James and I had been struggling. Cheryl explained that she and John had seen a therapist, which was how they had helped their relationship. Their marriage and family therapist, Lynn Heitler, LCSW, had done nothing less than save their marriage.

Lynn practiced different techniques that helped couples open up their stream of emotions as well as their lines of communication. John said he had uncovered some issues he had been struggling with for years, and he had improved in a short period of time with one particular technique called EMDR (Eye Movement Desensitization and Reprocessing). I liked the sound of this treatment, especially after learning about a woman who had used this therapy to work through her pain after the traumatic death of her husband. The technique directly addresses the problems caused by intense trauma and grief and works in instances where other therapies have failed. As the weeks went by, it became more and more apparent that this was the route I needed to take next.

I was feeling better physically, but I continued to have bouts of anxiety. I didn't know how to deal with the stress; I only knew how to internalize it. I worked on relaxing, but I was having a hard time. One evening, while reading in bed, I stood up, only to find that my vision was filled with white spots. I held on to the side of the bed; something was happening that was out of my control. I yelled for James. I began shaking uncontrollably and I couldn't stop. James called an ambulance and we went to the hospital.

Neither one of us knew what was happening to me. When we got to the hospital, the medical staff started me on an IV and gave me all the usual tests. I started feeling better with the IV, and thought that I must have been dehydrated. The doctor came in and explained that I had suffered an anxiety attack. I didn't know whether I should feel relieved that that was all it was, or bad that I had actually had this happen. It didn't matter, because another attack occurred not long after the first. We called Dr. Klepper, who instructed James to keep me wrapped in a blanket and to give me something warm to drink. With this help, James talked me through it. He learned later to give me baking soda mixed with water to drink, which always helped me move through the attacks more quickly. He had learned this trick from his father—the mixture works to get your system back into pH balance quickly and naturally. Apparently, anxiety attacks are not unlike being in shock, and when your body is deprived of sleep, in combination with high stress and low cortisol, strange things happen.

This sequence of events prompted my call to Lynn Heitler. I knew I needed to try a different avenue. I also knew that if James and I had any chance of staying together through all this, and if I was going to deal with the root of my anxiety attacks, I had to start with my own emotional repair.

I met with Lynn one-on-one first. We talked about the past couple of years and all the events that had brought me to the point where I was that day. It was a beginning, and I felt like the appointment was long overdue. Then James and I began seeing Lynn together and individually. Along with addressing my pent-up anxiety, I worked on getting over my anger toward James and his dad. I certainly recognized that I had a love–hate relationship with James's father. I felt a great deal of underlying resentment toward him and I seemed to be taking it out on James at times, especially when he talked to me in a way that reminded me of his father. Although Dr. Vance had always pointed me in the right direction for the missing pieces of Jamie's treatment, and I was grateful for that, I still struggled with my feelings about him. I felt some anger toward him for contributing to Jamie's initial hospital stay, which I obviously considered to be the first cause of his current condition.

Lynn believed my treatment was also addressing post-traumatic stress disorder, which she felt was caused by Jamie's health complications, his near-death experience, his subsequent hospitalizations, and even the death of the little boy down the hall in the hospital. It had been too much for me in too short a time. The fact that I could never talk about the hospital event without completely breaking down spoke volumes.

Lynn knew that using EMDR with me would be a key piece in my recovery puzzle. The work we did required reliving the experiences that had affected me. EMDR involved shifting my eyes from left to right and right to left as they followed a moving light on a board, and as Lynn walked me through each event of the past, we addressed the fear, the anger, and the pain I had experienced. This process helps the mind release negative patterns of thinking and remembering, better equipping us to deal with our emotions. After about five visits, I felt myself letting go of the traumatic feelings I had always harbored after Jamie's hospitalization. Eventually, I could even discuss the experience with other people, finishing the story without any tears.

When James and I worked together with Lynn, I started to feel the anger and resentments I had held on to for so long toward both James and his father decrease. These dark and heavy feelings had exhausted me over the years, and it felt extremely good to see past them. We continued to work with Lynn, and we focused on strengthening ourselves and repairing the wounds of our relationship.

On another front, Dr. Klepper was working wonders on my physical health. During one of my appointments, I discussed with him my continual struggle with Jamie's supplements, asking if he worked with kids. He encouraged me to bring Jamie in. From then on, he was regularly involved in Jamie's treatment as well.

Jamie and I had fun during those appointments, not so much because of the visit but because the doctor had a trampoline outside his office. Before each appointment, Jamie, Jack, and I had a blast jumping up and down, holding hands, and bouncing high into the air. It was a positive mood to set before the visit, because we laughed and laughed.

Dr. Klepper's primary function became monitoring the products Jamie was taking. He is a brilliant checks-and-balances person for supplements, and he used an advanced and accurate form of muscle testing to reveal some of Jamie's body's inner workings. Between Dr. Klepper and Dr. Grossman, we had a very workable system. This lifted a huge load from my mind, because I no longer had to stress over the choices and decisions I was making on my own. All the different products from Wobenzym, Ortho Biotic, Pharmax HLC Maintenance, Primal Defense, and the many other new brands of probiotics and enzymes were working to heal Jamie's gut. While his intestinal tract was on the mend, his brain was being treated with vitamin A and high doses of omega-3, omega-6, omega-9, and other essential fatty acids.

With so much progress under our belts, I planned to go ahead with the next step. The protocol implemented by Dr. Grossman for putting Jamie on an oral supplement called Captomer, made up primarily of DMSA, a chelating agent, would help pull metals from his body. I knew this was exactly what Jamie needed. This was the first form of chelation that we used, and the beginning of our experience with one of the most controversial therapies thus far.

Santa Barbara was always on my mind. I continued to think about all the benefits it could bring. Even though James and I were working on our problems with Lynn, I still felt disconnected. I needed soul nourishment. Of course, James didn't want another financial burden, but I felt I *had* to go. He wasn't happy about it, but he went along with my plan, hoping it would give me the time away that I felt I seriously needed, making our reunions and time together more appreciated. I might have been somewhat selfish in my motivations, but I truly believed that the ocean air could help Jamie. I asked Dr. Allen if being

A nurse testing Jamie's breathing capacity

in California could accomplish that because of the lower altitude and increased moisture. He thought it was "definitely a possibility."

We did what we needed to do to make the temporary move work, and I went ahead and rented the house I had chosen during our summer visit. James and I agreed on a new work schedule for him. He would work for two weeks, come out and stay for a week, and then return to work for two more weeks. During this time, I took a break from work.

In Colorado, Jamie had a lot of new programs and a new school under way, which made me a little hesitant about making the change to California. I knew that it sounded crazy to leave when we were *also* on such a good path with the new treatments and supplements at work, but Dr. Grossman and Dr. Klepper were available over the phone if I needed them. I felt that having Shelley as a speech therapist from the beginning would give me the head start I needed to find even more quality therapists. And I knew the trip was only temporary, and that we could jump right back into G.E.M.S. when we returned.

Before we left, I took Jack and Jamie to see Dr. Allen. We talked again about our ongoing issues, including Jamie's breathing. He wanted to share with me information about a new, inhaled steroid called Flovent. I heard the word *steroid* and didn't need to hear any more. Jamie did not need any more steroids! It immediately sounded too scary to try. He suggested I contact a pulmonary doctor through National Jewish Hospital in Denver, a prominent treatment facility for lung and asthma conditions. I made the appointment but ended up leaving without, I thought, the slightest bit of useful information. This was unexpected, considering this hospital was one of the most prominent respiratory facilities in the United States. I was discouraged until Dr. Allen provided me with the name of a pulmonary doctor, Gwen Kerby, MD, at Children's Hospital Colorado. I was able to connect with her quickly and during our first appointment we had a helpful discussion.

"Krista, I really think you should try giving Jamie the Flovent."

"I've heard about it," I explained, "but I really don't like the idea of giving him a steroid. I was actually hoping that our upcoming stay in Santa Barbara would bring some benefits to his breathing."

Dr. Kerby replied, "You know, I don't believe that a change in environment is going to help him. But I feel confident that the Flovent would help his breathing immensely."

"All right." I felt my thinking shift. "I'm willing to try it. But it's inhaled, right? That's another one of my concerns, because if it works systemically, it will be way too hard on his body."

"There's no need to worry about that. Flovent doesn't work that way. It enters the mouth, travels straight into the throat, and keeps the swelling down right at the spot."

That was the information I needed. I was still a little hesitant, but I decided we would give it a try.

Everything was in place for our trip to California, and I was energetic and looking forward to leaving. The simple act of making a life change had a huge impact in itself, but the idea of running on the beach, strolling through town with Beth, wandering through the greenery and abundant flower gardens of Santa Barbara, and taking in the smell of the salty, moist ocean air made the move even more thrilling. I was ready.

A girlfriend bought me a new Shakira CD to listen to on the road. I loved it. I put it on and grabbed the boys, trying to get them excited about our trip the next day. Acting wild, I jumped up and down on the ottoman and danced around the living room. They looked at me and laughed as I sang the words to "Ready for a good time" loudly.

CHAPTER

11

Santa Barbara

We were packed and ready to head to the West Coast. I was extremely excited; it felt like a new beginning. Our neighbors across the street weren't happy that we were leaving because they had two boys Jack and Jamie's age, and they had been playing together almost daily. We also had to leave our two dogs behind, but James would be back every couple of weeks and a friend of mine would take care of the dogs in between.

Taking our time along the way sounded like the best idea, so we planned to make several stops to help break up the long road trip. I drove one vehicle and James drove another because we were taking so many things, and we needed the room.

We started driving and made it as far as Green River, Utah, when Jamie began experiencing severe stomach cramps. I was hoping the pain would pass, but it came and went for two hours, and we thought it would be best to pull over at a little hotel in Richfield, the only option for miles. I felt he should at least be able to lie down and be more comfortable. Of course, he couldn't verbalize the pain to me, but he continued clutching at his stomach. We went to bed hoping he would feel better in the morning.

In the middle of the night, I heard something that woke me up. I looked at the twins' bed, but Jamie was missing. I opened the bathroom door to turn on the light and saw him lying next to the bed, writhing in pain. I tried to comfort him, but even the slightest touch to his stomach caused him to flinch. That sent me flying into panic mode: we were in a small-town hotel at four in the morning, and there was no hospital for miles. I decided I needed to get him medical attention. The closest large medical facility was back the way we came, in Grand Junction, Colorado. The best option I could see was to try to make it to Las Vegas.

I was hoping that Jamie didn't have appendicitis or something life-threatening. Unfortunately, my mind was geared toward fearing the worst. I got ready to make the drive, putting Jamie in the back of my car, trying to make him as comfortable as possible with a blanket and pillow. James asked me if I was okay going alone all those miles to Las Vegas in the early morning hours. I said I wasn't sure, but I just had to do it. I didn't feel good about taking Jamie anywhere other than a large hospital that was well-equipped with specialists, in case he was experiencing something complicated.

Las Vegas was a good three to four hours away. James stayed behind at the hotel with Jack and Carla and a plan to be right behind us when the sun rose. He worried about what I would do if something happened to us on the road, but I had made up my mind and my adrenaline was running full force.

As I drove, I sorted through the onslaught of thoughts coming at me. Did Jamie have food poisoning? Was he constipated? Was there a major problem with his digestive system or something else internal? He hadn't thrown up and he didn't have a fever. I was driving about one hundred miles an hour, literally. There weren't many people on the road, and I felt that the urgency of Jamie's condition justified the risk of speeding. I was actually *hoping* I would get pulled over, so the police could help me get to the hospital quickly.

When we got into Las Vegas, it was seven in the morning. I took Jamie to Sunrise Hospital, the children's facility he had been to when we were visiting the Vances the previous year. Jamie had fallen asleep. I pulled him out of his car seat and held him over my shoulder. As I hurried in, he moaned weakly. We sat in the lobby for only a few minutes before they took us back to be examined. They gave him an X-ray and an ultrasound because they were concerned about appendicitis. The young doctor came in shortly afterward and informed me in his direct, dry manner that Jamie was just terribly constipated.

"Are you sure that's all it is?" The idea had crossed my mind, but I was still surprised.

He showed me the X-ray and I could see the problem for myself. He questioned me about Jamie's diet, and any new changes I might have made to cause a change in his system. I thought about the DMSA in Captomer. Dr. Grossman had said that one of the possible side effects was gastrointestinal irritation. The supplement must have been the cause. I felt horrible that Jamie was having this kind of pain from it! The doctor gave him an enema and shortly thereafter he was running around. I was extremely relieved and apparently so was Jamie.

James arrived as we were just leaving the hospital. I told him what had happened and everybody was happy to hear the good news. We stayed in Las Vegas for a while to visit James's parents. Jamie was fine, no more pain. We were ready to head to Santa Barbara the next day.

I woke up and went running as the boys slept. I put on my earphones and turned the music up loud; it felt exhilarating as I ran through the streets of Summerlin, Nevada, feeling the heat and taking in the sights. Working out chased away anxiety for a couple of days or at least a few hours. My body felt lighter as I ran faster, the stress dripping away with the sweat. I felt energized, and yet I had a wonderful sense of tranquility and clarity.

When I got back from my run, I called Dr. Grossman and told him what had happened on the road. I let him know that I wasn't going to give Jamie any more Captomer. He thought that was the right decision and told me he would do some research to find a better chelating agent.

As we traveled through Ventura, California, we passed so many buildings and homes. Then we crossed over a bridge and the scenery quickly changed: during the last twenty-five miles to Santa Barbara, we were surrounded by only the beautiful blue ocean on one side and the green California hills on the other. It was a sight I had seen thousands of times in my life, but this time was different. My senses were really heightened. I could smell the ocean air, and felt the warmth of summer still lingering in the air on this beautiful September day. I wanted to jump in the ocean, squeeze my toes in the sand, and feel the heat coming up from the earth. Even James was excited. We were on an adventure—and I love adventures!

As soon as we were close, I called my friend Beth. She was eager to get together. "Let's meet at Intermezzo as soon as you get here and get a drink," she said. "Oh, I forgot—you guys don't drink."

I laughed. "Oh no. We are *so* drinking. I'm going to drink. I'm going to drink every day, as much as I possibly can!" This was an exaggeration, of course, but it had been awhile since I had gone out drinking, and I was ready to relax and have some fun.

We got settled into our new home, where we could look out over the ocean from every room. The house sat about five miles from the shoreline, and the vast ocean expanded far into the horizon on each side. Watching the sparkle of sunlight on the water throughout the day was as beautiful as watching the golden sun disappear into the water in the evening. And there was something about breathing in the ocean air and taking in the soothing presence of the water that brought tranquility to my being. I walked outside and took a deep breath, closing my eyes to say a silent prayer of gratitude.

I really wanted to see Beth, so I left right away, while James and Carla finished unpacking. James planned to meet us later. The boys were completely wound up, running around the house to explore their new surroundings.

I walked into Intermezzo and Beth was sitting there looking beautiful, as usual. We were happy to be with each other. No matter how much time had passed between visits, we found we never missed a beat. She had been my closest friend since we were teenagers. We had so much in common, from our taste in things to our mindsets and lifestyles.

We began our visit with a yummy martini. I don't think I had ever had one before. It was a boysenberry martini—so California fresh! I got really lightheaded with the first one, but it felt good. James showed up after a while and tried a martini while the three of us sat and chatted. We talked about Jamie and Jack and why we had chosen to come to Santa Barbara, enjoying one another's company as we giggled about Beth's current "no-boyfriend" status. The topic of clothes was a given, especially after seeing the top Beth was wearing because I loved it! She said there was a new store in town that had the cutest clothes. I admitted that for the last few years my wardrobe wasn't the most stylish it had ever been. With my busy life of doctors' appointments, I hadn't been shopping that much, and Colorado had more of an outdoor-wear style. But even though my options were mostly conservative, I still tried to dress in an up-to-date style.

Beth felt the need to break the news to me: "I know were not teenagers anymore, but we need to keep up on the fashion, Krista." By *we*, she meant *me*.

"I think I get it—we need to go shopping!" I replied with a laugh.

She and I planned to meet up in a few days to hit the new boutiques, and I was completely ecstatic.

James gave us both "the look" and said, "Okay, okay. You should go and have some fun."

But before clothes: much-needed groceries! I went grocery shopping at our local health food store, Lazy Acres. I really enjoyed shopping there. It was different and fun, with quality fresh foods (almost as pleasurable as the newest fashions on the rack—but not quite!). Speaking of new, I noticed a new brand of soy milk in an individual box. *Pretty cool*, I thought. *The boys would love this*. Soon enough, all our cabinets were filled with our usual healthy fare.

Right up there with my other priorities was linking up with Shelley Greenbaum, the speech language pathologist that the Santa Barbara homeowner had told me about. I gave her a call and we were able to meet her soon after. She was as bubbly in personality as she was in appearance. Packaged in a petite, thin frame, with curly blonde hair and sky blue eyes behind artsy eyeglasses, Shelley was a highly intelligent, slightly quirky, and truly kind teacher who was more skilled at connecting with children than anyone else we had worked with.

With energy and enthusiasm, Shelley laid out proposed goals for Jamie's treatment that involved growth and advancement through the use of games, activities, and listening exercises. He would begin with lightweight earphones because of his sensory issues (and even those initial earphones sent him into a total meltdown at first). He graduated to several other headphone versions, which got heavier and heavier until he could tolerate the pair he would use at home, which had the best functioning ability for his listening program.

The program played a variety of sounds that worked to develop his eye contact in coordination with his listening ability. Shelley was constantly testing him to measure his growth, and he was showing regular progress. I definitely noticed little changes in him right away. He met with Shelley twice a week for a half hour each time. I could tell from the beginning that this charming and dynamic woman would mesh well with Jamie. Her work did wonders for him, and she adored him as much as he obviously adored her.

One day after a session with Shelley, I was walking to the car and holding hands with Jack and Jamie. While stepping off the curb into the parking lot, I noticed that Jamie was looking up at me. This was unusual and caught me off guard. I smiled sweetly at him, and he quickly looked away. This small interaction was exciting because his reaction showed that our exchange had registered with him. The first two weeks came and went in a flash, and before we knew it, it was time for James to return to Denver. Luckily, there was a direct two-hour flight, so traveling back and forth was fairly convenient.

James came back every couple of weeks. While he was gone, I worked with Lynn Heitler over the phone, both one-on-one and through conference calls with James. He worked with her in person when he was in Colorado. These weren't the easiest sessions, and oftentimes I didn't feel like doing the work. But I wanted our relationship to get better, so I stuck it out. I didn't realize it at the time, but I was getting the space and opportunity to rediscover my love for him.

I was also busy setting up all our needed treatments. I got in contact with Julia, one of my longtime friends, and she and I got together for a visit. She had been a colon hydrotherapist for years and knew many alternative practitioners in the area because of her work in the field. She recommended a few she thought I might like.

The first appointment I made for Jamie was with Dr. Leo Smith. He used a technique where he evaluated a person's condition through examining the skull, eyes, and emotions, using a certain kind of brain exercise. It was quite an alternative practice, and I wasn't at all familiar with the technique. I tried him a couple of times to see if there was any noticeable change. I tried to keep an open mind with each doctor, hoping I might uncover something special. But this time nothing materialized, so I moved on.

After I got the boys to bed each night, Beth and I would go out. We met with friends, or she would plan work-related meetings for her floral design business and I would come and join the group. We often just hung out and got a bite to eat at Blue Agave in downtown Santa Barbara. They had good food and a nice bar; it was a very happening place. She'd lived in Santa Barbara her entire life, and it seemed like she knew everybody in town! I hadn't drunk alcohol regularly in years and I was really a lightweight. I had to limit myself to two drinks. Beth always joked with me because it took me an hour to finish my first cocktail.

Beth was single and although I was still very much married, we talked to a lot of guys in the bars. It was definitely part of the fun. She had once been married to a fireman and knew a lot of firefighters in town. One night we ended up at Blue Agave, and a couple of those friends came in. She flirted with them, and I found myself doing the same. I enjoyed the attention and it seemed harmless. I knew James trusted me, and he wanted me to have fun. I loved having this freedom, and each time James came back, I appreciated him more for giving it to me.

Beth loved wine and she had such a refined palate for it. Being around her, James started enjoying wine for the first time. One night when the three of us had planned to have dinner at our house, James came home with several cases of alcohol. One full case contained a variety of wines he had selected for us to try. We laughed when he walked in the door with his arms full of wine and liquor. This was a scene I had never witnessed in all the years I'd known him because he had been raised Mormon and had never really been a big drinker. He had sweetly made an effort to make Beth happy. Over the course of the night, he proceeded to open about six bottles of wine. If one wasn't that good, he'd open another. To this day, Beth reminisces about that night, and we all have a good laugh about it.

Carla and I were still trading off nights getting up with Jamie. She handled three nights in a row and I took two or three. When James wasn't there, I brought Jamie into my room so I could sleep across the foot of the bed throughout the night. During his fits of waking, he would sit straight up in bed, as though he were possessed. It was incredibly frightening. He would start crying as if he were having a

James, Beth and I, having some fun with the self-portrait

horrible nightmare. Whenever I took care of him, I would get about three hours of sleep. My saving grace was always the break, where I could catch up by getting two or even three nights of sleep in a row. My sleep was still not sound or uninterrupted, so I started taking valerian root, which definitely helped relax me.

One night I had half a beer in combination with the herb, and I slept like a baby. After that, I was sold on the combination and slept much better. I know, I know . . . don't try this at home! I was simply desperate for a good night's sleep! I figured some beer and a little herb couldn't hurt. And although a psychiatrist that Lynn Heitler had recommended had given me sample packs of Ambien and Serzone for anxiety, I didn't want to take them.

After a month or so, I started looking around at schools for the boys. I thought it might be okay to put Jamie in a preschool, if only for the socialization it provided. I just needed to find one that could handle his special needs, even if it wasn't specifically equipped for autism. I had gotten some ideas from my workout friends at Studio E, a dance and fitness center. One school seemed really cute and I liked the director. They had a large playground and playing outdoors was something the boys had always loved; that added some weight to my decision to give it a try.

I spoke with the director about the possibility of hiring an assistant who could help Jamie in class when he needed it. She liked the idea and suggested I look into getting support from the state, which offered that kind of help in certain circumstances. I did as she suggested and completed the requisite mountain of paperwork. I thought the effort would be worth it until I found out that Jamie would be entered into the California education system databank with a permanent "autistic" label, just like in Colorado. That still wasn't an acceptable option for us, especially if it was only to fund two hours of therapy a week.

Each day, I picked the boys up and spoke with the teacher about how everything was going. After two weeks of this routine, I checked in once again with the teacher. Right in front of Jamie, she answered, "He is not a good listener. He can't sit still and he's acting out with exceedingly 'autistic' behaviors."

That offended and upset me on many levels. It surprised me that she would give such negative feedback abruptly after two weeks of only positive observations. It had come out of nowhere. Obviously her comments and her communication style were not appropriate, and her outlook was not going to work at all. It became evident that this was not the kind of person or environment for us. I gathered up the boys and left, and I never looked back.

Once again, I was on the lookout for a school. The next time I spoke to the owner of our house, I happened to mention my frustration. She suggested I look into a school only a block away, a Jewish preschool called B'nai B'rith, where she had sent her own children. They loved it.

I couldn't believe the school was so close. I had driven by the building without realizing what was inside. I contacted the director and was pleased because this particular school was open to all our conditions. They were willing to take Jamie and the assistant I wanted to hire for him. The grounds of the preschool were the best I had seen. Not only did they have tons of playground equipment on an expansive property, but also the grassy yard was filled with caged guinea pigs, rabbits, and mice. There were cats, too, for the kids to hold. (When the other animals were let out of their cages, the cats were tucked away into their own cages.) The classrooms were assembled nicely, set up for a variety of engaging activities. The boys' teacher was gentle and kind, and full of empathy for what Jamie was going through. All I needed was to find someone who could work with Jamie in the classroom.

My search ended when I found a wonderful assistant, Emily Potts. She began coming over every morning and walking the boys to school, staying with Jamie in his class, and then walking them home in the early afternoon. In addition to assisting with classroom activities, she was also able to implement The Son-Rise Program techniques she had learned from me, both during the school day and at home. Her presence was vital in supporting Jamie through activities like "circle time." He would dart out the door every time the kids sat down and faced one another; he would be overwhelmed by the structure. Emily was there to calm him, staying outside with him until he was ready to take part in the next classroom activity.

Through the months, she brought joy to the boys' lives and helped me feel at ease while Jamie was at school. After school, she helped them at home with different learning activities, turning everything into an entertaining game. She was the perfect fit for our family, and I couldn't have been more pleased with our arrangement.

Emily and Jamie

When December rolled around, the boys celebrated their fourth birthday. I decided it was the perfect occasion for a get-together. My brother, Dana, and his family came down from San Luis Obispo; my mother came from Northern California; and my stepfather (whom I refer to as my

Jamie in the playground at B'nai B'rith

Chase palm Park in Santa Barbara

Hanging with Jack and a friend at the park

dad) and his wife Della also made the trip out. My sister Laura joined us from her home in nearby Santa Barbara. It was fun to get together, and my family was happy that we were much closer and could meet easily.

I also invited my old friends from town and some of the boys' new preschool friends. The highlight of the party arrived in the form of a huge, bouncy castle for everyone to play in. Jamie kept to himself most of the time, but enjoyed the sensory stimulation of jumping around and hitting the walls inside the castle. I hired an entertainer, who led the kids in songs and games, although Jamie wasn't interested in those activities. When everyone was around him, he was like a deer

in the headlights. I now realize, looking back at the photographs taken that day, that it was one of the last times Jamie displayed that kind of behavior in a larger group.

A couple of weeks later, Christmas Day arrived. I decided scooters would be fun presents for the boys because Jack was already interested in riding bikes and his coordination had really developed. I knew it would probably take a while longer for Jamie to ride one, but I never allowed myself to sell him short about his abilities. James and I worked to teach Jamie how to push with one foot while riding with the other, but he was far from being able to do it; he just didn't have the coordination or the focus. He tried and tried to keep up with Jack over the coming months, but he just couldn't ride the scooter. What was beautiful about him was that *he* didn't know he couldn't do it, and he kept on trying. I relished the fun I was having in Santa Barbara. I appreciated every day that went by.

With James out of town, it was time to shop! Beth took me to one of our favorite shops, Blue Bee, and I started collecting my new wardrobe. After her first comment on my lovely Colorado duds, Beth introduced me to the store's owners, John and Marti, and we hit it off immediately. It was energizing to have Blue Bee visits to look forward to. The distraction of shopping was relaxing and fun for me. One early evening after meeting at Intermezzo, we started drinking our usual martinis. We still argue about this: I swear she had four or five, but she says she had only three. I had two. Either way, we reached full giggle mode. We declared a fashion emergency and headed straight for Blue Bee. It was a short walk from Intermezzo in downtown Santa Barbara. So we headed over, laughing the whole way, saying to each other that it might be more dangerous for us to shop while intoxicated than to drive, but we went anyway. We had so much fun, and we didn't leave until about ten o'clock. That was probably the most fun I ever had shopping, and it had been a quick and lovely escape, temporarily, from my ongoing stress and worry. That night I fell into bed relaxed and happy.

The networking in Santa Barbara worked well for me. One day, Beth had an appointment and she wanted me to go with her so I could talk to her event coordinator, Tamara, about finding a doctor for Jamie. Tamara has a daughter and was happy to share the information she had about the doctors in the area. She told me about Dr. Luc Maes, ND, DC and his wife Barbara. They became good friends of hers, almost like family, because of the way they seemed to deal with all their patients—very compassionately. Dr. Maes, who is from Belgium, is a naturopathic doctor specializing in homeopathy.

Colorado digs . . .

He helped Tamara's daughter through allergy and asthma problems, and Tamara was impressed by his work with children. I returned home without getting his number, which I ended up regretting a few days later.

Later that week, Jamie started getting sick; he had a bad cough and a runny nose. He had the symptoms for days, and it seemed like they would never go away. I called Dr. Klepper and he tried to help us over the phone, but what with the distance between us, and his not being able to examine Jamie in person, it was difficult. I worked with supplements to kill the bacteria, but Jamie was still sick. Dr. Klepper thought the illness might be some kind of allergy. I decided I needed to take Jamie to a regular pediatrician because I wanted to make sure he wasn't fighting any serious infection. Of course, when I went to the appointment, the doctor immediately wanted to give him an antibiotic. He began questioning me about Jamie's vaccines and whether he was up on them. I told him he was not. After that, I had to sit and listen to a lecture on the importance of vaccinating. I felt that some vaccines were

Back to my Santa Barbara girl dress code, after makeover at Blue Bee with Beth

helpful, but I didn't think they were good for Jamie right then, especially when he was sick. I didn't even want to talk about the subject because I knew where we were headed. I wasn't going down that road with another new doctor.

I called Beth and got Dr. Maes's number, dialing it from the car on the way home. His wife, Barb, took the call. Their office was backlogged, but when she heard that Jamie had been sick for about three weeks, she made a place for us a few days out in the schedule.

There were obvious differences between Dr. Maes and most other doctors; this was evident from the minute

Jamie with his constant runny nose and James

we walked into his office. Unlike the cold and unwelcoming environments of many medical spaces, Dr. Maes's office was warm and homey. The building was a renovated historical home with wall-to-wall wood floors, soft couches, and autumn-colored rugs. This reflected a holistic awareness, or perhaps it just showed how much the patients were valued. Jamie seemed to feel comfortable from the start, and so did I, and considering the many, many offices we had entered over the years, this was worth acknowledging.

Dr. Maes made a wonderful first impression with his warm welcoming voice and endearing smile. Barb assisted him in his office, and they worked well together. She really complemented his style, and it was lovely to be around such a pleasant husband-and-wife team.

Initially, Dr. Maes simply watched Jamie, trying to get a feel for his demeanor and mannerisms. Then he and I spoke at length about Jamie's daily life: diet, sleeping patterns, history of behaviors, and so on. With Jamie far away from the Colorado doctors, Dr. Maes wanted to keep up with his changing chemistry, so he made some slight changes to Jamie's daily routine.

His treatment focused first on Jamie's diet, where he advised the complete removal of soy. He suspected Jamie was reacting to it, especially after drinking it daily. Great. He had gotten so attached to the little soy milk boxes, and now I would have to take them away.

My son's continuous cold and allergy symptoms went away almost immediately after I stopped giving him soy. Dr. Maes explained that sometimes sensitivities to certain foods turn into a problem after too much is taken in on a daily basis—but that doesn't necessarily indicate a food allergy. I was learning new things every day.

We worked with Dr. Maes during several long appointments. Over the next couple of months, he added and took away supplements, evaluating the need for each one as well as its impact on Jamie's wellness. There was also a strong focus on Jamie's sleeping problem because it had such severe consequences for everyone in the family. Dr. Maes gave us two homeopathic remedies that brought no apparent change to Jamie's sleep patterns. Then he gave my son a strong dose of a third homeopathic; this one was called stramonium. After spending a lot of time researching remedies, the doctor had a lot of confidence in this one.

Their extensive time together helped the doctor get to know Jamie well, and it was apparent that his treatment plan worked even better because of this relationship. In fact, we all developed a wonderful bond with one another. We felt a strong union with the doctor and his wife. They were as warm and sincere as Tamara said, but even beyond that they were genuinely concerned about Jamie's health and truly invested in his improvement.

Following his third homeopathic remedy, which he received on a Thursday, I didn't hesitate to call Dr. Maes at home early Saturday morning after Jamie became hyper and hysterical. Barb answered the phone, and she had obviously been sleeping.

"Sorry to wake you, Barb."

"Hi, Krista. It's okay. It's just eight o'clock on Saturday morning!" We both laughed and she handed the phone to her husband. I explained about Jamie's behavior.

His response surprised me. "That's exactly what we're looking for."

"What are you talking about?" I asked, astonished.

He explained, "When a patient experiences a temporary increase of his symptoms after the prescription of a single homeopathic remedy, it's considered a good sign. It's an indication that the remedy is right on and deep-acting, with a good prognosis for the patient."

For eight o'clock in the morning, I thought that was a pretty good answer. "So it looks like the third time is a charm, right? he continued. Let's wait a couple weeks to see how his body responds."

Dr. Maes and I continued speaking on the phone almost every day, even weekends and evenings, during the next few weeks. He was an incredible help to us, and his presence and accessibility were consoling. How often do you find a doctor who puts your needs first and understands that problems do not arise only between the hours of nine and five?

Jamie had continued taking Flovent every day, and it was a "so far, so good" situation. I credited the weather, with days that were mild and sunny. At the very least, it made me feel better knowing the temperatures were more conducive to staying well. What was amusing was that it always seemed to rain on Sunday morning, and by noon it was sunny again, making Sunday the perfect day to sleep in, for our much-needed rest. One Sunday evening, I was putting the boys down and everything seemed like a normal night. But at about eleven o'clock, Jamie started coughing. It was the kind of croupy cough that put my hair on end, the kind that had always started his breathing episodes in the past. I thought, *Oh no! James isn't here! How am I going to manage this alone? What am I going to do? It's been so long since he had a breathing attack!*

I was alarmed and unprepared, so I called Beth. "Hey. What are you doing?" I asked as calmly as I could.

Beth sensed my nervousness and answered, "Going to bed. Why? What's wrong?"

"I'm afraid that Jamie is going into a breathing episode. I need your help. Can you come over? I think I need to call 911."

Without hesitation, she replied, "I'll be there in five minutes."

As promised, she arrived in no time. I called 911 and then grabbed Jamie and wrapped him up in a warm blanket. We sat outside in the backyard on a chair, with Jamie on my lap and his head against my chest. I looked out to the ocean, saw the lights from the ships, and showed them to Jamie, knowing this would distract him from his routine panic. I saw the mist in the air, and I prayed it would help him get through this quickly. After ten minutes, shortly before the ambulance came, he fell asleep. The moist night air and the calming discussion had definitely helped. I picked him up and went back inside until the paramedics arrived. Jack woke up from all the commotion and Carla comforted him.

Walking through the kitchen, I crossed the path of the most handsome firefighter ever. He was gorgeous—six-feet-five, black hair, blue eyes, a chiseled face, and perfect lips. Beth came in and we exchanged a look as our jaws dropped in disbelief. We couldn't help but laugh out loud. Had Jamie not been much improved, the mood would never have struck, but it was funny how our habit of being around good-looking men these days had turned us both back into little schoolgirls.

When we got to the hospital, the doctors gave Jamie the steroid dexamethasone; he didn't need the racemic epinephrine that time. It was exciting knowing he had done without it. It was obviously because the Flovent had made such a huge difference in his throat, having kept the swelling down from the start.

Beth stayed at our house that night until Jack fell asleep, and then she joined us at the hospital. She was so sweet to wait with me until we were released. We drove home together and laughed again about the cute, adorable *married* fireman and how we noticed him right in the middle of our emergency.

I fell into bed, relieved that the night had not been as dramatic as I had feared it would be. I had trouble sleeping, though. Maybe I was overtired or had gotten too wound up from all the excitement. I thought about the sample of Serzone, and after the hours that had passed and my desire for deep sleep, I figured I'd give it a try. After about twenty minutes I started shaking, and I felt like my head was going to spin right off. I was dizzy and lightheaded and had an inexplicable surge of energy. Was the drug having the opposite effect than it was supposed to? I stayed up until the wee hours of the morning, drinking water and pacing around the house, trying to mellow out by flipping through the channels and breathing deeply.

I finally fell asleep. Since that incident, Serzone has been taken off the market because of problems with side effects. Well, hmmm! First, Jamie took Prilosec and his hair fell out, causing a caution label for possible hair loss in children; then he took Propulsid and it was pulled off the shelves after eighty children died while taking it; then I took Serzone and had a bad reaction and it was taken off the market. We did not have a good track record with medications, but I have to say that Flovent had restored a little bit of my faith in them.

When James next returned to Santa Barbara, Carla and I let him take a sleep shift with Jamie. Carla and I were both exhausted by this time, so the ability to make up sleep was welcomed. James didn't seem to mind. He could sleep anywhere, anytime, thank goodness.

When he was in town, James started going out with Beth and me during the evening and during the day. He and I began practicing Bikram yoga and working out at Studio E together. This was a good time for us to really enjoy being together.

Studio E was definitely one of the brighter parts of my Santa Barbara stay. A couple named John and Cindy Ebadi ran it. I have known Cindy since I was eighteen years old. My mother, sister, and I had regularly attended her renowned two-hour workout class. She was still kicking my butt all these years later. Only a select few had the endurance for her workouts. Not surprisingly, the same girls had been working out with her since the beginning of the classes. Aside from the unsurpassed workout, just being in the facility was an experience. It was an aesthetic treat from one door to the other, with walls painted by a local artist who had a knack for creating Egyptian goddesses in bright colors. Every couple of months, the art on the walls was changed to the work of a different featured artist. The floors were beautiful wood and the building had an eclectic feel, like the updated factory buildings in lower downtown.

I was energized the minute I walked in the door, but the most empowering moments came after forty-five minutes of jumping, with fifteen minutes to go, when I pushed myself to the absolute limit, kicking my legs as high as I could to the beat of Lisa Stansfield's "Jackie" (gotta love that eighties music!). I might lose my breath, but I would drive through the pain, fatigue, and sweat. It gave me the strength and confidence to make me feel like I could take on anything!

The possibilities for taking things on continued to abound. One opportunity surfaced when I received a fax from James's dad about "Metal-Free." It was a new product that used glutathione, lipoic acid, N-acetylcysteine, and other ingredients to pull metals from the body, while being gentle on the insides. Glutathione, the most abundant antioxidant in the body, is fat soluble and water soluble, so it has antioxidant activity throughout the entire body.

I was unsure about the product's source and validity, so I asked Dr. Maes about it. It just so happened he had it available in his office and knew the company to be reputable. He agreed that Jamie should try it, especially because—unlike the DMSA, which Jamie took in pill form—it was a sublingual spray, which went right into the system instead of through the stomach.

Before beginning the process, he would need some baseline tests on Jamie. The doctor sent me away with several take-home testing kits so I could gather stool, urine, saliva, and hair samples, which would measure Jamie's levels at that point, much like the initial tests that Dr. Grossman had conducted.

In hindsight, the gathering of samples was a comedy of errors. I began by chasing Jamie around the house while he screamed and ran away in fear. When I finally caught him, he struggled while I held his hands down. I was able to cut a piece of his hair while trying not to gouge out one of his eyes as he wriggled in resistance. Next, there was the oh-so-pleasurable

Jamie still with his distant and empty stare, at the park with cousin Bailey

collection of the stool sample. How does one neatly pick up a piece of poop? I do not recommend a spoonlike tool, as the sample is likely to roll off onto the floor, completely grossing everyone out. Trust me when I say that this technique will not go smoothly. Ah, then there was the urine. Boys who realize the fun in making circles in and around the gathering cup are much less interested in cooperating than they are in entertaining themselves and making a mess of the bathroom.

Ultimately, the frantic chasing and mess-making sufficed, and I gathered the samples and returned to Dr. Maes. He calculated some baseline measurements, and then had me begin giving Jamie the chelating agent in a much higher dosage than would be necessary on a regular basis. Then the doctor could conduct a purge test to reveal the amounts of heavy metals coming out of Jamie's body.

Two weeks later, Dr. Maes ordered another round of testing. This time, I was cleverer with my sample collection. While Jamie was playing and distracted with toys, I cut a piece of hair before he noticed what I was doing. Also, I found the perfect set of tongs to control the capture of the stool sample. No rolling! *(Note to self: Throw tongs away before next dinner party.)* Making a game out of aiming urine into the testing bottle was my final trick.

The lab tested the samples again. A couple of days later, Dr. Maes received the faxed results, which revealed that metals, including tin, antimony, mercury, and aluminum, were dumping heavily out of Jamie's system. There was the mercury! I had just known that it was in there! I was shocked, amazed, and delighted to see those metals coming out of his body without any stomach problems or other consequences so far.

Seeing the results made me even more motivated to continue using the chelation treatment. Jamie was completely content and committed to following my everyday regimen, which included his twice-daily spray of chelating agent. It was as if he knew exactly how well it was working for him. Along with the spray, he worked happily with his listening program. I was always tickled as I watched him in the kitchen, wearing his oversize earphones, listening to his therapeutic music, and drinking his supplement-filled bottle at four years old. He was such a good sport about it all.

After Dr. Maes gave us new supplements and added caprylic acid, Jamie no longer took his bottle so readily. I had to change around my daily mixing experiment to see how I could stir his supplements into rice milk and make it enticing enough for him to actually drink it. I taste-tested the mixture myself and it made me gag. I wondered how Jamie would ever swallow the entire bottle of caprylic acid down. There had to be an easier way to get Jamie to take his supplements.

The next morning, after I worked out, I made a protein smoothie and took my supplements—all part of my usual routine. A light went on in my mind. I had a great idea for how I could show Jamie to do the same.

I called to the boys, thinking that, as always, it would help to have Jack there for modeling. "Jamie, come over here, please. You see how Mommy takes her supplements? Watch, okay?" I put a couple of pills in my mouth, exaggerating a gulp to show them going down. Jamie and Jack giggled at how silly I was.

"Jamie, let's try this." I got on the floor with him and motioned with a pill, explaining, "You can take your supplements just like me. See, you put the pill in your mouth and swallow it with your drink of water." Again, I performed my best dramatic "gulp." "Then it goes down your throat, into your esophagus, into your tummy, through your intestines, and out your poopy."

While I explained, I took my finger and touched their throats, tickling my way as I moved along the pathway of the pill. Jamie and Jack laughed hysterically. I repeated my instructions twice and had the boys rolling on the ground, giggling. My little show had Jamie so excited about the pathway of the pill that he wanted to try it, too. I put a vitamin in his mouth; he copied my gulp, and easily swallowed the pill down. He even did it without Jack doing it first! Jack and I cheered, and Jamie was proud of his accomplishment. Then it was Jack's turn, but this time, he was following Jamie's lead.

From that point, Jamie was able to take his supplements in pill form. I was ecstatic that I would never again have to mix or taste-test for either of them. The boys ran off and I sat on the floor, leaning up against a cabinet. Again, the littlest things kept me going. I fell into deep thought for a long time about what had just happened, and how even that small step would propel us all closer to our goal. Our lives were changing so much for the better. It was one of those unforgettable moments of gratitude.

Nearly a month later, one late afternoon, I had just finished a shower, and was getting dressed in my room. I would be meeting Beth soon. A little voice behind me asked, "What are you doing?"

I turned around to see Jamie standing there looking up at me. Searching around, I wondered if Jack was hiding from me, trying to play a trick.

I called out, "Jack? Jack, where are you?"

Jamie stood there waiting, looking around with that wonderful, innocent look of his. My heart skipped a beat. For a second, I was paralyzed in disbelief that the question had actually come from Jamie's mouth. My shock turned to sheer joy and I broke out into happy, crazy laughter. For the first time in over three years, Jamie had spoken to me! I grabbed him and squeezed him tightly. Looking into his face, I noticed that something about him was very different. It was as if some of the cobwebs in his brain had been brushed away. There was a moment of true connection between us. I ran to the phone to call James, Dr. Maes, my mother, Beth, and anyone else I could think of to tell them that Jamie had spoken!

I was unbelievably excited and couldn't sit still. I was reluctant to get ready, even after a couple of hours had passed. Although Beth and I had plans to go out that evening, I just couldn't leave then; I knew there was something else I had to do. I felt like I was wading through a cloud. At the time, Jamie was only partially potty trained. Specifically, he would use the toilet, but never to poop. Our ritual had always been to put a diaper on when he indicated that it was time for him to go.

On that night, an hour after he had spoken, he signaled that he needed a diaper. I decided that I wouldn't do it anymore. I told him that even though I was on my way out the door, I was not going anywhere until he used the potty. In fact, I told him that he was going to use the potty from then on. What was with my new determination? Jamie's speech had me standing taller than ever, and I was ready to grab him by the hand so we could take on the world together! He was resistant, mostly because he always feared the loud flushing noise and swirling water of the bowl, and because sitting on the toilet gave him too much sensory overload, but I felt strongly that right then was the time for us to work through it.

It was about seven o'clock and I was already late, but I called to tell Beth I would be even later because we were on a roll and had moved on to pooping in the potty. How could she argue with that? Finally, by about nine o'clock, Jamie had visited every bathroom in the house and tried to go at least six different times. He tried various stances, until he stood over the toilet with his feet planted on the floor, one hand on the cabinet and the other hand on the wall, in the four-post stance. The mission was finally accomplished while leaning in this position. He had done it!

It had been an evening of wonderful accomplishments. I realized that much of our success came from my believing that Jamie could do it, and holding him to my expectations. He was very proud of his success. I cheered so loudly, and with such excitement, that I almost scared him. I hugged and kissed him until he couldn't take it anymore. He fell fast asleep, along with Jack.

I made it to the party that night in a state of elation. I must have emitted some kind of vibe because I was attracting a lot of attention. The house where everyone had gathered was filled with all of our regular friends from town, including Brad, a guy who always hung out with us. We were talking at a table, just like we always did, and I didn't feel like things were any different than normal. We ended up together, just the two of us, after everyone had gotten up and left the balcony. We had been talking for a while when, suddenly, he leaned over and kissed me. It was definitely a surprise, and I didn't know how to react. I realized at that moment that it didn't feel right at all. I pulled away and jokingly said, "What was *that*?"

He said, "I've been wanting to do that for a long time."

I told him kindly that I wasn't interested. I felt bad that it had happened and that I might have provoked it in some way. The moment really put things in perspective for me. I knew I didn't want to do anything like that to James or our relationship.

After that incident, I walked outside, away from it all. Had I wanted that to happen to me? Had I brought it on myself? Maybe a part of me had been looking for something else. I had felt so much hurt during my relationship with James over the years. Maybe I had wanted to get back at him in some way. I remembered several times when he had taken his father's or a friend's side instead of mine. All the pain from those moments rushed in. But we had also been through so much. I needed to look at how much he had worked on making himself a better person. And he had encouraged me to go and play and laugh and have fun again. He hadn't stood in my way. It seemed like he truly wanted me to be happy.

At that moment, I realized how I felt about him. My heart was more open, and there was a lot less pain. All these guys were sweet and we had fun together, but I only wanted to be with James. I had found my ground with him again, and I wanted to see where it would take us.

The nightlife I had created with Beth was fun, and it was essential to my mental well-being. It took me to a happier place. But the times we had together weren't nearly as important as all the extraordinary things that were going on with Jamie. The joy I felt about his spoken words and his potty training far outweighed my social life, and my primary focus on him had never changed.

We were in a groove with treatments and therapies. Each time I took Jamie to see Shelley, I was more and more impressed with her. She was extremely organized; she knew exactly where Jamie needed to go next because she continually assessed his progress. She is an outstanding therapist who really helped Jamie further his language skills, especially in combination with the effects of chelation.

Shelley referred me to Serena Sutherland, OTR/L, CHT, an occupational therapist in Goleta who specialized in sensory integration. Jamie met with her in the special therapy room she had created in the garage of her house. I was unsure what to expect from someone who worked from her home, but I was impressed with what I saw. The room was filled with beanbags, and thick pads covered the entire floor. She had padded swings, wooden swings, and other physical attractions to engage her young clientele. Jamie and Jack both loved being there. It was too bad that we began seeing her only toward the end of our time in Santa Barbara, and got only about six visits under our belts, because she had amazing insight into children and was extremely effective with her sensory work.

After the powerful addition of Metal-Free, along with the incredible advancements Jamie had made in eye contact through the listening program, the continued nutrition and supplement program took him even further. These treatments, combined, had the biggest impact on Jamie's improvement we'd seen so far. I was incredibly excited to have him actually look back at me. Our ability to communicate back and forth was getting better all the time. Each month there were more and more additions to his vocabulary.

During our last week in Santa Barbara, we had a day just like the many other days we had spent there: a joyous occasion filled with outdoor activities. One of Jack's favorites was riding his scooter around the big circular driveway. James and I watched the twins as they played with their scooters.

It began to rain, and the boys moved into the garage. Jamie stepped up and down on his scooter, holding the handles or moving it from side to side, as he had always done. Jack rode around, pushing off, going faster and faster in a circle in

My first glimpse of some contact with Jamie after several years. The driveway at the rental house

In Santa Barbara after the scooter ride

the big garage. Jamie stopped to watch, but this time it was different. He turned and began to push his scooter around the circle, too, trying to keep up with Jack. You could see his determination as he moved his foot over the ground, hanging tightly to the handles. Jamie slowly worked up a momentum. He pushed himself around, put his foot up, and then pushed again and again until he went faster and faster. It was as if something had just clicked, and his body suddenly knew how to do what his mind wanted it to.

"He's got it, he's doing it! Great job, Jamie!" we yelled with excitement, cheering him on.

Jack was thrilled that Jamie could ride along with him. We all jumped up and down as if we were watching an Olympic gold medal being won. And there should have been a medal, because we had just witnessed the greatest physical achievement of Jamie's life.

CHAPTER

12

Something Is Working

The nice thing about returning home from Santa Barbara in April was that we had all spring, summer, and fall to look forward to. Almost an entire year would go by without snow, which for me was something to get excited about.

I had obviously collected way too much stuff in Santa Barbara because I had to send at least eighteen large boxes home. I can blame it on the length of the stay, right? We had spent seven months there. It was hard to leave; our lives had taken such unexpected turns during that time. We had found new friendships, gotten used to new practitioners, and come to adore many people there. And it had been wonderful to have that much time to spend with Beth. When we left, there were many tearful good-byes, but I knew we would be back, and we would all see each other again soon.

James and I were ready for a new start. We felt refreshed and our relationship was better than it had been in a long time. Almost everything that had been troubling me had faded.

I was excited about the drive back because we were going to stop and visit my mom in Palm Desert, California. Visiting her was something to look forward to. My mom is always working on her current house, making continual changes. Her favorite hobby is committing much of her time to taking an old, ugly, unstylish house and turning it into something beautiful. I have seen certain homes she has purchased and have had serious doubts about her vision for them, but with her incredible taste and flair, she has turned the neglected property into a palace every time. Her home was sure to impress and astound.

The first morning there, I arose and suddenly realized Jamie hadn't woken up during the night. I was panicked and ran around asking James and my mom if they had heard or seen him. I peeked into his room to find that both he and Jack were still sleeping. After three weeks, Dr. Maes's third homeopathic remedy had actually worked! Finally, at four years and three months of age, Jamie had slept through the night!

Jamie slept through the next night, and the night after that. And I could actually sleep through the night, too. I didn't know what to do with myself. Habit continued to wake me, so I got up anyway, just to check on the boys. My body was used to the rhythm. It was strange to think this might really last. It was such an amazing visit at my mom's—one we would never forget.

We headed through the desert back to Colorado. As we drove, I revisited my memories of Santa Barbara. I went through a lot of emotions, both laughing and tearing up. We

After the first full night's sleep, Yeah!

crossed over the mountain passes, and I noticed the shadows of the clouds hanging over the peaks and the amazing formations of rocks, with their vibrant colors. It was strange that all I had thought about on the way to California was one goal: getting there. Now, as I was leaving, I could see things I hadn't noticed before. What a joyous awakening!

I called James on my cell phone. I could see his car in the rearview mirror as we caravanned, but I felt like talking. He was in the mood to talk, too, and we stayed on the phone for hours as we drove through California to Arizona and then Utah and then on to Colorado. We talked about the wonderful months we'd had, our new friendships, and the progress Jamie was making. We even talked about us.

"What are you thinking?" he asked, as he often did.

"I was just thinking about how you bought those bottles of wine that night with Beth. You were so cute." We laughed. "I was also thinking about Jack and Jamie and how much they love each other."

"Do you know how much I love you?"

"No. How much?" I replied coyly.

"I love you more than I can ever say. And I want you to know that I can now see what you've done with Jamie. You've done an incredible job."

I giggled with embarrassment as I squeaked out, "Thank you."

Things between James and me were definitely looking up. We were much closer. I had succeeded in rediscovering my love for him. I valued him as my partner, and I appreciated the fact that we had been able to keep our family together through all those tough times.

We arrived home. It was exciting to see our black labs, Emoi and Jaro. The neighbor boys were also a welcome sight, and Jamie actually ran over first to see them. He and Jack were at the neighbors' house for a while as we unpacked the car.

Kelly, their mom, came out to see us. "Hey, guys! How is everything? It's so good to see the boys. They've really grown! And I can't believe how much Jamie has changed." She was clearly astonished. "He's looking right at me, and he's talking—responding to us!"

"Yes, he's done really well, but we still have so much work to do!" I replied.

"Are you sure he needs it? He's come so far!" She was surprised that I wasn't yet satisfied.

Her question frustrated me. Kelly was consistently positive, but I knew she could never understand what I had been through, because I hadn't really shared many of my emotions with her—or anyone other than James, for that matter. Jamie was better, obviously, and it was astonishing, but I wanted him back *completely*. I recognized that what was great was still not quite good enough. I had come this far, but I knew we could keep going even further.

Did I want him to be more like Jack? Was that my goal? I guess it was. At least I wanted Jamie to be able to communicate and to understand things the way Jack understood things. I wanted him to have every opportunity Jack had. There had been a point when I thought Jamie wouldn't be able to have the kind of life I wanted for him, but that worry was drifting further and further away.

After getting settled back into our house, we renewed our momentum. The supplements, chelation, and nutrition regimen that Jamie had going with Dr. Maes were working in full force. I planned for Jamie to continue his various treatments, including speech, occupational, and music/listening therapies, but once again I needed to track down some quality specialists in Colorado who could pick up where we had left off in Santa Barbara. I felt grateful about the fact that we already had Dr. Grossman.

Jamie continued to do well in all areas, including his sleep habits. So far, he had slept through the night every night since we had left Santa Barbara. This miracle never escaped my recognition. I started the boys back at G.E.M.S., but after a couple of weeks I noticed Jamie was no longer benefiting from it. He had changed so much that instead of blending with the group, he stood out. His focus and his language were much better, and he had fewer and fewer repetitive behaviors. There was a particular cadence at school, and it was no longer the fit it had been before we left for California. I talked to Joan about my observations, and she was disappointed, wanting the opportunity to continue her work with Jamie, but also keeping his best interests in mind. Luckily, having worked with Shelley Greenbaum (the speech therapist from Santa Barbara) for a while, she had set the perfect standard for us.

Serena Sutherland referred me to a woman who had created a specialized OTSI (occupational therapy with sensory integration therapy) called the Wilbarger Protocol, a technique of skin brushing. The Wilbarger Deep Pressure and Proprioceptive Technique and Oral Tactile Technique (formerly referred to as the Wilbarger Brushing Protocol, or WBP) are techniques developed by Patricia Wilbarger, MEd, OTR, FAOTA, a clinical psychologist and an internationally recognized expert. This process of applying deep pressure to the skin with a special brush was created to address the problem of sensory defensiveness.

When I contacted Dr. Wilbarger's daughter, she referred me to one of her protégées, Kristy Phelps, OTR, BCP, an occupational therapist and clinical director/founder of a group called Unique Prints Pediatric Therapy Services. After working with Serena in her amazing therapy room in Santa Barbara, I was intent on finding something similar in Colorado. I had gone to see at least three locations, but hadn't found anything even close. The places I saw had only a few toys and didn't seem designed to capture the interest of kids like Jamie. But when I met Kristy Phelps and toured her treatment area, I knew that it was the place.

She had a program incorporating OTSI, speech therapy, Samonas sound therapy, Jin Shin, massage, and craniosacral therapy, and she was beginning the incorporation of a new program called brain gems. She also had a fantastic treatment room. It was a large play space covered with beanbags, along with wall-to-wall bouncy mattresses and air mattresses. There was a fun obstacle course where kids could climb a wall, go down a slide, and jump onto the mattresses and beanbags.

All the kids enjoyed entering into this world of their own through a cute little trap door. I was sold because I knew that Jamie would be, too.

I took him in to meet Kristy. She did a long evaluation with him and, when the work was done, let him loose in the playroom. He had an absolute blast, jumping, swinging, and playing. Jamie was at the point where he wanted and needed to have constant sensory input. I was anxious to get her working with him. She never really saw his severe behavior—only eight months earlier he wouldn't have even let anyone touch him. She put him on a program where he came for five to six hours a day, four days a week. We kept this schedule for three weeks at a time, with one week off in between. At home, we did our own skin brushing, with the instructions and skin brushing kit that Kristy had given us.

I liked her not only as a therapist but also as a person because she was quite optimistic. With her combination of therapies and her positive attitude, she was successful at meeting the needs of each child she worked with, and Jamie was no exception.

After several months of rotating through our rigorous therapy schedule, Jamie's improvement signaled to me that he could handle a preschool setting seemingly well, so I considered finding a place for the boys in the fall. For many months, G.E.M.S. had been a perfect and familiar place, but I wanted to give Jamie the opportunity to attend a regular preschool near our home instead of one geared toward special needs. I figured that being around "regular" kids would also be better for him at this point in his progression.

One day I drove by a church preschool called Abiding Hope. I liked what I saw and thought it would be worth checking out. The director had just the attitude I was hoping for when I met with her about Jack and Jamie. I had tried to get Jamie's assistant in Santa Barbara to join us in Colorado because we had all become quite attached to her. She had considered it, and I was hopeful for a time, but in the end she just couldn't leave her home. In order to begin the boys at Abiding Hope, I wanted to find another assistant, and I mentioned this to the director, who thought it sounded like a fine plan.

I found an assistant through an ad in the newspaper, and the boys began at the new preschool with her help. After a week or so, I had a conference with the teacher. Apparently, Jamie was doing fairly well. The teacher also added that she really didn't think he needed an assistant because he was interacting just fine on his own, and she was fully prepared to provide him with the extra support he needed. I loved hearing this news.

Following the recommendation of the director, Jack was in a different class than his brother. He had a cute young teacher with short blonde hair and smiley eyes: the typical profile of all the boys' teachers over the past few years. Jamie's teacher had the opposite appearance. She was a shorter woman, masculine and frumpy, with an intimidating demeanor, but she was a good balance of strict and sweet. I thought her looks might be a deal-breaker with Jamie, because her image was so drastically different from that of previous teachers, but that's what I get for drawing conclusions. Jamie didn't even see her exterior, and he gelled with her from the start.

He changed as often as the weather. At this point, he was about 80 percent better than he had been when he was diagnosed at nineteen months. He was more aware of his surroundings and was capable of having some engaging conversations. It was thrilling to interact with him. However, he was still not *all* there.

For example, one day I was sitting at the desk in the kitchen when the boys came in to tell me they were going next door.

I stopped Jamie in his tracks and looked him in the eye. "Jamie, are you going next door?"

He answered "Yes, and I want to . . ." but then he lost his words, as if they were getting tied up in his thoughts.

I said, "Okay, sweetie, have a fun time, and Jamie . . . I love you."

He just looked at me and walked away.

Jamie still lost his focus after a few moments of conversation, and he was still a bit disconnected from his words. More than anything, I wanted to feel an emotional link between us. I longed to hear Jamie tell me he loved me, too, understanding the meaning behind the words.

Once again, my father-in-law shared some information he had gained from a medical conference he had recently attended in Texas. He had learned about a young specialist named Max Collins, DC, who was practicing in South Carolina. This particular doctor had developed a specialized light treatment to detoxify the body.

Dr. Vance felt strongly about his discovery. "Krista, I believe this is something worth your while."

I was skeptical. "What is this treatment exactly? I've never heard or read about anything like this."

"I know, but this is something really special," he said. "It works to pull heavy metals from the body. I saw how it was used. I think you should look into it."

"Well, Jamie is much better, but I know he needs more help."

The more I thought about it over the next couple of days, the more intrigued I became. The idea that we might have another avenue for heavy-metal detoxification that would be even quicker and more efficient would definitely be worth investigating. I gave Dr. Collins a call but didn't hear back from him. I waited for several days and then called again. No return call. I called again and again, every day for two weeks. Not getting a return call made me even more determined to get hold of him.

Finally, one night at about eleven o'clock, I was making my way up to bed. Everyone else in the house was already sleeping when the phone rang. It was Dr. Collins. He had finally found time to call me back, even though it was one in the morning, his time. We stayed on the phone for two hours! He did an impressive job describing the way his blue light diode therapy worked, and through the technical jargon I managed to understand its basic design for detoxifying the body of heavy metals and radiation—the two main causes of every human disease, according to him.

I spoke with James the next day about a potential visit to Dr. Collins in South Carolina. Of course, I pushed the fact that James's father was the one who thought we should see this doctor. We had been home from Santa Barbara only a couple of months, and I knew it was another expense that would cause James stress. I had researched the costs, though, and the hotels were inexpensive. I shared my gathered information about the possible discounts and probable expenses, and James was quite pleased that I had shown concern about the financial aspects of the plan. He knew I felt that we really needed to go, so he decided we should see what it was all about.

As we flew into Charlotte, North Carolina (no more RVs, ever!), I looked out the windows and couldn't see much below except for a lot of flat, green country. We exited the plane and took a shuttle bus to pick up our rental car. It dropped us off outside a small building. I was sure it was no less than 90 degrees, with 100 percent humidity. We waited outside, dripping with sweat, laughing and looking at each other. We were sharing the same thought: *What are we doing here?*

We drove for about an hour to get to Columbia. It was a decent-size college town, but quiet compared with Denver. There wasn't a lot of traffic, although we were right in the middle of rush hour. It was hard to get our bearings without the mountains to identify "west"; James and I were used to this kind of a landmark, which functioned as a compass. We got a little lost, but finally found the exit to get with Dr. Collins's property. He had suggested some hotels off the exits near his home, and I had made a reservation at the one closest to him. We arrived, and were a bit disappointed—to say the least. It didn't seem clean and was run-down. We might have been a little spoiled, but it felt like we were in some kind of time warp that had sent us back a couple of decades. The only buildings in sight were a Piggly Wiggly and a Bojangles' Famous Chicken 'n' Biscuits. I'd never even heard of those places.

We went into the hotel and I asked to see a room. They showed us their suite, which was a big, drafty room with a smelly, old Jacuzzi right in the middle of it. I knew there was no way we could stay there for a week. We needed a place that was at least clean, with somewhere to work out and a nearby Starbucks, maybe? No such luck.

I talked to the young woman at the front desk about finding different accommodations. When she spoke I noticed she had only a couple of teeth. She looked a little more rustic than I was used to, but she seemed nice, apologizing because she didn't know of anywhere to send us. We called Dr. Collins and he directed us to a strip of businesses about fifteen minutes away. This area was more populated, with many more choices. We grabbed some water at a local market, and the cashier was also missing most of her teeth, the remainder of which were black and rotted. I hadn't seen many people with all these dental issues before. *We'd better not drink the water*, I thought.

We found contentment at the Fairfield Inn. There were restaurants, stores, and a mall nearby, and we managed to locate a much-coveted coffee shop in one of the bookstores on the boulevard. We had a two-bedroom suite with a kitchen—plenty of room to get settled in—and the only tub was in the bathroom, right where we preferred it. There was an outdoor pool, too, and the boys were so excited about that.

We headed toward Dr. Collins's home and office. Before we got there, I told James that if we pulled up to his house and it was a shack, and if all his teeth were missing, we were going to turn around and take a vacation on the coast. He laughed while nodding in agreement. As we neared Dr. Collins's street, we drove up the road and actually saw a run-down shack on the corner. I thought my worst fears had materialized and we had traveled all that way for nothing. But we realized we had not reached the correct turn yet, and we continued on, laughing on the one hand—but a bit worried on the other. We called Dr. Collins to recheck our directions, and he reassured us that we were right where we needed to be.

A moment later, we arrived. What a relief not only to find the building but also to see that it was actually an attractive Victorian home. A new office building had just been built on the property, and there was a parking lot full of cars. We entered the office to find quite a few people in the waiting room. It had beautiful wood floors, white shuttered windows, and subdued yellow walls. The air in South Carolina was humid, but the ceiling fans in the doctor's office created a nice flow of air that added to the calming mood inside. It was an environment that felt good, and we relaxed in the comfort of it.

I still wondered about Dr. Collins's character. I was curious about him and wanted to know more before we actually met him. I walked down the hall to wash my hands and happened to pass the open door of the examination room. I was able to catch a peek at Dr. Collins. My concerns eased when I saw a nice-looking, fit man with a pleasant smile and a warm voice. He had a magnetic energy about him. I couldn't wait to get back and share these observations with James. We anxiously waited two hours for our turn.

While we waited, I relaxed outside in the hot sunshine and humid air, and Jack and Jamie played in the grass. When we were finally ushered in, we met Dr. Collins, a young, vibrant man with glowing skin. Instantly, I knew we had not come this far for nothing.

Jamie was first up. He got on the table and the blue light diode was placed on his head as the light turned on and started running its programs from the periodic table. Dr. Collins listened, moved Jamie's limbs, felt his skin, and examined his body as if he could see through to his insides. He had a unique way about him. I would say it was something equivalent to having a sixth sense, a true vision into the body; he saw it as a whole instead of separate, independent parts. He understood the systems within so well that he could draw conclusions by gathering information in ways that mainstream medical practitioners never did. To this day, I find his abilities unbelievable.

When Jamie's examination was done, it was my turn. Dr. Collins believes in treating the entire family. He likes to treat mother and child together, at the same time, because of their strong link to each other. My initial examination really surprised me. I lay down on the table, and he touched my stomach through my clothes. He said he could tell that I had had quite a few surgeries for female issues. He was right. I wondered how he knew that merely by touching me, and he explained that he knew there was scar tissue because it was blocking the energy from that area. . . . Okay.

Over the next couple of appointments, Dr. Collins treated Jamie and the rest of the family with the blue light diode twice a day, and performed certain manipulations on Jamie's body. Each cycle of light lasted for eight minutes. Dr. Collins also had Jamie lie on my stomach while he simultaneously put the light on my head and Jamie's. We spent about two hours each day with the doctor.

Because Dr. Collins was also a chiropractor, I spoke to him about the problems I had experienced after my last adjustment two years earlier, when I had suffered from vertigo. My vertigo had finally gone away, thanks to the intervention of skilled health care practitioners. But at first I didn't want Dr. Collins to work on my neck because the idea of another adjustment made me nervous. I had never seen another chiropractor after the last catastrophe. He gently reached up and placed his fingers on the exact spot where I had felt the pain. I had to ask him, "How did you know where it was?"

"I can see it by the way you hold your head."

I wasn't sure if I felt like crying or laughing, but I was completely caught off guard by his perceptiveness. I don't want to call him psychic, but he definitely has a vision into his patient's bodies—a unique and special style. I can say this with confidence because I have seen my share of doctors.

After the third or fourth visit, he wanted to adjust my neck because he could tell that my body's rhythm was ready.

I was still a little nervous. I felt comfortable with Dr. Collins, and I let myself trust him. Afterward, I had absolutely no pain at all. He had worked gently and with ease. My neck went right into place, and I was amazed at how good it felt.

James got on the table for his examination. He told the doctor that his only real problem was that his knee had hurt since college, mostly when he exercised it. It had been injected with saline a few times, years earlier. That had helped, but then the pain had returned and continued. As Dr. Collins worked with different pressure points, he determined that James's knee hurt because of his teeth. Well, of course, everyone knows that. *What?* Well, the mercury in the metal amalgam fillings of teeth affects certain organs, which affect certain joints in the body. I had known about the harmful properties of metal fillings for years and had already had mine replaced, but James hadn't yet done the same. He decided to get it done when we got back home, and after several months his knee never bothered him again.

During our seven-day visit, we got to know Dr. Collins and his family, which was really a treat. He was like one of those small-town, house-call–making doctors of the past whose interactions with every patient were so warm and personal you felt like you were watching a father talk to his children. Dr. Grossman, Dr. Klepper, and Dr. Maes created the same kind of relaxed environment. It is extremely conducive to healing when a doctor really gets to know his patients, and that was how he treated our family—he knew how to treat each one of us as an individual with unique needs. Others must have felt the same, because everyone in the packed waiting room happily waited hours to see him.

After witnessing a bit of his life, I realized why it had taken him two weeks to call me back. We gained a lot of respect for him during our visit. James (and even I, for that matter) had been skeptical from the start, but had all our concerns laid to rest.

How does the blue light diode work? Everyone wants to know. Dr. Collins explained that his childhood had been full of sickness, and that this had eventually led him to explore the fringes of alternative medicine. He believes that growing up in the South exposed him to an overabundance of toxic metals in the water—such as lead, mercury, arsenic, and copper—both through drinking tap water and from swimming in the bacteria-contaminated local ponds. He had spent a large part of his life feeling ill, to the point where he was often nauseated and vomiting on a daily basis. He also had a lot of skin problems, which left him with bumpy, scarred, and chronically irritated skin.

After college, he decided to open a Mexican restaurant in Saudi Arabia. (I know, I'm not joking, very out of the ordinary.) He liked the idea of being overseas and was a big fan of cooking. While he was there, a friend introduced him to a local healer. He decided to visit her in the hope of finding a treatment that would improve his overall health. One of the treatments she created was meant to help his skin. It was a concoction of herbs with a consistency similar to mud. She gave him a supply and told him to put it on his face every day. After a month, his condition was gone. This permanently affected the direction of his life; it started him thinking about alternative healing and the power of Mother Nature's elements.

The idea of the blue light diode came from his hobby of scuba diving. During his many diving trips, he witnessed fish swimming through various channels of light under the water. He had already learned from a friend of his, a researcher at NASA, that being at certain depths underwater alters the body's makeup. He was driven to study these two principles. He worked underwater, taking his blood at different depths to monitor the changes, and saw that the metals in the blood were much higher as he moved deeper and through different lighting, inducing his body to detoxify. His work centered around manipulating the changes that light and pressure can bring to the system in a way that promotes the shedding of outside materials as the body works to clean, or rejuvenate, itself. This is the theory that drove the design of the blue light diode, which Dr. Collins took years to create. It is still a work in progress.

Aside from the whole world of treatment and healing that opened up to us, we also made a nice vacation out of our visit to South Carolina. James and I would run to the gym, work out, and stop by the bookstore to have coffee. I loved the humidity because it turned our workout environment into a sauna, giving us a good sweat, which I always enjoyed.

One day, we rented a boat to take the boys waterskiing. They had never been on a boat before. They didn't like it at first and found the lake daunting. We had them bundled up in life jackets and couldn't wait to get out on the open water.

But each time we accelerated past the wake, a mere 10 to 15 miles per hour, the boys screamed bloody murder. They were beside themselves with fear. We kept slowing down, trying to calm them, telling them that once we got out on the lake, it was going to be fun! We went back and forth like that for a while. It was so funny at one point that I had to take pictures of them screaming, knowing they would find it hilarious when they got older.

Each time I jumped in the lake, the boys would call to me, wildly alarmed, begging me to get back in the boat. But after a while their panic lessened a little, so James and I started skiing, taking turns driving. The boys were so impressed when they saw me get up on the skis that they forgot their fear, and we ended up having an awesome time together.

In the evenings, we would visit with Dr. Collins and his wife, Lora. They had four kids: a girl—the eldest—and three boys, who liked to play with Jack and Jamie. The Collins boys would show our boys the bugs outside, play all kinds of games, slide back and forth between the trees on their homemade zipline, or jump around on their broken-down swing set.

The fourth day he used the light, Dr. Collins called me into the room where he was working on Jamie. He told me to feel Jamie's liver, so I placed my hand on the lower right side of his stomach, where the doctor indicated. My son's skin was hot to the touch. It was like that area of his body had its own little fever. Dr. Collins explained that there was a parasite leaving his body, being pushed out because of the correction of Jamie's DNA by the light. I had never felt or seen any effect like that before. It was mind-boggling.

James and I were both stunned by Dr. Collins's treatment. The laser had sounded strangely bizarre when I first learned of it, but all his treatments, his explanations, and his general way of working with us couldn't have felt more legitimate. After we listened to and understood his theories, it all made a lot of sense. If we help the body, it can heal by ridding itself of harmful substances.

At the end of the week, Dr. Collins and his family invited us to their house for dinner. The visit was as comfortable as it would have been had we done it every Sunday afternoon. The meal was unbelievable: vegetables from their garden, homemade wheat tortillas and bread, hand-prepared pinto beans, and sides of freshly made salsa and guacamole. The boys didn't love the food, but it was heavenly to me, because it reminded me of the food at home. The Collinses inspired me with all their recipes. We said our good-byes, and the next day headed for the airport to go back home.

When we returned to Denver, Jamie became very sick with a very bad cough. Dr. Collins had warned us that this could happen. He said that in two months we would see the changes the laser had brought, and we might see a recurrence of his sicknesses before Jamie got better. I knew that sometimes you have to get sicker before you heal. Dr. Collins believed that Jamie's body was beginning to let go of all the medications he had been given throughout his different hospital visits. His improved sleeping habits had continued, but after he got sick this time, he started to wake up during the night again. Once the sleep problems kicked in, I had a little bit of a breakdown, calling Dr. Collins in a nervous panic.

"I'm going to go crazy if you don't help me. He's been sleeping through the night for four months now. I can't do this anymore! What can I do?"

"Remember, Krista, the light is working or we wouldn't be seeing such a drastic change. It will get better once the parasites are completely gone. You can help the process by giving him some black walnut tincture. After eight days of the herb, he should be sleeping through the night again. Don't worry, everything is going to be okay," he said with confidence.

I didn't find his advice that helpful, but I followed his directions. I had trusted him this far, and—despite my reluctance—even James encouraged me to keep trusting him. So for eight days I gave Jamie drops of the herb. On the eighth day exactly, just as Dr. Collins had predicted, Jamie resumed sleeping through the night. Words cannot describe my relief. Crazy, isn't it?

Two more months went by and, yet again, there were major improvements in Jamie's behavior, just as the doctor had said there would be. Jamie held his eye contact for longer periods of time and his language became more and more improved. His vocabulary grew with each passing week.

One afternoon, the boys were playing outside with Emoi and Jaro, while I was gardening. A loud roar from a jet flying overhead suddenly filled the sky. I immediately glanced at Jamie, expecting his need for attention. His eyes watched the jet cross over, followed by its trail of white vapor, and I heard him murmur, "Cool plane." This was quite a notable change from the earlier days of extreme panic!

A few weeks later, we went to Santa Barbara for two weeks to visit Dr. Maes. We saw him at the office a few times and we also had him, Barb, and their kids over for dinner and a swim. We had become good friends and our families enjoyed each other's company, even outside the office.

Dr. Maes couldn't get over the change in Jamie, who was now much more engaged with the other kids, excited to be swimming and playing. He didn't hesitate to jump right in the pool. The layers of his emptiness were disappearing, as he showed his ability to blend in with all the kids and take part in activities around him.

During this stay, I also made several appointments to see our previous speech therapist, Shelley. After her first five minutes with Jamie, she asked, "What did you do? This is not the same child I saw four months ago." She was shocked at how different he was.

Seeing Jamie through someone else's eyes made his growth seem even more valid. Shelley had seen Jamie at the peak of his autism, and if anyone could make the claim that there had been a drastic improvement, she could.

She wanted to know exactly what had happened. "What did you do that he's so much better? It's amazing!"

"You wouldn't believe me if I told you."

"Yes, I would. Please tell me," she replied.

So I explained about our trip to South Carolina for the innovative light therapy, and also told her about the effects of Metal-Free. The evidence was right in front of her, and what else could possibly explain it?

If one trip had been good, another would be even better. I decided to go for another visit to Dr. Collins. When October came, we headed back, this time staying two weeks. Even though James was able to stay with us for only one, I still wanted him to come.

We arrived in town for the second time and quickly got back into the daily routine we had established on our first trip. The weather was still nice and felt great, but it wasn't nearly as hot outside. James and I had a ball with every workout, at every meal, and over every cup of coffee.

The first Sunday we were there, we decided to drive an hour and a half to Charleston to take the boys on a horse-and-buggy tour of the town. The homes and the history were fascinating. After the buggy ride, we walked around the area; there was something going on in every corner of town. We saw a haunted house where you could walk around and see the ghosts that lived there. (The boys wanted to pass on that particular attraction.) We stopped to eat at a little Italian restaurant in a rustic, worn yellow house that was punctuated with an abundance of flowers in window boxes. We sat outside and James and I drank wine out of short crystal glasses. Charleston was a beautiful little town on the ocean, and I loved the feel of it. Overall, the people in South Carolina were kind and polite. We had a pleasant trip, and it was fun to take Jack and Jamie with us.

Each evening, returning for our second treatment of the day, we were lucky to get to know Zoe, the Great Dane who waited with everyone else at Dr. Collins's office. Zoe was being treated for cancer. She was a sweet dog, and we sympathized with her condition, but at the same time it was sort of funny that she was there with all the humans. Jack and Jamie would lie with her and pet her, and she was quite gentle with them.

During that trip, we had dinner with Dr. Collins and his family several times. I always enjoyed it because theirs was probably the cleanest, healthiest food in town, and it was always delicious. His wife, Lora, made the most amazing dishes, using her own recipes for hummus, homemade soy milk, fresh granola, and flaxseed chips. We laughed as they morphed into an ordinary married couple, arguing over who was the better cook and who did most of the cooking.

A mile away there was an outdoor organic vegetable and fruit market. We made a point to visit it regularly and bring back the goods to the Collins family. They were much obliged, and transformed the mouthwatering produce into dinner for us all.

Before James left, we hit the zoo in town—a must-see attraction for us. Although built on a smaller scale than most zoos, the size added to its appeal. It had a attractive tropical area, elephants that had been trained to eat from the hands of their visitors, and a beautiful botanical garden. Jack and Jamie just loved it. They would run from one animal to the next, acting like they had never seen a zoo before. It was fun to watch Jamie's amusement with all the animals.

The night before we were to return to Denver, around two in the morning, Jamie woke me up out of a deep sleep when he started having difficulty breathing. He vomited saliva as he struggled for air, screaming and gasping for breath. I had all the equipment available to help open up his airway, but as I opened up the nebulizer, I couldn't remember how to work it because we hadn't needed any treatments since being in Santa Barbara. I acted quickly, calling the hotel operator and telling her I needed 911. The paramedics came in and they were sweet and patient with Jamie in the ambulance, talking to him until they managed to calm him down.

On the way to the hospital, I realized that his breathing had returned to normal. I thought that perhaps the situation had arisen more from his panic or a Pavlovian response than an actual physical problem. We ended up spending several late-night hours in the hospital, where Jamie was given steroids and kept for observation. It eased my worries that, once again, he had not needed racemic epinephrine. But at the same time, I was concerned about the heavy mucus in his chest. They released us early the next morning, and Jamie and I took a taxi back to the hotel, where we found Jack and

Jamie winning the battle over autism

Dr. Collins's office in South Carolina

Carla awake and concerned. I was exhausted, but the fact that everything was fine again helped me bounce right back.

I called Dr. Collins but couldn't get hold of him, so I just drove over to his office. I explained what had happened. He examined Jamie and gave him another treatment. We discussed the fact that Jamie was experiencing something like a Herxheimer reaction, where the body goes mildly through the sickness again in its process of healing.

We decided that he was doing better and was okay to travel that day. After giving Dr. Collins's family hugs and kisses, we waved good-bye and rushed to get to the airport in time to make our flight.

Once again, the doctor told us to expect positive changes after a couple of months. Although Jamie's behavior and language continued to improve, this time I was more blown away by it than ever, because the changes were more advanced and came faster all the time. Everybody was healthier and happier than we had been in a long while. Had the roller-coaster ride really come to an end?

A few months later, the boys told me they wanted to go play across the street. I went to the door with them, watching as they walked to the neighbor's house.

I yelled after them, "Bye, boys. Have fun and be careful. I love you!"

Jamie turned and yelled back, "I love you, too, Mom!"

That was the first time I felt the depth of his meaning as he spoke the words.

CHAPTER 13

Healed

One late afternoon, I sat next to the tub, giving Jack and Jamie a bath. They always loved their bath time when they were little, and were reluctant to leave the warm water where they could splash and play. After about thirty minutes, Jack decided he was done and got out, but Jamie still wasn't ready. He and I talked and laughed, and I suddenly became aware of what was happening between us. We were just going over the events of the day, back and forth in conversation. I thought, *Look at us!* Jamie was completely connecting with me. There wasn't a missed beat between us. At that moment I knew he had returned to me.

It had been about four months since we had gone to see Dr. Collins for the second time. I was overwhelmed by what I saw happening right in front of me. Even now, I can hardly write this without tears coming to my eyes:

By August 2002, Jamie was completely recovered from autism.

We finally found peace after all the suffering we had endured. I was relaxed to my very depths, content knowing what we had accomplished. I had many perfect moments during the years that followed. Life became even more precious to me.

It took me an entire year to get back to health again, physically and emotionally. What an unbelievable year. I got back into the best shape I had been in a long time, and I had a lot of fun doing it. So not only was I able to experience my own recovery, but our whole family also found equilibrium. After years of focusing on Jamie's needs ahead of everything, it was a nice feeling to have a more balanced life.

One of the many special events that followed Jamie's recovery was observing as his personality became more distinct. We saw over and over again how pronounced his determination was. For example, Jack had been riding his bike for a while without training wheels. One particular evening, there was barely any light left in the sky as the sun was going down. The boys were still playing outside, and Jamie came in and asked if we could take the training wheels off his bike. James was surprised, but immediately went outside and began taking the wheels off. Jamie had gotten a huge amount of his coordination back at this point, and I really hoped he would be capable of balancing the bike. I sat apprehensively on the grass while James got him ready.

"Are you sure about this?" I asked him again.

"Yes, Mom. No problem."

He got on his bike as James, Jack, and I gave him directions, all at the same time.

"Be sure to pedal fast!"

"Steer away from houses . . . and cars!"

"Don't get your feet stuck in the pedals."

Jamie just listened, nodded, and gave us the thumbs up. James took the signal and started him down the street, holding the back of the bike and running by his side long enough to keep him steady.

I yelled after him with urgency, "Keep pedaling, Jamie! Don't stop pedaling!"

James let go, and Jamie rode his bike all by himself on the first try. We were all elated, and hollered down the street with support.

"Awesome, Jamie!"

"Great job, Jamie!"

We clapped and yelled, watching him travel up and down the street. He continued riding until it was completely dark. He didn't want to stop. Jack joined him as James and I watched our boys riding their bikes together. It was a moment to remember forever.

Another strong trait of Jamie's that we love is his innocent nature and warm attitude toward all people. We were on vacation once at a club in Northern California during the colder months of the year. Jamie saw the pool area and wanted to get warm in the Jacuzzi. He got in and scooted around the large hot tub, slowly moving until he was sitting right next to the only other person there, an elderly man. For a few seconds, there was a comfortable silence between the seventy-year-old and the six-year-old.

Then the older man said, "Pretty warm."

James with the boys, taking off the training wheels

"Yeah," Jamie replied. Then he began to ask a series of direct questions about what he had observed, and the gentleman responded to his inquisitive observations. It was like they had done this a hundred times before and were just running into each other again. Those moments may be overlooked by most and seem almost trivial, but their significance will never be lost on us. Time passed, each day bringing changes in Jamie. His body and mind seemed to be reawakened, experiencing regular daily events as if it were the first time. He kept up just a few of his therapies, such as visiting Kristy Phelps each month for five days in a row. Jamie also continued his involvement in speech therapy once a week. In addition, Jenny, a young woman who had worked at G.E.M.S., came

Boys and me at the beach in Santa Barbara

Loving life

over to do music therapy with both boys. The therapy was more like a music lesson, and the twins had great fun with it, playing the guitar, drums, violin, saxophone, and piano. I had kept Jamie on Metal-Free for a total of five years. The combination of therapies had helped to make his repetitive behaviors, sensory issues, and communication problems fall away by the age of five. I continued to see him grow and develop over the next couple of years. It was extraordinary to see the butterfly emerge from his chrysalis.

I began trying some sports for the boys, knowing not only that they would love the activity but also that it would further build their strength and coordination, an especially good focus for Jamie. They began with swimming and tennis lessons. I remember how I just loved watching them swim. They had always enjoyed the water, and swimming came naturally. During their lesson, I used to hide around the corner so they wouldn't see me watching. It was phenomenal to see them move through every graceful stroke. Jack was an exceptionally quick swimmer and still is. Jamie didn't have the speed Jack did, but he was smooth and strong. As his coordination advanced, he became agile at all his physical activities.

At around six years old, they both showed an impressive knack for tennis. They would lob every shot over the net and chase down each ball with tenacity. These early years were only the beginning of the Vance brothers' tennis careers.

CHAPTER

14

Life Goes On

James and I had survived the threat of divorce and were going strong. We weren't perfect, of course, and we still argued a lot—but fortunately, not so much about major health crises. And, of course, we still fought about money. I think he regretted that I had not lost my love of shopping, because with less money required for Jamie's treatments, more could be spent on clothes. (I know, I have a few issues. . . .)

One Saturday night, James and I decided to go out for dinner at our favorite sushi bar. We met there at the end of the workday and were looking forward to a relaxing time and some light conversation. We were talking about work and the kids when things took a turn for the worse. We started to argue. I was hurt and emotional from the start. We both got angry and continued arguing back and forth, not caring that we were in the middle of a restaurant. Sometimes it seemed like all our hard work had gone right out the window. Frustrated, I got up and left, driving home in my car. It had started to rain outside, and I wasn't sure if it was the weather or my own tears that were making it hard to see the road. I wasn't really listening closely at first, but then I started to catch the song coming over the radio. It was the latest song from Celine Dion and was called *A New Day Has Come*. I had to pull over because my crying turned to sobbing as I caught the meaning of the words.

The song was telling my story and expressing the feelings about everything we had been through. At that moment I felt a range of emotions all at once, from grief to joy, and ultimately, optimism for the future. I couldn't stop crying and I sat in the car for an hour, releasing a great many things along with the tears. When I was done, I started my car, wiped my wet eyes, blew my nose, and cleared the mascara from my smudged cheeks. I found strength again, remembering the words.

James called on my cell phone to apologize. I said I was sorry, too. Maybe it was just PMS. But we moved on, just like we have always done.

The unforgettable words from our wedding day always come to my mind. The man who married us said as part of the service, "In your relationship the most important thing for you to do is to yield." I always tell myself this, and I remind James: Remember to *yield*. Of course, I prefer when James does the yielding. I have a hard time doing it, but I still try. If one of us yields, the compromise is made and everything works out fine.

Through the years, one unfaltering bond between James and me has been the love we share for our boys. With most things in our life mended, we decided to have another baby. I daydreamed about adding a daughter to our family.

Dr. Klepper must have given me the wrong diagnosis; I was crazy after all! I decided to go through in vitro fertilization a second time. At first, I worked with Dr. Grossman to do a mercury detoxification on my body, using glutathione and DMPS. I knew I didn't want to pass on any mercury toxicity to my baby. After twelve weeks of IV treatments, my urine test showed I was chelating a ton of metals, especially mercury. I don't know who had more metals in their system—Jamie or me.

Amy S. Holmes, MD, gives us these "Reasonable Rules for Life" for during and after treatment for mercury toxicity. It seems to me that a woman trying to conceive would benefit from these guidelines, too:

1. No fish and no seafood (supposedly, salmon is okay).
2. No amalgam (metal) fillings in teeth. Use white composite material instead.
3. No more thimerosal-containing vaccines. . . . For almost every possible vaccine given, there is at least one brand that does not contain thimerosal.[1]

In my opinion, if you need a tetanus shot, you should get one at your doctor's office, not at a hospital. Your doctor will be able to give you a thimerosal-free tetanus shot; a hospital probably won't be able to do this. If you choose to get a flu vaccine, you should, in my opinion, ask for a thimerosal-free flu shot.

When the detox process was finished, I began the fertility and in vitro process. I will spare the gory details, except the one that involved injecting my lower abdomen with a fertility drug intended to stimulate my eggs and ovaries for about a six-week period. Sometimes when I did the injections, the boys were with me in the kitchen. Jamie was quite intrigued by the whole process and wasn't afraid to actually insert the needle into my skin. They were both fearless, watching curiously what I went through, helping me where they could along the way. They were very aware of the fact that we were trying to make a baby. I used to amuse myself with an imagined scenario in which Jack and Jamie argued with their teacher at school about where babies really come from.

One day, I came home from the doctor after taking a pregnancy test. I told the boys we would hear back soon. They were really excited. When the phone rang the next day, it was the doctor's office. They gave me the news; I was pregnant. Mission accomplished. Thank you again, Dr. Schoolcraft! James wasn't home at the time, but I yelled for the boys to come downstairs. We held hands in a circle and jumped up and down at the idea that a baby was on the way.

Jamie said, "Nice job. It was all because of our help, huh, Mom?"

"Of course it was. Of course!" I said, as I kissed them all over.

We were scheduled for an ultrasound the next day to find out how many fertilized eggs there were. I had actually asked the doctor to put just one embryo in. I wasn't sure if I was prepared for twins again. He suggested we put in two.

He explained that two eggs would be a better bet for me to get one baby. I was afraid of having twins again after all we had been through. As I lay down for the ultrasound, I was happy and nervous at the same time. James seemed excited, and I saw him whispering to the nurses. I was curious about what was on his mind and what he was sharing with everyone else in the room.

The gel went on my belly along with the cold probe. The technician searched around until we saw one heartbeat. Everyone in the room responded, "Awww . . . so precious." I was only two weeks pregnant, but the baby already had a heartbeat. The technician continued moving the scope around, and I was thinking to myself, *What more could she be searching for?* And then, there it was. The second heartbeat. I was paralyzed. I couldn't believe it. Two eggs, two babies. James had tears in his eyes when he looked over at me.

Later, he confessed that he had secretly wanted twins again and that was what he'd been whispering about. I thought he was out of his mind, but my fear and surprise later turned to gratitude and anticipation.

We went home and told the boys the news. They were unbelievably excited about having twin siblings, just like themselves. We got some sparkling apple juice and four wine glasses and made a toast to another set of twins. We toasted again a couple of months later, when we found out that this time we were having girls. The boys couldn't get over the idea that they would soon have two sisters, and I was thrilled that I would have the little girls I had been hoping for.

Change was a constant for us. It certainly kept things interesting. The next big change in store for us all: It was time for the boys to start kindergarten. I couldn't believe it. Jamie was going to kindergarten! I began checking out a few schools to see what they were like. During one of my tours, all of a sudden I didn't feel well. I ran to the bathroom and threw up my strawberry-smoothie breakfast. At least it didn't taste that bad the second time. Good old morning sickness had arrived.

Before I had a chance to decide on a school, change came to visit again. We found a business opportunity that would require our family to relocate to Las Vegas. But by the end of my first month of pregnancy, I was put on bed rest for a placental tear and massive bleeding. That was really hard for me, because not only did I have to give up my beloved workouts but I was also unable to play with the boys and drive them around the city for the first time in their lives. Luckily, my mom came out to take over for me, working with our current nanny, Brittany, to manage the house and the boys.

When it came time to move, I was twenty-two weeks pregnant. I had never gotten off bed rest because of further complications from placenta previa, so I had to be airlifted by a medical jet from Denver to Las Vegas. James was handling all the moving logistics, and traveled there a day earlier. My mom took the boys, Brittany, and me to the airport. Brittany was moving out with us to help with the boys while I stayed on bed rest. Jack and Jamie were excited to get to come along for the plane ride, and to them it was an adventure beyond what they could have imagined.

The plane was staffed with two pilots and a nurse. We took off quickly and after forty minutes landed in Nevada. The boys made the most of every minute, laughing and playing the whole way, while I stayed horizontal on a mobile stretcher. We landed at an executive airport and as they wheeled me off the plane I saw a huge crowd of people waiting for us. James had come with all of his family, and they were holding welcome signs and cheering. It was such a cute thing for him to do, and the vivid memory still brings a smile to my face.

We arrived at our new home on July 9, 2003. I spent all my waking moments either lying down—bored and half crazy—or at the hospital, because I was hospitalized every three to ten days for heavy bleeding from the placenta previa. It was a pregnancy filled with complications, and one thing I just didn't do well was lie around all day. I started to feel sorry for myself. I couldn't believe this was happening to me. I thought I had already paid my dues. I guess it's true: Life isn't fair.

At seven months pregnant, and after twenty-nine weeks of bed rest, I was watching Federer versus Nadal in the U.S. Open tennis tournament in my usual position. I got a little too enthusiastic, cheered a bit too intensely, and started bleeding and cramping. I ended up going into the hospital to try to stop the contractions. I had so much bleeding that, after three days in the hospital, the doctors had to deliver the girls by emergency C-section.

Sofia and Gabriella Vance graced us with their presence on September 9, 2003. They were confined to the neonatal intensive care unit, just as Jack and Jamie had been, due to complications from premature birth. Jack and Jamie were so excited about their new sisters and wondered when they would come home. They loved going to see them in the hospital with me. Jamie never worried that he would lose my attention to the girls. Instead, he was enthralled with them and their every move. The girls stayed in the hospital for ten weeks, while I returned home after a week. It was great to finally be back home and moving around—a privilege that I didn't take for granted.

One morning I woke up and went into the kitchen to get something to drink. Jack and Jamie walked in with Brittany and just stared at me. Brittany gasped and put her hand over her mouth. I was puzzled by their reaction until they

Boys looking upon
their sister Sofia for the first time
through the window of the NICU

explained that they were just surprised to see me standing up, a view they hadn't seen for seven months. I had actually interviewed and hired Brittany from my bed, and she brought to my attention the fact that she had never seen me in an upright position. It was pretty humorous.

The girls came home and we relished our new family of six. Gabriella and Sofia became the center of all our attention. The four of us enjoyed watching their growth and the boys were completely absorbed with their sisters.

Jamie, Sofia, Gabriella, and Jack

As the girls grew, Gabriella showed a physical delay on the left side of her body. Tests revealed that she had mild cerebral palsy—another challenge for our family and a personal challenge for me, as I changed the direction of my efforts toward another quest for recovery.

When the girls were five years old and in kindergarten, they and their brothers attended the same school. That was the first—and last—year that all my kids would be in the same school. I visited the school often to have lunch with them, and greatly enjoyed the time I had with them under one roof. That year, I saw Gabriella move all the way across the monkey bars on her own for the first time. I was overjoyed and started crying among all the kindergarteners on the playground!

Now that the girls are ten, Gabriella is doing incredibly well. She has been involved in physical and occupational therapy since she was eighteen months old. Several months ago, I found a wonderful clinic in Los Angeles called the NAPA Center (Neurological and Physical Abilitation Center), where she receives intensive physical therapy. I take Gabriella every month to the NAPA Center for one week. (Sofia goes along, too, to keep her sister company.) During the summer, we go for three weeks. Gabriella does four hours a day of intensive therapy. With the help of some incredible therapists and her giant-size determination, she gets stronger and stronger each day. Meanwhile, I continue with my research for the newest treatments for cerebral palsy, including stem cell therapy and hyperbaric oxygen therapy, which we will start soon. We continue to use the Collins blue light diode.

She also receives cranial osteopathy from Kathryn Gill, MD. Dr. Gill treats me also; she is a brilliant practitioner. This is Dr. Gill's definition of cranial osteopathy:

> Structure determines function; this is the basis of Osteopathy. This healing science creates changes throughout the body, affecting every tissue and every organ. Osteopathy works to prevent and to treat dysfunction, and to improve well-being. A distortion in the position, density, motility, fluid content, or temperature of an area of the body will cause that area to function abnormally. The effects of this dysfunction will appear in other nearby—and even distant—parts. Furthermore, an aberration in the position of organs, vessels, nerves, or bones can cause extensive dysfunction as well. For example, if any part of the respiratory system (such as the chest wall, lungs, or diaphragm) is displaced, this will affect breathing. And breathing affects the function of everything in the human body.[2]

I think what Dr. Gill and the other doctors in her office give to their patients is completely and utterly priceless. I'm truly grateful.

Gabriella and Sofia are incredible together. They are like little replicas of Jack and Jamie, only in girl form. Sofia is always helping Gabriella, in the same way that Jack helped Jamie. Having these four children to love is an amazing gift.

Jamie healed

Jack . . .
my rock

CHAPTER
15

Meet Jamie Now

It is love–30 in the second set. The mood is intense, as the score is 4–3 in favor of the other team. Jack and Jamie seem to be a little off today, making small mistakes that aren't typical for them. During this second set, they seem to have lost their communication. There is obvious tension between them. Jack is shaking his head with frustration. They both know what an important match this is.

The weather at this tennis tournament in St. George, Utah, is hot, and a lot of final matches are going on around the boys, making for an elevated level of noise—and a big distraction. Jamie is up to serve. I notice him straightening up, standing just a little bit taller, as he walks with a confident stride over to his brother to exchange a high five. Jack is a little surprised at the timing, but as their hands meet, you can see that Jamie's vibe has just passed on to Jack. Jamie turns and walks to the baseline. Game on.

After a gentle toss in the air, the ball drops and Jamie slams it hard into the opponent's court. It is too fast to be

returned; it is an ace. Wow! We stand up and cheer. He calls out the score: 15–30. Looking at Jack, I can see he is fired up and ready to go. Jamie serves again. Another power shot to the opponent. This time it is returned, and Jamie addresses the arrival with a fierce backhand to the other side. The next return goes to Jack, who moves quickly, hammering it over the net for the point: 30–30.

The boys make one killer shot after the next before anyone can stop their heat wave, and the score changes to 40–30. Jamie serves again, but this time he misses it. I feel a brief pause in their push until the second serve flies over, a great slice. Jack rips the return over again, the opponent pipes it back to Jamie, and Jamie puts it away. They win the game. Yeah!

It's 4–4 and then it's 5–4, Jamie and Jack. The twins are on a roll. They have suddenly meshed, playing off each other, winning each point. What an amazing team. Both boys had seemed to be ready to wave the white flag, but it became obvious that Jamie just wasn't going to let it go. He was on fire, and he passed the torch to Jack. I was excited to see their bond showing in their teamwork on the court. Throughout the rest of the match, Jack and Jamie played incredibly hard until they claimed their victory, taking the National Doubles Championship title for the tournament.

I was very proud of their drive and determination. Earlier that day, Jack had won in his age group for singles in a two-hour match, and he had been exhausted from the start. Things would have gone differently with the doubles if Jamie hadn't decided, all of a sudden, that they both needed to step it up and rise to the challenge. I was thrilled to watch Jamie's leadership and initiative take over the game.

Jack and Jamie are fifteen now. Jamie is ten years post-recovery. He has gone more than four years without any breathing episodes. During the first ten years of his life, he had thirty-six hospital visits. A day doesn't go by that I don't appreciate where he is now and how he got here.

I thought it would be fun to know Jamie from a different perspective—his. So in my most recent interview with him, he shared with me that one of his favorite things to do is play with his friends: Lauren, Jace M., Riley, Kiley, Luke, and

Jack, of course. Ava, Nicholas, Bailey, Casey, Jace V., Jaxon, Brooke, Doug, Tanner, and Olivia, his beloved cousins, also share the top slots for kids he loves to hang out with. Jamie and Jack adore their sisters, Sofia and Gabriella. The time they spend together, playing and talking, warms my heart and makes me incredibly appreciative of the fact that they have one another.

Jamie also describes himself as a kid who loves tennis (of course), basketball, football, rollerblading, skiing, swimming, and surfing. He enjoys music almost as much as sports. Michael Jackson, Taylor Swift, Usher, Bruno Mars, Flo Rida, Katy Perry, Celine Dion, U2, Coldplay, the Beach Boys, Rihanna, Madonna, Taio Cruz, and Nickelback are just a few of his favorite artists. The subjects he prefers at school are boys' choir, art, science, and physical education. He names Hawaii and Santa Barbara, California, as his favorite vacation spots.

You will find Jamie and Jack today being very jazzed about heading off to a four-hour tennis session, with their huge tennis bags slung over their shoulders. Then maybe jumping in the pool for some laps afterward. Wow, makes me tired just writing about it! They are growing taller and stronger every day. And as each day goes by, I feel shorter and shorter. Feeling excited and scared about all the changes at the same time.

At fifteen years old, Jamie is 6'2" tall and 145 pounds of solid muscle. It's endearing to me that he doesn't realize how strong he is yet. My sweet gentle giant. Jamie does well in school and looks forward to it. I'll never forget how my heart jumped after the first few weeks of the boys' first-grade year, when Jamie's teacher said, "He's doing well, just like any other first grader!" Jamie's report card for the first half of first grade was filled with mostly A's and B's. That was years ago now, but I still receive positive feedback from teachers every year. Last year a teacher asked me, "Are you Jamie and Jack's mom?" When I said yes, she told me that she was impressed with their kindness and their willing spirit. She said, "The boys volunteer to clean cafeteria tables. And they guide autistic kids to class and help them out at lunch and recess." Both Jamie and Jack continue to make the honor roll.

Jamie and Jack also have a wonderful comedic side. They're jokesters who love to make each other, and everyone else, laugh. On days when the boys are out of school, they get up and play on the computer, go outside to the basketball court and shoot hoops, or ride their scooters to the nearby park for a couple of hours. Jamie loves Mario tennis on the X-Box 360, and, of course, Jack and Jamie can't get enough of computer games, YouTube, or iTunes downloads. Both boys enjoy watching *iCarly, Wizards of Waverly Place, Shake It Up, Johnny Test, Tom and Jerry* cartoons, *World of Adventure Sports, Fear Factor*, and other Nickelodeon and Disney Channel favorites.

This past couple years, our house has been filled with music. Jack and Jamie have excelled at playing piano. Jamie enjoys playing "The Star Wars Theme," while Jack's favorite is "Pirates of the Caribbean," but they both love "Heart and Soul" and "Für Elise." They also have been taking singing lessons. They continue to have more confidence in their voices and we get to reap the benefits of hearing the vocal talents of all four of our children. (Thanks, Melissa, our sweet nanny.)

Beyond his many talents, Jamie has a heart of gold. Recently, he displayed his compassion for others when all the neighborhood boys were engaged in a competitive game of flag football. Lauren, an athletic girl, and one of the boys' closest friends, was playing, too. The other boys weren't treating her fairly, and were excluding her because she is a girl. She ended up getting upset and walking away from the game to stand by herself. Jamie saw that her feelings were hurt, and he left the game to check on her. She resisted talking to him, but he continued to try to get her to open up.

"Come on, Lauren. I can see you're upset. Just talk to me. I'm a good listener. It's just me, Jamie."

They eventually talked it over and everything was better. Even Lauren's mom commented to me about Jamie's gentleness and consideration that day.

Jack and Jamie are very personable. James and I love how respectful they are with us, and the ways in which they try to do well. Almost every weekend they try to please me in some way: for example, by making their room neat and clean. But also, I think they might have an underlying agenda to make a little money, especially when I bring home new flowers to plant and they ask, ever so sweetly, if I need their help. They have a good life, and many reasons to be self-absorbed, but they stay humble and often put other people before themselves.

As we become adults, we develop boundaries and become guarded, but children are often unself-conscious and open with others. Jamie definitely is, which is amazing, especially considering his behavior before his recovery. It seems like it was just a short time ago when I was the only person who could touch him. Not anymore. He is comfortable around everyone now, especially when it comes to touch or affection. He is awe-inspiring to me, as is Jack, each in his own perfect way.

I could write another whole book devoted just to Jack. He was an integral part of Jamie's healing. He is and always has been happy, supportive, sweet, and reassuring. One day, Jamie will be able to fully understand what an enormous part Jack played in his recovery, not only as a helper, role model, partner, and friend but also as the brother whose unconditional love stayed with him every step of the way. Even though he is Jamie's twin, Jack has taken on the role of an older brother.

As a family, we are all close. One of the things we do together is travel. We are always going to tennis tournaments in California; first, because it's so close and we can all spend time together without too many distractions; and second, because we get to enjoy the beach. We recently went to Hermosa Beach. I took a run along the Strand, and the boys rollerbladed alongside me. I couldn't believe how naturally rollerblading came to them.

Working to keep healthy in all ways is an ongoing task. Of course, that doesn't rule out the occasional accident. About five years ago we spent Thanksgiving on the big island in Hawaii. While playing in the ocean, Jamie cut his knee on some coral. I had to take him to the hospital for stitches. At first, it was a worry and somewhat of an inconvenience because it was forty minutes of lost beach time and a wasted piña colada. But I quickly remembered past reasons for hospital visits . . . and was overjoyed that the only reason for this one was a quick fix, not a life-threatening emergency. I could relax—except for the small part where I had to carry a 120-pound boy on my back from the parking lot to the door of the hospital because he had forgotten his shoes.

The doctor in the emergency room highly recommended a tetanus shot. I immediately questioned the need, saying, "Are you sure?" I really didn't want him to get the shot. Then I learned from the doctor that the bacteria that live in coral reefs can cause both tetanus and staph infections. I called Dr. Collins, Dr. Maes, and James in a panic. Sure I overreact at times, but can you blame me? I needed to know the right thing to do.

Dr. Maes suggested that Jamie get the injection, and we could deal with any potential aftereffects later. My worst fears from all the stories of vaccines had surfaced and were staring me in the face, but I had to do it. Yikes! When it was over, we walked out happily. Everything had gone smoothly, except for the two stitches in Jamie's leg and the sore area on his shoulder where the needle had gone in. We looked forward to getting back to the beach: Jamie to his snorkeling, and me to a new piña colada.

I learned the tetanus shot would require two follow-ups to be effective. I was disappointed but still concerned about his wound from the coral, so back at home, four weeks after our trip, I took him into the doctor's office for the second injection. A few weeks later, I noticed the slightest decline in his focus. He also seemed a bit more hyperactive. Of course, I am ultra-aware of every difference in him.

I suspected that it was the tetanus vaccine that had brought about the change in his behavior. I decided to put him back on Metal-Free for about a month to make sure that his body would detoxify any remnants of the medicine. I also gave him N-acetyl cysteine and extra krill oil. His focus returned quickly. He is obviously extremely sensitive to these types of immunizations; the first tetanus shot contained thimerosal and the second did not, but it did contain other types of preservatives, such as formaldehyde and chlorine.

For continued health these days and to combat illness, my kids take select supplements. In particular, Jamie takes allicillin (garlic) and Russian Choice Immune to keep his immune system strong, and Rehmannia 6 Formula—a Chinese herb and allover body tonic—to keep his kidneys and lungs healthy. He also gets the omega-3 essential fatty acid in krill oil. He takes a multivitamin and multimineral supplement called Vitavescence, and in addition he takes

Probiotic Synergy, both by Designs for Health. On occasion, when he or any of my other kids begins feeling sick, I add a packet of ProBoost to enhance their thymus gland function.

Most importantly, our entire family continues to eat organic, whole foods. Nowadays, Jamie is able to eat some wheat and some milk products. For the past three years, Jamie has been the healthiest of our four children. Maybe his body went through so much earlier that he has a higher tolerance for illness now, or maybe his immune system has just been forced to become stronger. We continue to see Dr. Maes in California, Dr. Klepper in Colorado, and Dr. Collins in South Carolina. We have to cross state lines a couple of times a year to see each doctor, but it is always worth the trip. I have never found any other doctors who can rival the care they give us.

Jamie occasionally has to deal with the aftereffects of his past traumas from hospitalizations and emergencies. He has a vivid memory of the panic he experienced so many times. When it surfaces, we work through it, and I see him getting stronger each time. It is miraculous that he has chosen never to give up. On the one hand, I feel like he lost three and a half years of his life that he can never get back, but on the other, I feel that his illness was the origin of a kind of unshakable determination that few individuals will ever know or understand. He had to do some very difficult things during his recovery. All those experiences have made him the boy he is today—resilient, loving, kind, and unassuming, Jamie gets excited over everything, even the smallest event. It's as if he appreciates the incredible gift his recovery has given him, and he never takes any of life's opportunities for granted.

I can't wait to see where the years take him. What will he be when he grows up? Who will he fall in love with? What will his children be like? I am excited for the future, excited that Jamie has every opportunity. Who could ever guess that ten years ago, he was autistic?

Now

Meet the girls . . .

CHAPTER

16

Lessons Learned

What seems like a lifetime ago, I was sitting in a restaurant called Morton's in Beverly Hills. Steve, my husband at the time, was having a meeting about a show his company was producing. The table was full of bigwig Hollywood producers. One writer–director, Marco Garibaldi, was looking at me and asking questions. "So, Krista . . . what do you think about this idea?" I cowered, possessing so little confidence in what I had to say that I only smiled and laughed without responding. I felt paralyzed, thoroughly intimidated by the group of people who were successful and talented. There were a lot of thoughts in my head, and there was a lot that I could have said, but I just couldn't make the words come out. I had always been very shy. I don't think that I said anything throughout the entire dinner except "hello" and "good-bye."

Obviously, having children and finding out that Jamie was autistic propelled me outside my shell. I have learned how to stand up and speak up because I had to in order to keep my head above water. Marco is still a friend and he and I have extra-long phone conversations, no matter where we live or the distance between us. He laughs at how different I've become over the years, teasing me that when he speaks to me now, he can't even get a word in. Certainly the battles I've waged as a mother have brought about incredible changes in me.

So far, life has been quite remarkable. I still eat healthily and do the best I can to stay well. Each day I get up and make a choice about how I will feel. I am filled with love and gratitude for my children. I can't help but laugh out loud when I realize just how lucky I am.

Being the mother of a child with any type of disability is immensely difficult. It's hard to describe or even find the right words for all the emotions that surface. It overwhelms me. In most articles about autism that I have come across, there is no mention of what goes on behind the scenes of an autistic child's family, especially with regard to the mother: first, what we go through to bring our children into the world, and second, what we do to give them the best possible lives we can.

Finding doctors who knew about autism and how to help me was difficult. Most doctors had the attitude that you had drawn the short stick and there was nothing you could do to change your luck. This mindset motivated me to put a great deal of effort, practically every waking moment, into finding doctors who understood and could do something to help us. It was very frustrating running into so many roadblocks at the most difficult time of my life. Not many people or many doctors shared my attitude about the ability to change what afflicted my son. I needed people on my team who felt the same way I did and truly believed that I could get Jamie back.

I learned to listen to my instincts because it meant sometimes *not* listening to well-educated and well-intentioned people.

On the other hand, there are some people who, after Jamie's full recovery, question whether he was truly autistic to begin with. There is a group of skeptics out there who are convinced that there is absolutely no cure for autism, and since Jamie is ten years post-autism and living a full life like other children his age, they can only respond by trying to invalidate the facts. But Jamie was never just delayed. From the time he was nineteen months old, more than one specialist diagnosed him as having symptoms of echolalia, repetitive behaviors, complete language loss, sensory overload, and a lack of social skills or emotional expression. Jamie isn't the only child to have overcome autism; there are thousands of documented cases of other kids who have done the same. In the end, everyone involved in Jamie's healing knows the truth.

The Kaufman family fields the same kind of skepticism. People balked at their book *Son-Rise: The Gift of Love*, saying that the recovery it depicted was a one-time miracle, a fluke. Although the Kaufmans created their own program and helped hundreds of other autistic children recover, their method was still criticized. Their second book, *Son-Rise: The Miracle Continues*, records ongoing cases of recovery—despite the program's skeptics.

If more professionals were more open-minded, more children would be helped. The science and art of autism treatments would evolve instead of being an individual parent's trial and error. We need more studies. We need more funding. We need research done on the many children who have recovered, in order to find out what has influenced their recovery. With all this evidence, and all the focus and attention on this illness, there should be more support and less doubt.

The strongest impact on Jamie's recovery was chelation. Of course, there is much controversy surrounding the therapy, not only to treat autism but for any kind of treatment. However, even the United States Food and Drug Administration (FDA) recognizes the effectiveness of chelation; it approved the use of chelation in the 1960s to treat lead poisoning.

At the time of this book's publication, chelation therapy has not yet been approved by the FDA to treat coronary artery disease, but some physicians and alternative medicine practitioners have already been using it for that purpose, according to the American Heart Association.

Up to now, there have been no adequate, controlled, published scientific studies using currently approved scientific methodology to support this therapy for cardiovascular disease. The FDA, the National Institutes of Health (NIH), and the American College of Cardiology all agree with the American Heart Association on this point.

The American Heart Association website discusses a new study of chelation therapy for treatment of heart disease:

> In August 2002, the National Center for Complementary and Alternative Medicine (NCCAM) and the National Heart, Lung, and Blood Institute (NHLBI), which are both components of the National Institutes of Health (NIH), announced the launch of the Trial to Assess Chelation Therapy

> (TACT). This is the first large-scale, multicenter study to find out if EDTA [ethylenediamine tetraacetic acid] chelation therapy is safe and effective for people with coronary heart disease. This placebo-controlled, double-blind study involves participants age 50 years and older who've had a heart attack, and is expected to reach a total enrollment of 1,950. Participants are representative of the U.S. population. TACT will be much larger than any prior study of chelation therapy—large enough to show if chelation therapy has mild or moderate benefits.[1]

Chelation is considered to be dangerous for children. The FDA not only cautions parents against its use with children but has also included chelation in its lists of top-ten fraudulent medical practices. Certain pediatricians claim that chelation is dangerous for children—that it should be considered child abuse. And yet parents who have used chelation claim that it has saved their children's lives.

It's time to sort out the facts from the claims. This would require more research and more funding. We are ready to take the challenge, because we are positive that the potential outweighs the risks.

Parents of many autistic children are demanding action. We look around and see that cases of autism are increasing as the environment of our world changes, but we also see that many autistic children are recovering. We don't want to accept that nothing can be done—not while there is evidence proving otherwise. Every child should have the opportunity to engage in the many options for therapies and treatments, and every parent should have access to information and education about the illness.

The FDA knows the risks of mercury, and in 1999 it began recommending the removal or reduction of thimerosal in all routinely recommended vaccines for children six years of age and younger, with the exception of inactivated influenza vaccines. It has already mandated the complete removal of thimerosal from some vaccines. If the FDA recognizes that the body absorbs metals, and there is an existing treatment to help the body remove those metals, why won't it validate the treatment?

On September 7, 2006, the National Institute of Mental Health announced that it would conduct a study "to address the widespread but unproven theory that autism may be treated successfully by chelation therapy, which seeks to remove heavy metals from the blood."[2]

On September 18, 2008, it was reported that plans for such a study had been canceled: "Federal officials have abandoned a proposed study of a controversial alternative therapy for autism, leaving parents who believe in the treatment disappointed and angry."[3] Rebecca Estepp of the autism support group Talk About Curing Autism responded to the announcement: "We are dumbfounded and saddened that this study . . . will not happen. . . . When does the anecdotal evidence get so large that they have to listen to us?"[4]

A change is coming, but how many children will lose their chance to recover while we sit and wait for profit and politics to move out of the way?

I don't pretend to understand everything that has happened. It has happened for a reason. I wish I could have been superhuman on many occasions and made it through without having made any mistakes. I would try something and it would either work or not. Over the years, Jamie's life has given me a passion for learning, and I feel like I have improved my own life because of all we've been through. Overall, I knew my efforts wouldn't fail, because I put my love for Jamie first.

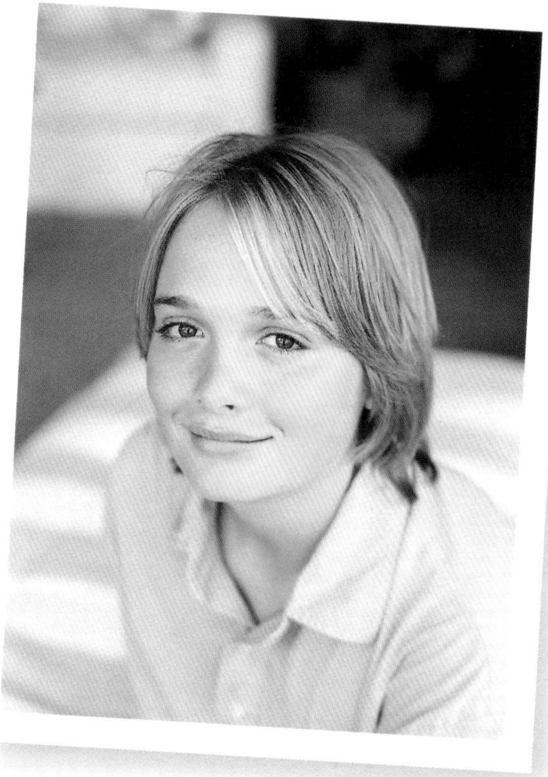

Meet Jamie Now.

In the last fifteen years, I have probably learned the most in my life about the human spirit. I learned so much about the anatomy and physiology of the human body, too. Because of my determination and perseverance, along with my desire for Jamie to be "normal," I pushed Jamie, my family, and myself to places we never knew existed. The people with whom I surrounded myself were vital to our ability to accomplish what we did.

This is the most important advice that I could give to another mother: Surround yourself with the kinds of people whose hearts and minds are open to all things good and have the same goal for your child as you do. Always go for the tenth opinion. Keep searching until you find the open door. One in every eighty-eight children is labeled with some form of autism, and few are expected to recover. We need to expect that they will.

Jamie's Diet

(No gluten, milk casein, corn, white sugar, white flour, or soy)
Organic as much as possible, especially fruits and vegetables

BREAKFAST

Organic eggs

Turkey sausage
(Shelton Farms brand, which has no
antibiotics or hormones)

Organic brown rice bread

Melon or papaya (The papaya is for enzymes.)

Filtered water with lemon

—or—

Kirkman Labs pancake mix or Authentic Foods Pancake and Baking Mix

Kirkman Labs no-sugar maple syrup (to avoid a sugar high) or any organic Grade A maple syrup or organic agave nectar (agave syrup)

Small amount of organic rice milk

Turkey sausage (Shelton Farms)

LUNCH

Organic turkey sandwich (made with organic brown rice bread)

Banana, apple, or pear; occasionally, a 100 percent organic juice drink box or organic rice milk box instead

Occasionally, organic, gluten-free potato chips or organic corn chips with no flavoring other than salt

Filtered water

—or—

Organic peanut butter or organic almond butter sandwich (made with organic brown rice bread)

Carrots and celery

Filtered water

DINNER

Homemade organic chicken fingers
(See "Notes" for recipe.)

Vegetables lightly sautéed in organic olive oil with
Celtic sea salt (for example, broccoli and carrots)

Organic brown rice, sweet potatoes, or mashed potatoes
(I use organic rice milk and organic ghee—also
called clarified butter—in the mashed potatoes.)

Sautéed potatoes
(I use only organic coconut oil, organic olive oil,
lard, or duck fat.)

—or—

Organic brown rice pasta
(I use Tinkyáda or Pastaríso organic brown rice
spaghetti or Pastaríso organic brown rice fettuccine.)

Organic dark turkey meatballs
(Dark turkey has more fat, so it's tastier.)

Organic pasta sauce without sugar or honey added

Sautéed carrots in coconut oil

Sautéed broccoli in olive oil

Fresh cucumber with lemon and Celtic sea salt

Filtered water with thin lemon or orange slices

SNACKS

Organic nuts, especially almonds

Organic fruit (small amount)

Wheat-free, gluten-free rice crackers

Organic, gluten-free potato chips

Organic corn chips

Organic carrot sticks

Organic gluten-free pretzels (Whole Foods carries these or you can order them off the Internet.)

Organic gluten-free cookies (Pamela's Organic Spicy Ginger Cookies with Crystallized Ginger are good.)

Notes

- This is the diet we followed when Jamie's symptoms were at their worst.
- I would often make my own bread in my bread maker. You can find gluten-free bread mix at your local natural food store. One kind that we continue to use is Authentic Foods

Wholesome Bread Mix. Of course, it's probably less expensive to buy organic brown rice flour and mix it with other gluten-free flours. I would also buy Food for Life brown rice bread; you can find this in the freezer section.

- I would buy antibiotic-free, hormone-free turkey at Whole Foods. You can also find this turkey at your local natural food store.
- I would use safflower oil mayonnaise, which contains egg and a little bit of sweetener. If your child has an allergy to either ingredient, you will have to come up with something else—possibly mustard or tomato sauce. Plain olive oil or olive oil with balsamic vinegar is good, too.
- For chicken fingers, I used organic, free-range chicken breaded with a mixture of two or more of these: brown rice flour, corn flour, millet flour, and sorghum flour. I would use a little rice milk or egg whites to keep the flour mixture stuck on the chicken. You can fry it on high heat with coconut oil, but always use low heat with olive oil. (I never used canola or any other oils to cook with.)
- Jamie *loved* ketchup. When he was not in the kitchen, I would take a can of organic tomato sauce, add only Celtic sea salt to it, and put this mixture in an empty ketchup bottle. The taste was similar to ketchup but had no sweetener.
- I was told by one of our doctors that we could use organic ghee (clarified butter) or *raw* organic butter.
- I also used a lot of BodyBio Balance Oil (organic sunflower and flaxseed oils) and Udo's Choice Oil Blend (organic flax,

sunflower, sesame, and other oils), putting them on foods after they had been cooked.

- On occasion, I would make a smoothie using a variety of ingredients, including almond milk, rice milk, or hazelnut milk; almond butter; bananas; vitamin C; and flax oil and borage oil (a mixture similar to Udo's Choice oil or BodyBio oil). I also used a scoop of Metagenics brand Ultracare for Kids rice protein powder. Now I use Paleomeal Organic Whey Protein by Designs for Health. You can go through your health care practitioner for these protein powders. I would add something green (Green Vibrance from Vibrant Health or PaleoGreens from Designs for Health), and I would mix it with fruit—strawberries or blueberries or blackberries (or some combination of two or three of these berries). *Be sure that all the fruit is organic, especially the berries.*
- On occasion, I would use Kirkman Labs pancake mix. (Nowadays, you can get gluten-free mixes at Whole Foods.) I would also use Kirkman Labs sugar-free maple syrup. Or I would use agave nectar (syrup) or brown rice syrup for sweetener. If you can't use sugar, stick with sugar-free, but in my opinion, you should not use aspartame. I think this is the worst sweetener you could use. There is a lot of research about it. Check out the book *Sweet'Ner Dearest: Bittersweet Vignettes about Aspartame (Nutrasweet)* by H. J. Roberts, MD.
- Be very cautious about the other artificial sweeteners because you don't know how your child will react to this stuff. It's good to stick with no sugar at all or a small amount of agave

nectar (syrup), brown rice syrup, stevia, or xylitol. As far as xylitol goes, it is sweet but don't allow your child to eat too much of it because xylitol can cause bloating and diarrhea. The newest sweetener that I use is raw coconut sugar or raw coconut nectar (syrup). It's low glycemic (does not trigger a rapid rise in blood sugar). It's also delicious!

- Kirkman Labs has Fructooligosaccharides (scFOS), which is actually good for the intestinal tract. I would dip strawberries in the scFOS and it tasted yummy.

- When we worked on bringing the yeast down in Jamie's intestinal tract I had him on positively *no* sugar, fruit, fruit juice, or cookies. Getting the sugar under control really seemed to help him, and he seemed to hold strong. Then we slowly brought back some fruit and an occasional low-sugar cookie or a Rice Dream frozen vanilla bar. That was a special treat!

- In almost every natural food store you can get gluten-free products. Casein-free products are a little more difficult. If your child likes goat cheese or sheep cheese (the sheep cheese tastes like regular cheese but does not have casein), that is a good alternative. We pretty much had to stay away from all dairy, except organic ghee (clarified butter).

- For the past several years, I have given my children raw organic milk from Organic Pastures. Check them out at www.organicpastures.com.

- I always try to buy everything organic, especially fruits, vegetables, and meats. Using pesticide-, chemical-, and hormone-free food could have been the key to helping

Jamie get the load off his system. Today, most of our foods are still organic. It's fun to grow your own garden, too. I did this in Colorado. Veggies are *yummy*!

Organic Greens Recipe

A few years ago, Dr. Max Collins was in Las Vegas for a week of medical meetings. During that time, he would come to our house to treat us. Afterward, he would make little things for us to eat. He would take some red chard or red leaf lettuce or maybe a few leaves of kale or collard greens, chop them up, and serve them with a squeeze of fresh lemon juice. Sometimes he would add some olive oil or apple cider vinegar—or maybe both—to the chopped-up greens also. Every day for a week he made these yummy delicacies.

He would do an avocado, tomato, cilantro, salt, and lemon juice combination to die for, too. He suggested we have this guacamole-and-salsa dish for breakfast. (Wow! I was not up for that in the morning.)

I took the salad a step further and created a fresh organic greens recipe for our family and friends to eat every day. I vary it quite a bit, and we've come up with just how we like it. You can mix and match and take away to please your palate. I've included the base recipe and a bunch of options, too:

ORGANIC GREENS RECIPE

Kale (2 or 3 big leaves) *base*
Red chard (2 big leaves) *base*
Red leaf lettuce (3 leaves) *base*
Spinach (handful) *base*
Beet greens (handful) *optional*
Collard greens or mustard greens (2 leaves) *optional*
Watercress (2 leaves) *optional*
We usually pick five of the seven above and vary the recipe often. There are many other varieties of lettuce greens you might like to use.

Cilantro *or* basil (small handful) *base*
Cucumber (1) *base*
Carrots (3) *base*
Red bell pepper (1) *base*
Celery (1 or 2 stalks, leaves included) *optional*
Chop everything above into small pieces. Amounts will make a delicious bowl of about 8 servings.

Then add the following:
Olive oil (liberal amount—about 4 to 5+ tablespoons) *base*
Apple cider vinegar (1 tablespoon) *base*
1 lemon, juiced (freshly squeezed) *base*
1 lime, juiced (freshly squeezed) *base*
1 cup garbanzo beans *optional*
1 cup kidney beans *optional*
1 cup beets *optional*

Salt and pepper to taste (Real Salt brand sea salt, Celtic sea salt, or Himalayan salt)

With the kids, the only way I can get them to eat a lot of the salad is by also serving Blue Diamond brand gluten-free Smokehouse flavor Nut-Thins (other flavors available) or Natural Tostitos organic blue corn chips. The combination of greens and crackers or chips is incredible.

After the salad is made, I recommend that you help yourself to a good portion in a separate bowl and then add any extras you like, such as one sliced avocado, one sliced tomato, or a light dusting of cayenne pepper. Don't mix the avocado or tomato into the main salad, as these ingredients get mushy and the salad will go bad after a few hours.

We have fun and mix it up! Choose local and organic ingredients as much as possible. And vary the leaves and veggies—your body will thank you!

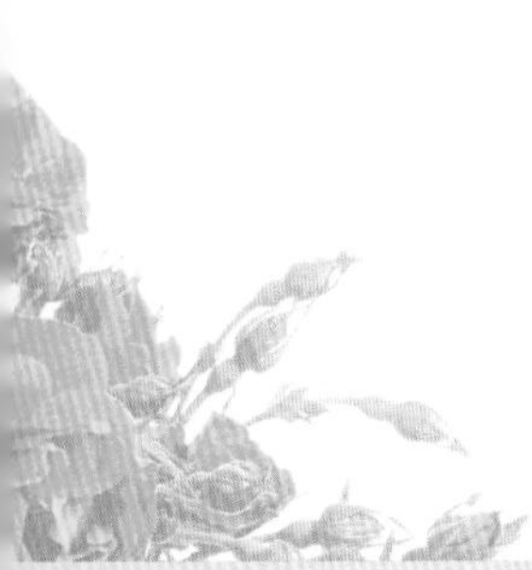

Resources

Autism Research Institute

Helped us contact a clinician in our area
Phone (619) 281-7165
Fax (619) 563-6840
www.autism.com

Dr. Max Collins, DC

Inventor of the Collins blue light diode

Bill Cunningham

White Dove Healing Arts
Phone (303) 828-4439
www.whitedovehealing.com

Embodied Resolutions

Maya Kaya, APP, SEP, RCST
Polarity Therapist
Somatic Experiencing Practitioner
Registered Craniosacral Therapist
Phone (303) 507-3583
Email: mayakaya@earthlink.net

G.E.M.S. (Growing Experientially Multi-Disciplinary Service) School in Denver

Joan A. Eckert, MA, CCC-SLP, Speech/Language Pathologist, Owner/Founder
Phone (303) 752-2977
www.denvergems.org

Genova Diagnostics (formerly Great Smokies Diagnostic Lab)

Phone (800) 522-4762

www.genovadiagnostics.com

Dr. Kathryn Gill, MD

Specializing in cranial Osteopathy
Santa Monica, CA
Phone (310) 576-2503

Dr. Garry Gordon, MD, DO, MD (H)

Gordon Research Institute
Longevity Plus
Phone (928) 474-3684
www.gordonresearch.com
www.autismanswer.com
www.longevityplus.com

Dr. Jay Gordon, MD, FAAP

Pediatrician
www.drjaygordon.com

The Great Plains Laboratory, Inc.

Phone (913) 341-8949
Phone (800) 288-0383
www.greatplainslaboratory.com

Rochelle I. Greenbaum, MA, CCC-SL Speech Language Pathologist

Phone (805) 569-9647

Dr. Terry Grossman, MD, (H)

Frontier Medical Institute
Phone (303) 233-4247
Phone (877) 548-4387
www.fmiclinic.com
www.grossmanwellness.com
www.liv4evr.com

Helios Integrated Medicine

2525 4th Street, Suite 205
Boulder, CO 80304
Phone (303) 499-9224
www.heliosintegratedmedicine.com

Kirkman Labs

Phone (800) 245-8282
www.kirkmanlabs.com

Dr. Gary Klepper, DC, CTN

The Ninth Wave

Dr. Luc Maes, BS, ND, DC, DHANP, CCH, DNBHE

Maes Center for Natural Health Care
Phone (805) 563-8660
www.maescenter.com

MAPS (Medical Academy of Pediatric Special Needs)

www.medmaps.org

Metal-Free

Phone (877) 804-3258
Email: webmaster@bodyhealth.com
www.bodyhealth.com

NAPA Center (Neurological and Physical Abilitation Center)

Phone (888) 711-NAPA
www.napacenter.org

Dr. Nicholas Nossaman

Classical Homeopath
Phone (303) 861-4181

The Option Institute™ and the Autism Treatment Center of America

Phone (413) 229-2100
Phone (800) 714-2779
2080 S. Undermountain Rd.
Sheffield, MA 01257
www.autismtreatmentcenter.org

Diane Osaki

Early Start Denver Model Director
Firefly Autism House
Phone (303) 709-3146
Email: osakiconsulting@mac.com

Helen Peak

Repatterning Therapist
Phone (970) 229-0765

Serena Sutherland, OTR/L, CHT, Occupational Therapist specializing in Sensory Integration

Phone (805) 964-1835

Dr. Keith Swan, DO, DABMA

Phone (303) 444-8337

Dr. Jerry Tennant, MD

Tennant Institute for Integrative Medicine
Phone (972) 580-1156
www.tennantinstitute.com

Unique Prints Pediatric Therapy Services, Inc.

Occupational, speech, music, and listening (Samonas) therapies
Kristy Phelps, OTR, BCP—Clinical Director
Phone (303) 773-1034

Dr. Jay Wilson, DC, ND

Phone (303) 449-7414

Notes

Chapter 6

The epigraph to this chapter is from Sallie Bernard,* Albert Enayati, BS, ChE, MSME,** Teresa Binstock, Heidi Roger, Lyn Redwood, RN, MSN, CRNP, and Woody McGinnis, MD, "Autism: A Unique Type of Mercury Poisoning," ARC Research, 14 Commerce Drive, Cranford, NJ 07016, http://www.vaccinationnews.com/dailynews/july2001/autismuniquemercpoison.htm (accessed November 7, 2010).
*Contact: sbernard@nac.net
**Contact: (201) 444-7306
njcan@aol.com

1. Robert Frost, "The Road Not Taken," in *Mountain Interval* (New York: Henry Holt and Company, 1920), http://www.bartleby.com/119/1.html (accessed November 28, 2010).
2. "Discover CranioSacral Therapy," http://www.upledger.com/content.asp?id=26 (accessed August 20, 2011).
3. "Quotations," "Wilma Rudolph Quotes," http://www.thinkexist.com/quotes/wilma_rudolph (accessed September 11, 2010).
4. Amy Morrison, "Balancing Biochemistry: An Interview with Stephanie Cave," *Mothering* 115 (November/December 2002).
5. "Chelation Treatments," http://www.chelationtreatments.org/chelation-therapy/what-is-chelation-therapy (accessed November 7, 2010).

6. Amy S. Holmes, MD, "Chelation of Mercury for the Treatment of Autism," http://www.healing-arts.org/children/holmes.htm (accessed November 7, 2010).
7. Morrison, "Balancing Biochemistry."
8. "Scientific Facts on Mercury," "Section 2.3: What Levels of Mercury Might Cause Harm?" http://www.greenfacts.org/en/mercury/l-2/mercury-2.htm (accessed January 18, 2011).
9. Jennifer 8. Lee, "E.P.A. Raises Estimate of Babies Affected by Mercury Exposure," *The New York Times*, February 10, 2004, http://www.nytimes.com/2004/02/10/science/epa-raises-estimate-of-babies-affected-by-mercury-exposure.html (accessed November 7, 2010).

Chapter 7

1. Steven Novella, "*The Lancet* Retracts Andrew Wakefield's Article," *Science-Based Medicine*, February 3, 2010, http://www.sciencebasedmedicine.org/index.php/lancet-retracts-wakefield-article (accessed December 7, 2011).
2. "Statement from Dr. Andrew Wakefield: No Fraud. No Hoax. No Profit Motive," http://www.ageofautism.com; June 6, 2013; posted on YouTube April 16, 2013.

Chapter 14

1. Holmes, "Chelation of Mercury," http://www.healing-arts.org/children/holmes.htm (accessed November 7, 2010).
2. Kathryn Gill, MD, email message to author, April 7, 2011.

Chapter 16

1. "Chelation Therapy," "AHA Recommendation," http://www.americanheart.org/presenter.jhtml?identifier=4493 (accessed September 12, 2010).
2. National Institute for Mental Health, Press Release, September 7, 2006, "New NIMH Research Program Launches Autism Trials,"

http://www.nimh.nih.gov/science-news/2006/new-nimh-research-program-launches-autism-trials.shtml (accessed November 30, 2010).

3. Salynn Boyles (reviewed by Louise Chang, MD), "Chelation Study for Autism Called Off: Controversial Trial Too Risky, Panel Says," *WebMD*, September 18, 2008, http://www.webmd.com/brain/autism/news/20080918/chelation-study-autism-called-off (accessed October 6, 2010).
4. Ibid.

About the Author

Krista Vance was born in Southern California and currently resides in Las Vegas, Nevada, with her family. She keeps busy with two sets of twins. In her spare time, Krista writes about alternative approaches to health. Her articles have been published in *Well Being Journal, Organic Family Magazine, and Alternative Medicine.*

Krista is a member of Autism Today and FEAT (Families for Effective Autism Treatment). She also supports the Autism Research Institute and their biomedical approach to autism.

Krista continues to devote her energy to researching the impact of nutrition and environmental factors on health and wellness. She relaxes by exercising, dancing, and enjoying time with her family.

Babolat
Babolat